THE SOCIAL SCIENCES

CONCEPTS AND VALUES

■ ■ ■ ■ ■ ■ ■ ■ ORANGE

CENTER FOR THE STUDY OF INSTRUCTION
SAN FRANCISCO, CALIFORNIA

RESEARCH, EVALUATION, AND WRITING

PAUL F. BRANDWEIN
President, Center for Study of Instruction
Adjunct Professor, University of Pittsburgh

NANCY W. BAUER
Extension Lecturer, Graduate School of Education
Michigan State University

Formerly Coordinator, Social Studies, Kg-12
Birmingham, Michigan

DANIEL J. DALY
Principal, Willard School, Ridgewood, New Jersey

JEANNE N. KNUTSON
Research Associate, Department of Political Science
Stanford University

W. ROBERT SCOTT
Principal, New Garden Elementary School
Toughkenamon, Pennsylvania

ELIZABETH LÉONIE SIMPSON
Research Associate, Center for Study of Instruction

AGNES McCARTHY WISE
Research Associate, Center for Study of Instruction

CONSULTING SOCIAL SCIENTISTS

BURTON R. CLARK, *Sociology*
Professor, Yale University

NATHAN GLAZER, *Sociology*
Professor, University of California, Berkeley

CHARLES HAMILTON, *Political Science*
Professor, Roosevelt College, Chicago

WILLIAM HOCHMAN, *History and Political Science*
Professor, Colorado College

FRED KNIFFEN, *Anthropology and Human Geography*
Professor, Louisiana State University

BEN WILLIAM LEWIS, *Economics*
Professor, Oberlin College

MARGARET MEAD, *Anthropology*
Curator, American Museum of Natural History

ANNE ROE, *Psychology*
Lecturer in Psychology, University of Arizona
Professor Emerita, Harvard University

HARCOURT BRACE JOVANOVICH, INC.
NEW YORK, CHICAGO, SAN FRANCISCO, ATLANTA, DALLAS

THE SOCIAL SCIENCES
CONCEPTS AND VALUES

ORANGE

CONSULTING SPECIALISTS IN EDUCATION

BARBARA B. CLARK
Environmental Education
Environmental Science Center
Golden Valley, Minnesota

ERMA FERRARI
Reading Specialist
New York City

JAMES C. GLEASON
Social Science Specialist
Ridgewood Public Schools
New Jersey

DARRELL F. KIRBY
Supervisor, Social Science
Boulder, Colorado

JAN McNEIL
Formerly Social Science Supervisor
Nova School
Fort Lauderdale, Florida

MORSLEY G. GIDDINGS
Educational Developer
Center for Urban Education
New York City

LISA HARBATKIN
Political Science
Center for Urban Education

MICHAEL KINSLER
History and Social Science
Center for Urban Education

ROBERT PRICE
Associate Professor, School of Education
University of Colorado
Boulder, Colorado

FRED ROSENAU
Far West Laboratory for Educational
Research and Development
Berkeley, California

LOUIS RUBIN
Director
Center for Coordinated Research
University of California
Santa Barbara, California

JANE WESTENBERGER
Conservation Education Specialist
United States Forest Service
San Francisco, California

LEE WILLIAMS
Social Science, Nova School
Fort Lauderdale, Florida

VIVIAN WINDLEY
Professor of Education
Department of Social Studies
City College of the City University
New York City

CONSULTING TEACHERS AND SUPERVISORS

POLLY ASH
Assistant Director
Clemmie Gill School of Conservation
Springville, California

MARION ASHWORTH
Supervisor
Beaumont, Texas

ROSALIND BEIMLER
Curriculum Coordinator
American School Foundation
Mexico City, Mexico

J. BYRON BURGESS
Assistant Superintendent of Instruction
Manhattan Beach, California

PHYLLIS I. BUSH
Project Director
Enterprise Elementary School District
Redding, California

ARMAND COLANG
Director of Social Studies
Seattle, Washington

HENRY P. GALLINA
Curriculum Coordinator
Lompoc, California

JOHN GRATE
Administrative Supervisor
Cincinnati, Ohio

RICHARD A. JENSEN
Superintendent
Los Lomitas School District
Menlo Park, California

LADYE JONES
Teacher
Metropolitan Public Schools
Nashville, Tennessee

ANDREW J. JOYCE
Director of Education
Palos Verdes, California

G. SIDNEY LESTER
Director
Marin Social Studies Project
Corte Madera, California

SISTER LUCIDA, C.PP.S.
Supervisor
Archdiocese of St. Louis, Missouri

RUTHE A. LUNDY
General Curriculum Consultant
Palo Alto, California

RAY OLIVER
Educational Director
Capistrano Unified School District
Capistrano, California

LILLIAN RAPHAEL
Principal
Los Angeles, California

SHIRLEY ROBERTS
Community Aide
Office of Economic Opportunity
Oakland County, Michigan

FLORINE SCARBOROUGH
Assistant Superintendent
Houston, Texas

DOROTHY K. SNYDER
Director
Los Angeles Children's Center
Los Angeles, California

NANETTE SULLIVAN
Teacher
Walnut Creek, California

MARILYNN WENDT
Curriculum Assistant
Bloomfield Hills, Michigan

Grateful acknowledgement is made to the following school systems for their help in obtaining photographs: Lancaster Independent School District, Lancaster Texas; Larkspur School District, Larkspur, California; San Francisco City and County Schools, San Francisco, California; Sausalito Public Schools, Sausalito, California; Tahoe-Truckee Unified School District, Truckee, California.

ISBN 0-15-377290-5

ACKNOWLEDGMENTS

For permission to reprint copyrighted material, grateful acknowledgment is made to the following publishers: **George Braziller, Inc.:** Excerpt from *Children of the Uprooted*, edited by Oscar Handlin, copyright © 1966 by Oscar Handlin. **Holt, Rinehart and Winston, Inc.:** Excerpt from "I Am the People, the Mob" from *Chicago Poems* by Carl Sandburg, copyright 1916 by Holt, Rinehart and Winston, Inc.; copyright 1944 by Carl Sandburg. Reprinted by permission of the publishers.

PHOTOGRAPH ACKNOWLEDGMENTS

Harbrace: 1, 2 top and bottom, 10 top and bottom, 12 bottom, 17 center and bottom left, right, 26 center and bottom, 28, 29, 34 top, 37, 38 left, 39 top, 44 left, 47 bottom, 52, 53 center and bottom, 58, 61 center left, 62 top, 64 bottom, 66 top, 76 bottom, 79, 87 bottom, 88 right, 91, 97 bottom left, 111 bottom left and right, 119 left, 121, 127, 130 bottom, 132, 133 left, 135, 137, 140, 143, 151, 153 bottom left, 159, 169 right, 170 top, 173, 177, 178 top and center, 218 top, 231, 265 bottom, 274 bottom, 276, 279 center left, second from bottom right, 284, 285, 288 top and center left, center right.

Harbrace, courtesy of: American Museum of Natural History: 3 bottom, 4, 8 bottom; Boy Scouts of America: 2 center, 17 top left; East Asian Library, Columbia University: 59 bottom center; Eldon Manufacturing Company: 172; The Huffman Mfg. Co., Azusa, Calif.: 135 bottom center; Koret of California, a Koracorp Company: 158 bottom; International Market Center: 145 right; Miller Ranch, Petaluma, Calif.: 122 top center; New York University Law School: 279 second from top right; San Francisco Fire Department: 61 bottom left; San Francisco Zoological Society: 143; copyright 1939 by G. Schirmer, Inc., used by permission: 59 bottom right; Smithsonian Institution: 59 bottom right, 162 center.

Harbrace by Jacques Jangoux: 73 top and bottom left, center top, top and bottom right.

Harbrace by Erik Arnesen: 10 second from top, 12 top, 30, 32–33, 34 center and bottom, 35, 36, 38 right, 39 center and bottom, 43, 44 right, 45, 46, 47 top, 48, 49, 53 top, 54, 57, 59 top left, 60, 61 top left and right, 62 bottom, 66 bottom, 68 bottom, 77, 93, 96, 97 bottom right, 120, 133 right, 144 bottom, 153 left top and center, right, 164, 166, 169 left, 191, 224, 225, 238 top, 252, 266 left, 279 left top and bottom, right top.

Harbrace by Erik Arnesen, courtesy of: Bank of America: 163; *Honolulu Star-Bulletin:* 262 bottom; Robert H. Lowie Museum of Anthropology, University of California. 24 second from bottom and bottom; Montana Historical Society: 203; John O'Connell Vocational School: 63 top, 135 page center, and 178 bottom; San Francisco Public Library, *Frank Leslie's Illustrated:* 212, 260 left, 272; Southwest Museum: 213 top; Leland Stanford Museum, Stanford University: 253 bottom; University of Oklahoma: 250 bottom; History Room, Wells Fargo Bank: 234, 237 bottom, 238 bottom, 251; YWCA: 63 bottom; page from Hermann Zapf, *Manuale Typographicum*, Frankfurt am Main, New York, 1968: 59 bottom left.

Abbott-Henderson from Rapho-Guillumette: 80, 87 top; Acme: 268 right; American Museum of Natural History: 5, 10 second from bottom, 220 center, 221; AMNH by Grace F. Ramsey: 3 top; Annan: 107, 108 top, 288 top right; Erik Arnesen: 105 left; Bancroft Library, University of California: 217 top, 235 top right, 236, 260 right; Bill Barksdale from *The Farm Quarterly:* 122 bottom; Marc and Evelyne Bernheim from Rapho-Guillumette: 20; Dr. Block Color Productions: 81; Dr. Block Color Productions, courtesy of: Denver Art Museum, 6, William Moore, 19 top, Peabody Museum of Harvard University, 162 top; Seattle Art Museum, 209 top; Brown Brothers: 31 center, 136 bottom, 176 left, 220 bottom, 244; Michael Buntin, 135 center right; Bureau of Reclamation, National Archives: 103 top; S. D. Butcher from Denver Public Library, Western Collection: 230 bottom, 246 top left and right; California State Library: 235 center right; Patricia Caulfield from Rapho-Guillumette: 88 left; Carnegie Library of Pittsburgh: 200; Chase Manhattan Bank Money Museum: 162 center; Cook Collection, Valentine Museum: 198 bottom; Jerry Cooke from Photo Researchers: 183 center; Joe Covelle from Black Star: 64 top right; Culver: 171 bottom; Denver Public Library, Western Collection: 105 right, 206, 213 bottom, 218 right, 243 right, 273 bottom; Richard Erdoes: 210; FACSEA: 59 center; Field Museum of Natural History, Chicago: 208; Florida Development Commission: 111 top left; A. A. Forbes Collection, Division of Manuscripts, University of Oklahoma Library: 69 bottom; Harrison Forman: 16; Arnold Genthe Collection, Palace of the Legion of Honor: 230 center; Getty

Oil: 205; Louis Goldman from Rapho-Guillumette: 183 left, top right; Ted Grant from National Film Board of Canada: 289 center; Charles Harbutt from Magnum: 124; Hawaii Visitors Bureau: 25 top; Grant Heilman: 82, 101, 111 center left, 241 top, 243 top left; Holland Tulip Time Festival, Inc.: 265 top; George Honeycutt from Gilloon Photo Agency: 264; © 1956, 1963 by Langston Hughes and Milton Meltzer, *A Pictorial History of the Negro in America*, Crown: 176 right; Indiana State Library: 179; Israel Consulate General: 183 top center, bottom center; Japan Air Lines: 73 center left, middle, right, and center bottom; Regina Kane: 218 center left, 243 bottom left; Kern County Museum: 184–185; Paul Knipping: 41; John Launois from Black Star: 288 center top, page center, bottom left, bottom right; Library of Congress: 103 center, 115 bottom, 130 top, 180, 255 right, 268 top left; Los Angeles County Museum, History Division: 235 left; Lowie Museum of Anthropology, University of California: 59 top right; Ray Manley from Shostal: 126; Steve and Dolores McCutcheon: 259 top; Metropolitan Museum, Gift of John S. Kennedy, 1897: 197; bequest of Grace Wilkes, 1922: 22; Roger Meyers for the Oklahoma Historical Society: 207; David Muench: 90; Josef Muench: 85, 259 bottom, 261; Museum of Fine Arts, Boston, George Nixon Black Fund: 199; Museum of New Mexico: 220 top; National Archives: 275; National Gallery of Art, lent by Peter Jay: 204 top left; *National Geographic* photographer, George F. Mobley, courtesy U.S. Capital Historical Society: 270 top, 196; National Portrait Gallery, Smithsonian Institution: 204 bottom left; Naval Photographic Center, Dwight D. Eisenhower Library: 270 center; Nebraska State Historical Society: 103 bottom; New Haven Redevelopment Agency: 144 top and center; New York Historical Society: 237 top, 267; North American Rockwell Corp.: 175; Oklahoma Historical Society: 104 and 246 bottom; A. Paladini, Inc.: 146; Pan Am: 149; Peace Corps: 174; Providence Public Library: 198 top; Rare Books Division, New York Public Library: 189 bottom, 190; Republican Congressional photograph: 271; G. R. Roberts: 158 top, 243 center left, 288 center; Irving Rosen from Shostal: 24 top; David Rubinger from Black Star: 183 bottom right; Joe Rychetnik: 263; Kurt Scholz from Shostal, 100, W. Ray Scott from Shostal, 125 left; Marilyn Silverstone from Magnum: 183 right center; Soil Conservation Service: 76 top, 78, 84; Soil Conservation Service from USDA: 115 top, 118 bottom; Sovfoto: 68 top; R. Burton Stratton: 188; Kryn Taconis from National Film Board of Canada: 289 top and bottom; Texas Highway Department: 145 bottom left; Title Insurance & Trust Company: 235 bottom; Tom Tracy: 18, 25 bottom, 24 second from top, 94 bottom, 108 bottom, 112, 116 top, 117, 118 center, 145 top and center left, 152 bottom; UPI: 26 top, 27, 31 bottom, 128–29, 138, 204 right, 262, 268 top right, center left, 270 bottom, 274 top; U.N.: 226, 268 bottom; Union Pacific Railroad: 254 bottom, 255 left, 256; USDA: 74–75, 76 center, 83, 116 bottom, 118 top, 119 right, 130 center, 248; U.S. Dept. of Commerce, Environmental Science Services Administration, Coast and Geodetic Survey: 92; U.S. Signal Corps, National Archives: 258 bottom, 273 top and center; Vermont Development Department: 170 bottom; Weather Bureau, National Archives: 257; Wide World Photos: 31 top; Elizabeth Wilcox: 14, 19 bottom; Wine Institute, courtesy of History Division, Oakland Museum: 230 top; Wolfe Worldwide Films, Los Angeles, California: 218 bottom left.

ART CREDITS

Mel Bolden: 9, 56 bottom, 102, 217 bottom, 240 left, 217; Gordon Brusstar: 51, 99, 100; Joseph Giordano: 228–29; Graphic Arts International from *The World Book Encyclopedia*, © 1968, Field Enterprises Educational Corporation: 67; Graphic Arts International: 7, 42, 69, 79, 91, 141, 142, 161 left, 165, 192 left, 201 left, 215 left, 216, 286, 291; Richard Harvey: 71, 181, 276; Robert Haydock: 154, 155, 192 left, 290; Norman Nicholson: 186, 244; Tom Quinn: 8, 11, 209 bottom, 250–51; James Sanford: 245; Hank Stallworth: 136; Portia Takakjian: 171, 189; Albert Pucci: 281, Table of Contents vi, vii, viii, Section Heads 3, 14, 22, 35, 41, 50, 56, 77, 86, 98, 107, 114, 131, 139, 151, 161, 169, 171, 187, 194, 201, 207, 215, 231, 240, 249, 257, 264, 282.

MAP CREDITS

Harbrace: 15, 23, 72, 89, 94, 97, 110, 114, 125, 152, 156–57, 182, 187, 195, 197, 202, 211, 219, 241, 254, 258, 292–93, 294–95; George Buctel: 123, 147, 283, 287, 296–97; Graphic Arts International: 232, 233.

Cover photographs: Front: Grant Heilman; Back: Santa Fe Trail Assoc., Great Bend, Kansas, photograph from USDA.

Title page art: Albert Pucci.

Title page photograph: Library of Congress, photograph from Minnesota Historical Society.

CONTENTS

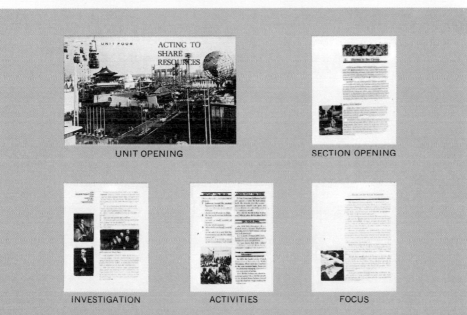

UNIT OPENING

SECTION OPENING

INVESTIGATION

ACTIVITIES

FOCUS

UNIT ONE

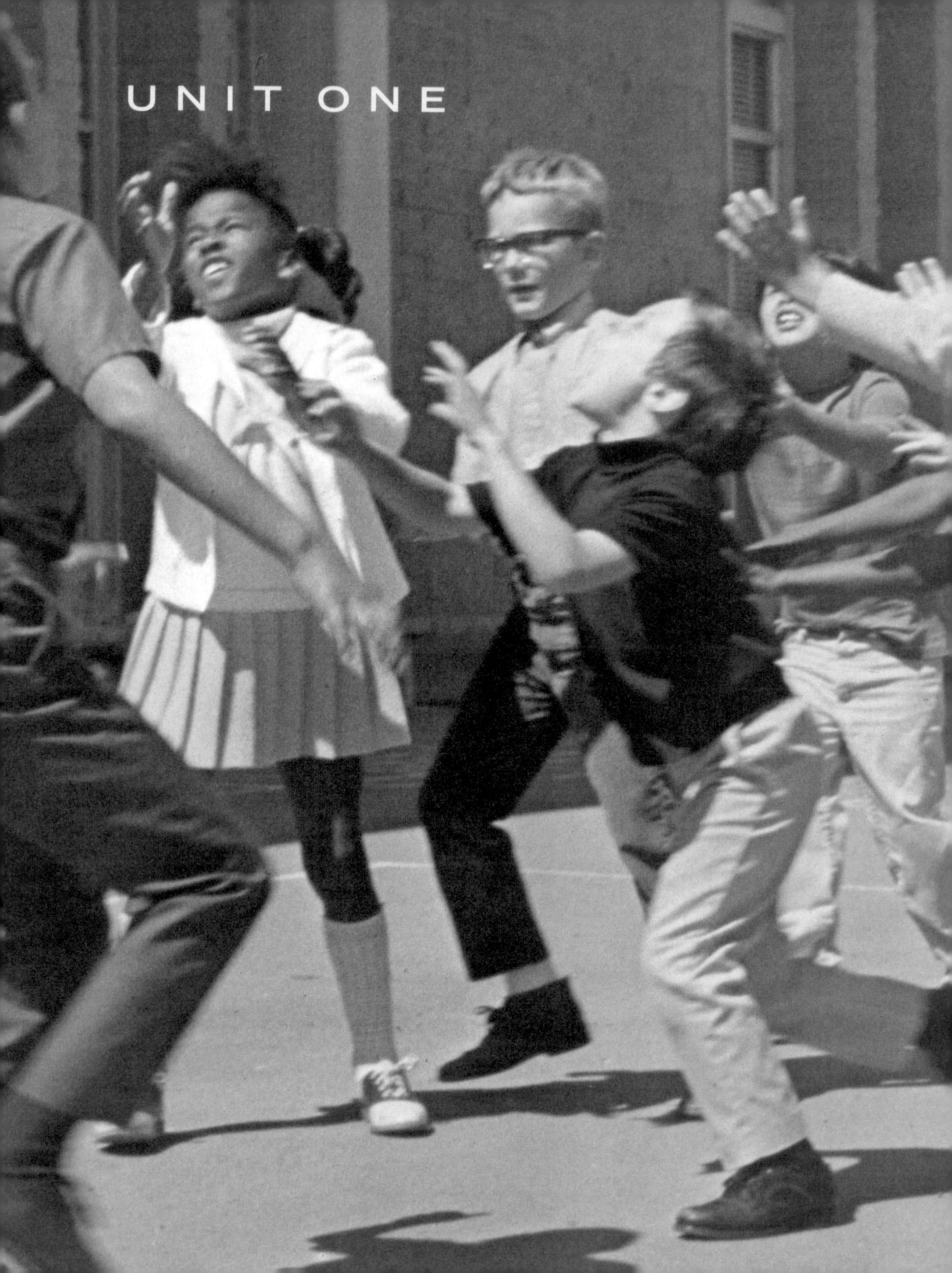

ACTING IN A GROUP

Introduction

Look at the pictures. ● What are the people in each picture doing? Do you do any of these things?

Look at the pictures again. Do you think the people in each picture came together by accident? Did they come together with a purpose in mind? How do you know?

The people in the pictures are doing different things. All the pictures are alike in one way, however. Each picture shows people in a group.

Everyone belongs to groups. To what groups do you belong? You belong to a family group and a school group. Of course, you belong to play groups, too. Maybe you are a Scout or a member of a baseball team.

Why do people belong to groups? How do people in groups act? In this unit, you will find the answers to these questions. You will study groups and the ways in which all groups are alike.

You will begin your study on the opposite page. There, you will begin to read about one group: a Blackfoot Indian tribe.

1.   The Blackfeet

Where is the upper Missouri River? Find it on the map on pages 296-297. Why is it called "upper"?

In the 1600's and 1700's, there were many buffalo in the region near the upper Missouri River. Long ago, this region had become the hunting grounds of the Blackfoot Indians, who followed the buffalo.

In their travels after buffalo, the Blackfoot Indians ranged all the way from Canada into the American Great Plains. When they found places with enough food and water, the Blackfeet set up villages. The Blackfoot women made tepees (tē'pēz) like these from animal skins. ● (See the picture marked with a dot.) The tepees were held up by strong poles. The women also used these poles to make drags, which held the families' belongings as they traveled. ▲

From the buffalo came almost everything the Blackfeet needed in order to live. The women used buffalo hides to make clothing and tepees. The Blackfeet ate buffalo meat. They burned buffalo fat in bowls for light.

HUNTERS AND WARRIORS

Making tepees and drags was part of a Blackfoot woman's **role**. Roles are the way certain people are expected to act in a group. A Blackfoot woman was expected to make tepees and drags, just as she was expected to clean and cook buffalo meat. All these activities were part of the role of a woman in the Blackfoot **culture**. Culture means all the ways of believing and acting that people in a group have. The Blackfoot woman had her role. You have roles in your culture, too. One of them is that of a pupil in class. What is expected of you in the role of a pupil?

Hunting was part of the role of a Blackfoot man. In the early days—perhaps for thousands of years before they saw the European explorers—the Blackfeet hunted buffalo on foot. Sometimes the Blackfoot men surrounded a herd and drove the buffalo over a cliff. ● Then they climbed down the cliff to get the animals. At other times, the hunters built a pen and drove the buffalo into it. Then they shot the buffalo with bows and arrows.

Sometime before 1750, the Blackfeet learned about horses and guns. The first European explorers had brought these animals and tools with them to America. Horses and guns changed the Blackfeet's way of hunting. On horseback, the Blackfeet could travel farther than they could on foot. With guns, they could shoot the buffalo from a distance.

The Blackfeet valued horses and guns. They went on raiding parties against other Plains Indians to get more horses and guns. So, in order to be a good hunter, a Blackfoot had to learn the role of warrior, too.

Each Blackfoot warrior expected himself to be brave. And, he expected other members of the group—other warriors—to be brave, too. People in a group expect themselves and other members of the group to behave in certain ways. These expected ways of behaving are called **norms of behavior**. Bravery was a norm of behavior for the Blackfoot warrior.

Boasting was another norm of behavior for the Blackfoot warrior. The warrior was expected to count coup (ko͞o), that is, to brag about how many horses he had captured or how many of the enemy tribe he had touched. Touching an enemy was a greater deed than killing him. The Blackfoot warrior painted his deeds on his tepee and his buffalo robe. ▲ These paintings were a record. We still use them today to learn about his life.

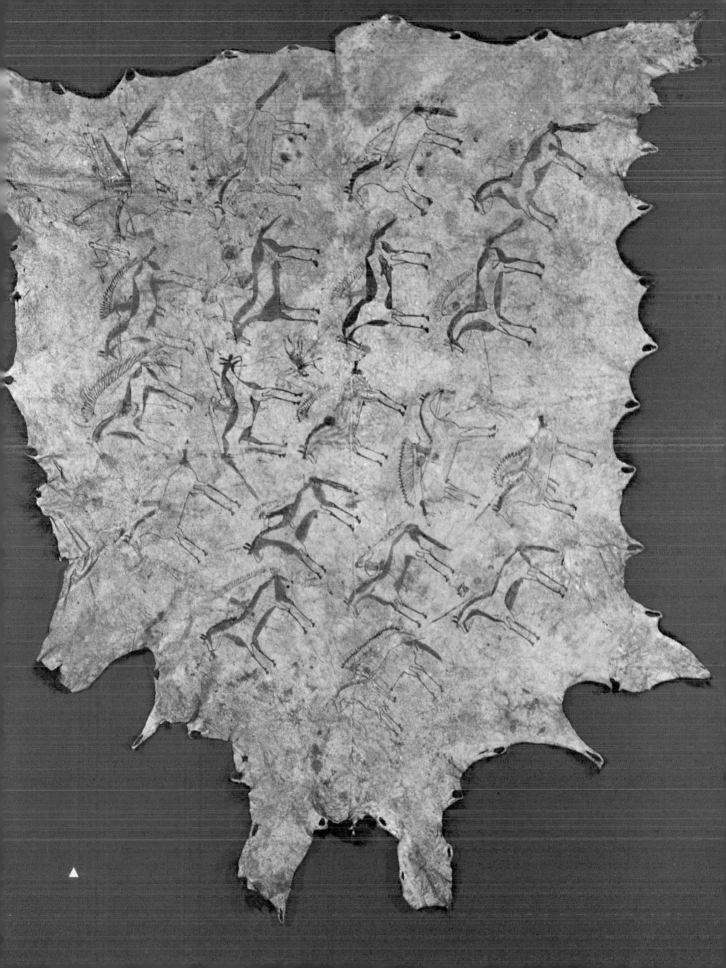

As a hunter, the Blackfoot man was expected to share his food with the very old, with the young, or with those who had been unlucky in the day's hunt. Sharing was another norm of behavior for Blackfoot men.

One kind of social scientist is a **sociologist** (sō'sē·ol'ə·jist). He studies how people behave in groups. A sociologist uses norms to describe how people are expected to behave in their roles. For example, a Blackfoot woman did not have the role of a warrior. So, she didn't have the norms of behavior of a warrior. And a warrior didn't have the norms of behavior of a Blackfoot woman.

WITHIN EACH TRIBE

A **society** (sə·sī'ə·tē) is the largest group to which people belong. Within a society, they share their way of life. Of what society are you a member?

Societies are made up of smaller groups. Sometimes these groups are called **communities**. The Blackfoot society was made up of three **tribes**. Each tribe lived apart from the others.

Each of the three Blackfoot tribes was made up of smaller communities called **bands**. Bands had from one hundred fifty to eight hundred people in them. Each band had a name, such as Liars, Biters, or Early Finished Eating. Study the chart. ● It shows how the Blackfeet were set up. What is the difference between a tribe and a band?

Some Blackfoot men were famous for their hunting skills and for their courage in war. They were also especially generous with food and horses. These men often became **leaders** of their band. The older Blackfoot leaders had a special role. They kept order within a band. They helped to solve quarrels. These older leaders also decided where and when a band should move.

These dolls, made by modern Blackfeet, are dressed like the Blackfoot Indians of long ago. The dolls' bodies are made of cloth. Their clothing is made from animal skins which have been decorated with beads.

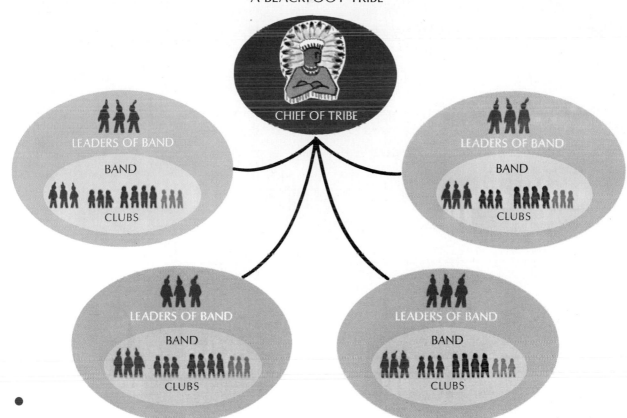

A BLACKFOOT TRIBE

CHIEF OF TRIBE

LEADERS OF BAND

BAND

CLUBS

LEADERS OF BAND

BAND

CLUBS

LEADERS OF BAND

BAND

CLUBS

LEADERS OF BAND

BAND

CLUBS

There was one man who was the leader of all the bands. He was the chief of a Blackfoot tribe. In the summer, all the bands of a tribe came together to make a camp for the great buffalo hunt. Then the chief chose the place for the camp. He also made rules for everyone. All members of the tribe had to obey him. If they didn't, they were punished.

THE SUMMER HUNT

At the summer camp, the members of the tribe placed all their tepees in one great circle. In the circle, there was an open space at the east side. The door of each tepee also faced east toward the rising sun. The horses were kept in the center of the circle.

The chief and the leaders of the bands planned the great buffalo hunt. One of the rules was that no man might hunt the buffalo alone.

On the day of the hunt, the hunters rode quietly to within shooting distance of the buffalo herd. They formed a great half-circle and waited for the signal from the chief. ● Everyone was silent. No one moved. As soon as the chief gave the signal, the hunters swooped down on the herd. They shot as many buffalo as they could before the herd scattered in all directions.

Later, the women prepared the buffalo. Recall that this work was part of the Blackfoot woman's role. If a woman's husband had shot no animals, she helped other women. For her help, she was given meat for her own family. Recall that sharing was a norm of behavior for the Blackfeet. No one was allowed to go hungry.

WITHIN THE BAND

Like other groups, the Blackfeet had special **customs**. Customs are habits followed by most members of a group. They are ways that people in a group have done things for years and years.

One Blackfoot custom was to live in tepees. Another was to ride ponies. You have customs in the groups to which you belong, too. For example, you probably have the custom of riding in automobiles or in buses. Did the Blackfeet have these customs? Your customs were learned at home and at school—both of which are part of your community.

Each Blackfoot boy and girl learned his role. He learned norms of behavior—the ways that he was expected to behave in his role. He learned the customs of his tribe, too. Where did the boys and girls learn these customs? Look back at the chart on page 7. It shows how a Blackfoot tribe was set up. Notice that each band was made up of smaller groups called clubs. Each member of a tribe belonged to a club.

The women and girls usually had just one club. Members of this club made the tepees and decorated hides with beadwork. ▲ They also did other work that was part of the Blackfoot woman's role. The girls learned from the women.

In becoming members of a club, the Blackfoot boys and girls learned some of the customs of their tribe. They learned, for example, all the customs that made up the summer hunt.

One Blackfoot custom was to sing songs at special times. In the clubs, Blackfoot boys learned some of these songs. They might sing one song as they rode off on a raid and another when they came home again. The members of a club might sing a song to say "good night" to each other.

The Blackfoot boys passed through one club after another, just as you might go through grades in school. They belonged to different clubs at different ages. For example, one club might be made up of boys six to nine years old. In one band, the first club the boys could join was called the Pigeons. In another band, the first club was called the Rabbits.

There were no tests to pass in moving to a new club. Each group of boys bought its new rights from

▲

You sing songs at special times, too. Do you sing songs at Christmastime?

Copy the two columns below on a piece of paper. Leave a good amount of space between the columns.

Discuss the role of each person listed in the first column. Then choose from the second column the norms each person follows. List the correct norms after each person.

PERSONS	NORMS
Blackfoot woman	promptness
you, as a child in a family	neatness
you, as a softball player ●	courage
housewife in your community ▲	speed
Blackfoot warrior ■	obedience
Blackfoot boy	sharing
telephone operator ⋈	boasting
Blackfoot chief	patience

Do people in your community have any norms of behavior that are like those of the Blackfeet? Which norms?

Are the roles of the Blackfeet and the roles of people in your community the same?

A Problem on Your Own

How are the roles in a Blackfoot family like the roles in your family? How are they different? The Blackfoot man had the role of a food-getter. Hunting was the way he got food for his family. Does your father hunt for food? Does he have the role of food-getter?

The Blackfoot woman cooked buffalo meat and made tepees out of hides. Does your mother cook and sew, too? Does she have the role of home-maker?

Roles may be the same for many people. How may norms of behavior be different when roles are the same? Name three ways.

●

▲

■

⋈

the group above it. The boys traded horses, hides, and
beads for the special costumes, songs, and dances that
belonged to the club into which they were moving. ●

In the clubs, the Blackfoot boys and girls also
learned about their roles. That is, they learned *what*
they were expected to do. They also learned *how* they
were expected to act. In other words, they learned the
norms of behavior of their roles.

Take a closer look at norms of behavior. Try the
investigation on the opposite page.

A GROUP FOR EVERYONE

In a Blackfoot community, everyone belonged to
a group within the community. There were clubs not
only for the young, but for people of all ages. No member could be put out of a club, although he could
choose to leave it. A group of men might decide to form
a new club. Sometimes a club was formed because
one man had a new song which gave great power to
those who sang it. He wished to share the song with his
close friends, so that they could sing it as they rode out
together on a raid.

There are many smaller groups within your community, too. To begin with, there are family groups. Then, there are school groups, work groups, and play groups. ● In each group, members learn their roles. In each group, members discover the norms of behavior followed by people in the group. In groups, we learn *what* we are expected to do and *how* we are expected to act as we do it.

━━━━━ **AT THIS POINT IN YOUR STUDY** ━━━━━

Do these statements seem correct?

1 All people have roles in the groups to which they belong.

You have the role of child in your family. What are the roles of other people in your family group?

2 In each role, people are expected to follow certain norms of behavior.

Bravery was a norm of behavior for a Blackfoot warrior. Bravery is also a norm of behavior for a fireman. ▲

What norms of behavior are there for the role of a policeman in your community?

What norms of behavior do you have in your role as a student? For example, is every boy and girl expected to be polite in a classroom? State at least two more norms.

Choose the ending for each of these sentences.

1   The Blackfeet found that the way to get the most buffalo for everyone was
    (a) to let every man try to kill one buffalo
    (b) to choose a leader and work together
2   In a group, a person learns
    (a) the cultural traits of the community
    (b) whichever cultural traits he chooses
3   Norms of behavior for a role are different
    (a) within a group
    (b) from group to group

USING WHAT YOU KNOW

1   Why did a Blackfoot boy become a warrior? Where did he learn the skills needed for raiding and hunting? Where did he learn what to do in the great buffalo hunt?
2   Name people in your community who do these things as part of their roles:

get food   prepare food

build shelters   teach children

make clothes   provide
                    entertainment

ON YOUR OWN

Find the word **environment** in your Social Science Dictionary.

1   Describe the environment of the Blackfeet.
2   Tell three ways in which the environment of the Blackfeet was like your environment. Tell three ways in which it was different.
3   Is courage a norm of behavior in your environment? Explain your answer.

IN TRANSIT

The Blackfeet passed their cultural traits, or customs, on to the young boys and girls. When they grew up, boys were expected to be hunters. They were also expected to be warriors. Boys in the Blackfoot culture learned their roles. Girls also were expected to learn the role that they would have as women.

The groups from which the Blackfoot boys and girls learned most were the clubs. In the clubs, they learned their roles. They learned norms of behavior for their roles, too.

What about boys and girls in communities that do not have clubs like these? To what groups do they belong? How are all groups alike? How may groups be different? To find out, turn to the next section.

2. Sharing in the Group

Think of Ikechukwu (ik′ə·chuk′wä) as a boy about your age. ● Ikechukwu is very much like many boys who live in the city of Lagos. Like many families in that area, his family belongs to the Yoruba (yō′rŏo·bä) tribe. Lagos (lä′gōs) is the capital of Nigeria. ▲ Nigeria is a country in Africa. ■

Ikechukwu's favorite game is soccer. In fact, soccer is a favorite game in Nigeria, just as baseball is a favorite game in the United States. Ikechukwu learned to play soccer at school. He is a goalkeeper for the school team. There are other boys who are also goalkeepers, so Ikechukwu doesn't always get to play. But whenever there is a match, he will try either to play or to watch. In either case, he is a member of the team.

WHAT IS A GROUP?

Like the other members of the soccer team, Ikechukwu knows many things about the group. For one thing, he knows the group's purpose. A purpose is sometimes called a **goal**. What is the goal, or purpose, of a soccer team?

Ikechukwu also knows that the members of the team depend on each other. In other words, they are **interdependent**. The soccer team is a group with many members. A group, of course, may have as few as two members. But whether the group is large or small, the members can reach their goal only if they can depend on each other.

A F R I C A

Ikechukwu knows that the members of the team **interact**. "Inter-" means "among" or "between." Interact, then, means "act among each other." It means more than that. It means that what each member of the team does affects, or changes, the other members—for better or worse! Interaction changes the way each member acts. Each member must change the way he acts if the other members do.

Ikechukwu's team is one example of a **group**. Sociologists say that all groups have these things in common:

First, they have a purpose, or **goal**—in this case, to play soccer. What purpose does a school band have?

Second, the members of a group **interact**. They act together. They change the way the other members act. What would happen if one boy on the soccer team tried to win the game all by himself? Does the way the drummer acts change the other players in a band?

Third, the members of a group depend on each other. That is, they are **interdependent**. In a soccer game, what would happen if one boy had the ball and threw it away? In a band, what would happen if one member didn't follow the leader?

NIGERIA

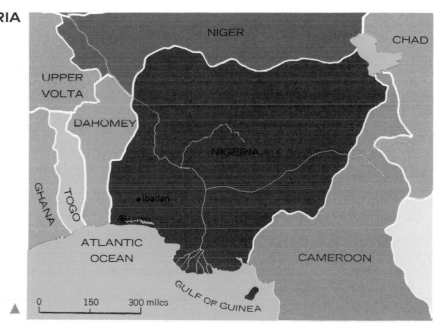

Fourth, the members of a group **share meanings**. In Ikechukwu's group, for instance, all the members know that good sportsmanship is a norm of behavior for the team. All the members know that the purpose of the team is to play soccer. The members of the team may not talk about the meanings they share. They may just take them for granted.

To learn more about groups, try the investigation on the opposite page.

IKECHUKWU'S GROUP

Ikechukwu's friends on the soccer team think of themselves as part of a group. The members of the team understand what it means to belong to this group. Each of them belongs to the team because he wants to play soccer. As team members, they all know how to act. They want to win, but they expect to lose sometimes.

The members of the team expect each other to behave in certain ways. They have certain norms of behavior. What are some of the things which are expected? One of them is good sportsmanship. They expect each other to lose well, without complaining, or to win well, without bragging. What other things do they expect of each other?

What is a **role**? If you do not remember, turn to page 3 or to your Social Science Dictionary at the back of the book.

Each team member knows what the other members' roles are, too. Like all games, soccer has rules. One boy is a goalkeeper, but he knows what positions the other boys play. He knows how each player will behave during the game. Among other things, he expects that his teammates will kick the ball or block it with their bodies or their heads. ● They expect him to guard the goal by using his hands or forearms or any part of his body. ▲ The goalkeeper is the only one who may touch the ball with his hands or arms. Of course, not all the roles in the group are alike. In your classroom, does everyone have exactly the same role?

AN INVESTIGATION into groups

Sociologists say that people are a group if:

1   They share a purpose.
2   They interact with each other.
3   They are interdependent.
4   They share certain meanings.

Perhaps, like Ikechukwu, you are a member of a team or a club. ● You are a member of many groups. One group is your class. ▲ Another is your family. ■

Choose a team or a club or another group to which you belong. For the group you choose, answer these questions:

1   What is the purpose of the group?
2   How do the members of the group interact?
3   Name at least two ways in which members of the group depend on each other.
4   Do they share norms of behavior? Do they value the same things?

A Problem on Your Own

What are some differences between a group and a crowd? Which of the following are groups? Which are crowds? ▻

      people attending a PTA meeting
      people at an art gallery
      people watching a movie
      a band marching in a parade

●

▲

■

▻◅

●

●

Are all these roles the same? How can you tell? Will the members of these groups have to depend on each other? ●

There are some norms which Ikechukwu's whole team shares. As you have learned, good sportsmanship is one of these. Another norm of behavior for the whole team is effort. The members expect each other to try very hard to make points for the team and to play with as much skill as possible. Still another norm is fairness. Ikechukwu's team tries very hard to win, but the members of the team will not cheat in order to win.

The team members think alike about these norms. They agree to them. If a member of the team does not try to live up to the norm, then he usually suffers some sort of penalty. If a team member does not try hard, his teammates may yell at him. Or they may not speak to him at all after the game is over. If a team member cheats in a game, the captain and the other members may decide not to let him play in the next game.

Most groups have some control over the way the members act. Groups punish or reward behavior. If a group member does not behave the way people expect, he may be punished in some way. Of course, if

18

he does behave the way people expect, he may be rewarded. How are you rewarded or punished in your family? How are you rewarded or punished in school?

IKECHUKWU AND OTHER GROUPS

Besides the soccer team, Ikechukwu belongs to a family group. He also belongs to the group which is made up of his classmates. ● He belongs to a church group and to a play group. He also belongs to the group which is his tribe, the Yoruba tribe. He is a member of an even larger group — the group which is his society — Nigeria.

Will Ikechukwu always be a member of the same groups? Ikechukwu will not always be a member of the group called students. That is a group he will outgrow, just as a Blackfoot boy outgrew the group called Rabbits. Ikechukwu may decide to be a member of one soccer team or another for many years. Or he may lose interest in the game and decide not to play anymore.

This vessel was made by members of the Yoruban tribe. It stands twenty-one inches high and is made of polychrome wood.

●

As he grows older, Ikechukwu will have other choices to make. He may decide to become a doctor or a storekeeper. In either one of these groups, he would learn a new role and new norms of behavior.

Someday, Ikechukwu will probably become a husband and father. Then he will be part of a new group—his own family. His role in the family will be quite different from what it is now, that of a child.

Ikechukwu may always be a member of the Yoruba tribe. Because he loves his country, Ikechukwu probably will choose to be a citizen of Nigeria all his life. ● But, if he chose, he could leave this group and become part of another society, another nation.

Ikechukwu will belong to many groups. In each group, he will learn to perform certain roles. He will learn to follow certain norms of behavior. In each group, he will work with people who share meanings and who work toward goals. Ikechukwu will always depend on other people, and other people will always depend on him.

▬▬▬▬▬▬▬ **AT THIS POINT IN YOUR STUDY** ▬▬▬▬▬▬▬

Do these statements seem correct?

1   All people belong to one or more groups.

Do you know any person who is not a member of a group? How do you know he is not?

2   In every group, the members share a purpose, interact with each other, depend on each other, and share meanings.

Do you know of any groups for which these four things are not true? Name one.

3   Members of a group do not always act exactly according to the norms of behavior of the group.

Tell about a time when you did not do what was expected of you. Were you punished?

Tell about a time when you did more than was expected. Was there a reward?

Choose the ending for each of these sentences.

1 A person may belong to
    (a) only one group at a time
    (b) many groups at once
2 Members of a group
    (a) agree on the group's goal
    (b) agree on everything
3 Group members depend on each other
    (a) to make new norms
    (b) to perform their roles

USING WHAT YOU KNOW

1 Mary is known as a "clown." This is her role within the group of boys and girls who go to school on the same bus. How do the other members of her group expect her to act? Can Mary change her role in the group? How?
2 A Blackfoot hunter was punished if he made any noise before the chief gave the signal to shoot at the buffalo herd. He would also be punished if he went up to the herd before the rest of the tribe was ready. Why was a hunter punished if he did these things?
3 (a) Three strangers traveling in the middle of the night in separate cars are stopped by large rocks which block their way. All three get out of their cars. Are they now a group?
    (b) Together, the three people decide to clear the road. One man finds a shovel and flashlight in the trunk in his car. He holds the flashlight. The others remove the rocks. When did the men become a group?
    (c) The road is cleared, and each man drives on in his own car. Are the men still a group?

ON YOUR OWN

1 List all the groups to which you belong. Think about your role in each group. Do you have different roles in each group? How many different roles do you have?
2 Most families have two parents, a father and a mother. Sometimes the family is made up of a mother and one or more children. Sometimes an aunt lives with them. Is the family still a group? Why?

IN TRANSIT

You have studied two groups—a Blackfoot tribe and Ikechukwu's team. One role is alike in both of these groups. It is the role of the leader. To learn more about leaders, turn to the next section.

3. The Leader of the Group

"First in war, first in peace, first in the hearts of his countrymen." This was said about George Washington. ● He was a general who led the Revolutionary army. He was also the first President of the United States. Notice the word "first." Why is every leader "first" in some way? As general, what group did Washington lead? As President, what group did he lead?

Some of the men who were trying to form the new nation asked George Washington to be its first king. He refused. He did not want to carry on the custom of having kings. If he was to lead, he wanted to be **elected**. That is, he wanted to be chosen by the people. And Washington believed that the people should be able to choose another leader if he failed to live up to what they expected of him.

However, some parts of what is now the United States were once ruled by kings. Kings of England ruled the thirteen colonies in America before the Revolutionary War. Russia owned Alaska until 1867, and so Alaska was ruled by the czar, or leader, of Russia. The state of Hawaii, too, was ruled by its own line of kings.

Are there any likenesses between leadership by a king and leadership by someone who has been elected? We can begin to find out by studying a group led by a king.

NEPHEW OF A KING

Kamehameha (kä·mā′hä·mä′hä) was the nephew of the king of the island of Hawaii. At the time Kameha-

What is a **custom**? If you do not remember, turn to page 8 or to your Social Science Dictionary at the back of the book.

meha was born, there were several kings in the Hawaiian Islands. ● Some kings, like Kamehameha's uncle, ruled over a whole island, while others ruled over parts of islands.

Like all the kings in the islands, Kamehameha's uncle had many followers called chiefs. These chiefs were wealthy landowners who had many men working and living on their land. Each worker gave part of what he grew to his chief. And each chief gave part of what he got to his king. So, the kings in the Hawaiian Islands were very wealthy.

When Kamehameha was a boy, he went to live with his uncle. He helped his uncle fight the king of the island of Maui. The kings of Hawaii often fought each other. The king who won would take all the land of the defeated king. Then he would divide the land among his own chiefs.

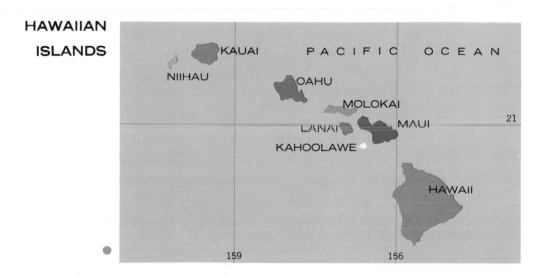

HAWAIIAN ISLANDS

KAUAI   PACIFIC   OCEAN
NIIHAU
OAHU
MOLOKAI
LANAI   MAUI   21
KAHOOLAWE
HAWAII
159   156

After some years, Kamehameha's uncle grew deathly ill. He called a council of his chiefs so that he could tell the name of the next king. According to the custom of the island, the king of Hawaii could give the kingship to anyone in the family. He could give it to his oldest son, to his brother, or to his nephew. However, the king chose to make his son the next king.

When the old king died, the new king took over all his lands. ● According to the custom, he divided these lands among the chiefs who were closest to him. He took some land away from Kamehameha and other chiefs. Of course, the chiefs whose lands were taken away became angry.

Kamehameha led the angry chiefs who had lost land into battle against the new king. These chiefs had a goal—to regain their lost land. Kamehameha was able to form them into a group so that they could work well together. A leader of any group must be able to help the members work together to reach their goals.

When the battle was over, Kamehameha and his friends had won a large part of the island. After many battles, Kamehameha defeated the young king and ruled the whole island of Hawaii.

Like all groups, the people of the island had customs that they followed in their day-to-day activities. There were rules about the building and use of canoes. ▲ People who did not obey the laws were usually punished. In your community, is a person who drives over the speed limit punished?

Because he was the leader of the group, Kamehameha had **authority** (ə·thôr′ə·tē). That is, he had the right to make certain decisions for the group. With this authority, Kamehameha could punish or pardon those who did not obey the rules.

Many of these rules had to do with the king himself. One Hawaiian rule was that a king could not be touched by anyone except a member of his family or another king. No one else could let even his shadow touch the king. The punishment for not following this rule might even be death. Another rule was that, when a king passed, the people near him had to fall to the ground and hide their faces. No one could look at him.

KAMEHAMEHA AND OTHER LEADERS

As a leader, Kamehameha was like other leaders in two important ways. First, he was able to help his followers work well together to reach their goals. Second, he had authority to make certain kinds of decisions for the group.

Through the years, Kamehameha defeated other chiefs and kings, too, until he ruled all the Hawaiian Islands. He lived to be over ninety years old. After his death, his son became king and called himself Kamehameha II. He became Hawaii's new leader.

Of course, Hawaii has no kings today. But the Hawaiian people remember Kamehameha. On holidays, a man dresses like Kamehameha and plays his role. ● The Hawaiians have also built statues of this great king. ▲

What kind of leaders does Hawaii have today? To find out, try the investigation on the next page.

▲

AT THIS POINT IN YOUR STUDY

Do these statements seem correct?

1   Groups have leaders.

Did the Blackfeet have leaders? Who were they?

Does Ikechukwu's soccer team have a leader? What does the leader do?

Who is the leader of a group to which you belong?

2   Leaders help the group take action together.

What action did Kamehameha help his followers take?

What action did a Blackfoot chief help his followers take?

3   Leaders have some kind of authority.

What authority did a Blackfoot chief have?

What authority does your teacher have? Which group does he or she lead? What action does your teacher help you take?

AN
INVESTIGATION
into
leaders

Those of you who do not live in Hawaii should try to do the first investigation. Those of you who live in Hawaii may already know the answers to it. If this is so, try the second investigation. Of course, all of you may want to do both.

A 1 What happened to the line of kings started by Kamehameha?

2 Can you name some of the people who are Hawaii's leaders today?

3 How did they become the leaders of Hawaii?

4 What is the difference between the way Kamehameha II was chosen and the way the leaders of Hawaii are chosen today? ●

B Make a chart with three columns on a piece of paper. In the first column of the chart, list the names of people who are leaders in the following groups:

> a leader of a sports team
> a school leader ▲
> a leader in your community ■
> a leader in your state ●
> a leader in the nation

In the second column of the chart, list one goal of the group led by each person.

In the third column of the chart, describe an action that each leader helped his group to take.

Where will you get the information to make the chart?

A Problem on Your Own

Today, there are not as many kings in the world as there were once. Can you explain why this is so? How have values changed since the time when there were many kings?

BEFORE YOU GO ON

Choose the ending for each of these sentences.

1 Leaders help a group to
   (a) reach a goal
   (b) do without a goal
2 Leaders have the authority to
   (a) decide only for themselves
   (b) make certain decisions for a group
3 A leader most often tries to see that people follow
   (a) the rules of the group
   (b) only his own ideas

USING WHAT YOU KNOW

1 How is the President of the United States chosen? How are the governors of the states chosen?

   In what way are these leaders like Kamehameha?
2 Write a paragraph on the topic, "The Role of a Leader."

ON YOUR OWN

1 A **hypothesis** (hi·poth′ə·sis) is an "educated guess" based on what a scientist has already observed. It is an explanation that a scientist forms before he rolls up his sleeves and goes to work to find out whether it is true. Some sociologists have made this hypothesis: Leaders have more energy than most people do. Why might leaders need this trait? How could you test this hypothesis?

2 You have studied the roles of leaders in different communities. For example, you have studied Blackfoot chiefs and King Kamehameha. Here is a picture of Mayor Carl Stokes when he was sworn in as mayor of Cleveland, Ohio. ● He is a leader in his community. Why do you think communities have their own leaders? Could the President and other national leaders do the work of community leaders? Why or why not?

You know that you learn from other people. In school, you learn the many things that men have discovered throughout history. Suppose that you had to discover everything for yourself. Would you make much progress?

But you learn more than facts from other people. You learn your ways of acting. Ever since you were born, you have been a member of different groups. Your family is one group. Your school is another. What language you speak depends on the group to which you belong. (If you were born in France, what language would you speak?) The kind of home you live in and the roles you learn also depend on the groups to which you belong.

As children, the Blackfeet also learned roles. They learned how to act in their roles — to ride horses and to sew buffalo hides. Nigerian boys and girls learn the roles expected of them. They learn customs from many groups to which they belong. ● Thus, we may make a statement about our concept, or idea, of **group: Members of a group learn the customs of the group.**

People learn customs from groups. They also learn how they are expected to behave. Among the Blackfeet, sharing food was a norm of behavior. Following the rules is a norm of behavior for all members of Ikechukwu's soccer team. We may, then, make another statement about the concept of **group: Members of a group share certain norms of behavior.**

Traits of Groups

One kind of social scientist, the sociologist, studies people's behavior in groups. Sociologists have found that all groups have certain likenesses. You have seen examples of these likenesses in each group you have studied in this unit. There are different roles in a group that fit together to make a family, a tribe, a club, or a team. We can make this statement about the concept of **group: A group is made up of people who interact and are interdependent. It is made up of people who share meanings and a purpose.**

Leaders of Groups

One role that seems part of every group is the role of leader. ● What are the likenesses among leaders? What does a leader do? You have studied different leaders—a Hawaiian king and a Blackfoot chief.

Each leader played a similar, or like, role in his group. Each leader had the authority to make certain decisions for the group. He could reward those who acted well, that is, those who acted according to the norms of behavior in the group. For example, a Hawaiian chief could give land to the warriors who had helped him. You saw that a leader also had authority to punish any person who did not follow the customs or rules of the group. For example, a Blackfoot chief could punish hunters who didn't obey during the buffalo hunt.

You have studied, then, evidence for this statement about the concept of **group: A leader uses his authority to see that the customs of a group are obeyed.** He helps the members of a group to work well together. A leader also helps members of a group to reach the group's goals.

When a human being is born, he does not know how to behave toward other people. He must learn how to behave. He learns from the people around him. There is, then, evidence for this important statement about the concept of **group: A person's social behavior is learned from the groups of which he is a part.**

AN ANALYSIS OF VALUES

You have learned that members of a group share certain meanings. ● They agree on norms of behavior and on the group's goals. Members of a group usually share **values**, too. Before you go on, you might want to look up the word **value** in the Social Science Dictionary.

Here are some values that members of one class said they shared.

We value:

    friendship

    interesting books

    a clean classroom

    people who help us

We don't value:

    taking without asking

    messy desks

    noise in the halls

    people who interrupt

With your classmates, make lists like the ones above to show values you share as members of a group. Where did you get these values?

Franklin D. Roosevelt ●

Louis XIV ▲

Mohandas Gandhi

Focus on the Social Scientist

Max Weber was a sociologist who studied leadership. He decided that governments could be divided into three types. Each type depends on the way a leader gets and uses his authority.

1 In the first type of government, authority belongs to the office, or role, of the leader. Whoever is elected to the office of President of the United States, for example, has authority. ● But he can do only what the laws permit. A leader in this type of government has authority only while he is in office.

2 In the second type of government, authority belongs to the person who is leader. Most often, this kind of leader is born to a family that has authority. ▲ In many countries ruled by kings, the oldest son of the king becomes king after him. Whatever kings did before him, he may do. In this type of government, a king is not controlled by laws. The people he rules cannot decide to elect someone else.

3 In the third type, there is a natural leader whom others follow. Such a person may be able to do many good things because people work with him and help him. ■ But sometimes, such a person may try to overthrow the government and rule in his own way.

Today, sociologists still find Max Weber's ideas useful. But any government may have more than one kind of leadership. A king may be born with his authority. At the same time, laws which control the king may be made by the people he rules. A natural leader may not try to overthrow the government. Instead, he may work to be elected as head of a group.

You have studied different leaders in this unit. Can you see each of them as one of three types? Can you tell which ones show a mixture of types?

■

UNIT TWO

ACTING AS
A PERSON

Introduction

All over this country, most boys and girls your age do these things.

In the early morning of a weekday, boys and girls wake up to begin the day's work. They wash. They dress. They eat breakfast. They go to school.

In the morning and early afternoon, boys and girls are in school. They study many different things: reading, social science, science, and mathematics. They take part in art and music; they learn to paint and sing. They spend time in play and in exercise. They go home.

In the afternoon and evening, they play with their friends. They do chores for the family. Many do homework. They watch television. They do things with their family.

What have we left out that *you* do?

All these things that you and other boys and girls do have one thing in common. Do you know what it is? It is shown in the pictures. It is also the first word on the next page. This important word is **learning**.

Study the pictures. ● What have the boys and girls learned to do? What have you learned?

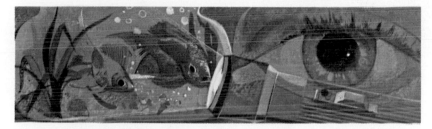

1. Learning to Respond

Put your finger on a very young baby's palm. The baby grasps your finger. ● He responds. The baby does not have to learn to make this response. He was born with it. That is, the response is **inborn**. Whenever a finger is put on his palm, the baby's response is the same. He grasps the finger. This is an inborn response of babies in your family and of babies everywhere in the world.

The finger on the palm is a **stimulus** (stim′yə·ləs). A stimulus is a change in the baby's environment. (Recall that your environment is all of your surroundings.) A stimulus can be small and simple, like the touch of a finger. Or a stimulus can be big, like the sound of thunder or the sight of an ocean.

"Stimuli" means "more than one stimulus."

Other examples of stimuli are listed on the left-hand side of the next page. To these stimuli, you make responses that are inborn. **Inborn responses** are those

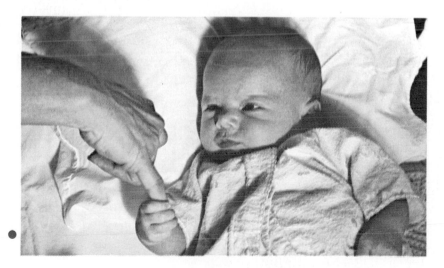

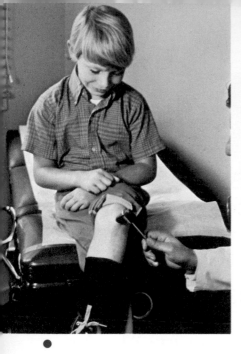

The Stimulus

Darkness meets your eye.

Light hits your eye.

The doctor taps you below the knee. ●

Your finger touches a hot stove. ▲

A cold wind blows.

You are hungry, and you smell food cooking. ■

The Inborn Response

The pupil of your eye widens.

The pupil of your eye gets smaller.

Your leg kicks out. ●

You pull your finger away. ▲

You shiver.

Your mouth waters. ■

that human beings do not have to learn to make. That is, they are responses that we are born with. Look at the responses listed on the left.

Human beings have many other responses that are inborn. But are *all* our responses inborn? For example, you often see traffic lights. You respond to this stimulus by stopping. You do this because you have learned something about traffic lights.

A CLOSER LOOK AT STIMULUS AND RESPONSE

Psychologists (sī·kol′ə·jists) are scientists who study how and why persons behave the way they do. Like other social scientists, they don't use the word **behave** the way we do. Usually, when someone says to you, "Behave!" he is telling you how he *wants* you to act. Psychologists use the word "behave" to describe all the ways in which people act. They use the word to describe the ways in which people respond to changes in their environment.

Psychologists study the responses which people make. Many of them are interested in what happens when people learn. How do psychologists know when you have learned something new? When you learn something new, your behavior changes. When your behavior changes, you have learned new responses.

As an example, let us look at a baby again. Suppose the baby is six months old, and his name is John. When someone says "John," he kicks his feet, turns his head, or looks up. ● These are some of the responses he may make to the sound of his name.

Did the baby know his name the minute he was born? Of course not. When he first heard his name, he didn't respond to it at all. It wasn't a stimulus for him. But in the six months since his birth, John has learned something. Now the stimulus ("John") leads to a response:

Stimulus	**Response**
Someone says "John."	John turns his head and smiles.

How did John learn to respond to the stimulus? How did he learn his name? Probably it happened this way: From the time he was born, his parents called him by name. Whenever they fed him, they called him "John." Whenever they showed him how much they loved him, they called him by his name. That is, whenever he was called by his name, something nice happened to him. He got a smile, a pat, or a kiss. Soon he began to know that the word "John" was connected to some of the good things that happened to him.

Can a goldfish learn by conditioning? Try to get a goldfish or a tropical fish to rise to the top of its tank whenever a light is shined. You might use a flashlight. Write down what happens.

1   Shine the flashlight on the water. Does the goldfish rise to the surface?

2   Then shine the flashlight on the water each day, just a moment before you sprinkle food in the tank. ● The food, of course, is a reward.

3   Will the fish learn to come to the surface as soon as the light is flashed? ▲

4   Would the fish stop responding to the light if you stopped feeding him afterward? What do you predict? How would you test your prediction?

A Problem on Your Own

Morrie was given a puppy which he named "King." Soon the puppy answered to the name "King." How do you explain this?

Each day, Morrie's father blew the horn of the car when he came home from work. When he heard the horn, Morrie ran to meet his father. Soon King came running, too. ■ How had King learned?

How did the baby respond to the nice things? He may have waved his arms or kicked or made happy noises. He may have reached toward the person who was giving him the hug or kiss.

Perhaps, one day, the baby's sister or brother or mother called "John." Then the baby turned his head or made some response. He made the response because he expected the nice things that always came with that sound. Of course, everyone was very happy. He had learned his name! They hugged him and made a fuss over him. ● The baby was rewarded. From then on, he responded whenever someone called him "John."

John learned to respond to a new stimulus. How do we know that he learned? His behavior changed. When people learn, they change their behavior in some way.

Psychologists call this kind of learning **conditioning**. They say that people are conditioned to respond to their names. ▲ That is, each time they make a response, something nice happens to them. Soon they learn to respond to their names. They learn to respond **automatically**, that is, without thinking.

To find out more about this kind of learning, try the investigation on the opposite page.

To find out more about this kind of learning, try the investigation on the opposite page.

AT THIS POINT IN YOUR STUDY

Do these statements seem correct?

1   Conditioning is one way of learning how to act.

Here are three stimuli: the telephone bell, a knock at the door, a quarter on the sidewalk. How have you learned to respond to each of them?

2   People learn most easily if they are given a reward.

If you wanted to change the behavior of a baby, how would you reward him? What kinds of rewards have you received for learning?

Choose the ending for each of these sentences.

1 A pigeon is given two lights at which to peck. One is yellow and the other is blue. When the pigeon pecks at the yellow light, he gets a grain of corn. When he pecks at the blue light, he gets nothing. The pigeon will soon learn to peck at the
    (a) blue light only
    (b) yellow light only

2 When the pigeon pecks at only the correct light, he will have become conditioned. A conditioned act is
    (a) a learned act
    (b) an inborn act

3 Conditioning works best when the response is
    (a) new
    (b) rewarded

USING WHAT YOU KNOW

In Ben's town, the firehouse siren always sounds at exactly twelve noon. When Ben was in school, the siren was always the signal for lunch. He and the other children always ate at twelve noon.

One holiday, Ben and his family visited his grandparents who lived in a large city. At ten-thirty in the morn-ing, Ben heard a fire siren. About fifteen minutes later, Ben felt very hungry.

How can you explain this? Why did Ben feel hungry at ten forty-five in the morning—an hour and a quarter before it was time for lunch?

ON YOUR OWN

1 Think some more about Ben and the fire siren. What responses like this do you make? Name at least two.

2 A rat is put into a box that has a bar in it. When the bar is pressed, food drops into the cage. The rat soon learns to press the bar. How has the rat learned? Now suppose that food no longer drops into the cage each time the bar is pressed. Soon the rat will stop pressing the bar. What does this tell about the importance of rewards in conditioning?

IN TRANSIT

Some things we do not need to learn. Some things we learn by conditioning. These are simple things. But we learn more than simple things. We learn complicated things, too.

What do we do when we learn? To find out more about learning, begin to read the next section.

2. Trying Again and Again

Try to run the maze on page 42. The way to do it is to take a pencil that has an eraser on the end. Place the eraser at the word "BEGIN." Then move it as fast as you can from "BEGIN" to "END." You may not cross a line. Try to run the maze only once.

How many trials do you think you would need before you could run the maze without making an error? When you tried to run it only one time, you probably made an error. If you practiced, do you think that you would make fewer errors? If you tried again and again, do you think you could learn to run the maze without making any errors?

LEARNING BY TRIAL AND ERROR

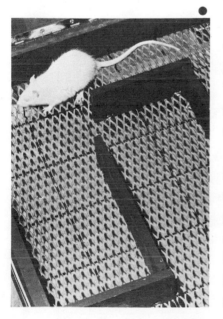

Psychologists have studied the way a rat found its way through this maze. ● The rat started at one end. At the other end, there was some grain—the reward. The rat was supposed to get to the food. Could he learn to do it without making any errors? Could he learn to do it quickly?

The psychologist timed the rat to see how long it took him to run the maze. The psychologist also counted an error each time the rat went into a blind alley and had to turn back. At first, the rat made many errors. But he tried again and again to reach the grain. Soon, the rat was making fewer errors. He was learning. Finally, the rat could run the maze without making any errors at all.

ANOTHER TRIAL

Look at the maze you ran before. Again, run the maze with the eraser end of your pencil. Try again and again until you can run the maze without making any errors. Ask a classmate to time you by the second hand on a watch. ● This time have him keep a record by writing down how long each trial takes you. Ask him to write down each time you turn into a blind alley. Are you both ready? Are you set? Go!

How long did the first trial take? How many errors did you make? Run the maze again and again. When you no longer make any errors, stop. Do you make fewer errors if you go slowly? How many trials did it take you to run the maze without making any errors?

Was it easier to run the maze the second time? Did you make fewer errors? Did you learn faster the second time? How do you explain this?

Try the investigation on the next page to find out more about the ways in which people learn.

ANALYZING THE RESULTS

The psychologist's experiment with the rat and your experiments with a maze both seem to show these things:

1   You had to try to run the maze before you could succeed. If you had not gone through the maze, you could not have learned how to run it. You had to be willing to make some errors if you wanted to learn.

2   Each time you tried, you found it easier to go through the maze. Practicing helped. Didn't you make fewer errors each time you practiced?

3   Being rewarded makes learning easier. The rat was rewarded by reaching the grain. What were your rewards for running the maze?

Perhaps you can see now that **trying to learn, practicing,** and **being rewarded** are all important acts of learning.

AN INVESTIGATION into learning by trial and error

In this investigation, you will learn how to tie a square knot. To do this, you will need two two-foot lengths of clothesline rope or heavy string. Take one length of rope in each hand. ● Cross the right-hand piece of rope over the left-hand piece. ▲ Pull it under and up. ■ Now cross the left-hand piece over the right. Pull the left-hand end through. ▻◅ Pull the ends so that your knot is tight.

After you have learned to tie the square knot, try to answer these questions:

1   Would you have learned to tie the knot if you hadn't tried?

2   Did you make errors when you first began to learn?

3   What was your reward in learning to tie the knot?

4   Now that you have learned to tie the knot, how can you learn to tie it faster?

●
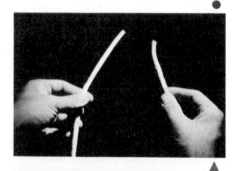

▲

■
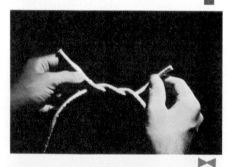

▻◅

▻◅

A Problem on Your Own

How do you think you learned to tie your shoe-laces when you were very young? What was your reward for learning to do this?

You've already learned to do many things this way. Perhaps you have learned some of these things:

1   You have learned to read. Why did you learn to read? What was the reward?

Suppose that you didn't want to learn to read. Suppose that you didn't try. Would you have learned to read as fast or as well as someone who wanted to read?

2   You have learned some mathematics. Suppose that you didn't practice doing math problems. Would you learn to do them as easily as someone who practiced? What is the reward for practicing?

3   You have learned to dress yourself. Why do you dress yourself? What is the reward?

LEARNING FOR YOURSELF

Suppose that a girl named Jenna lived in a community like yours. Like all of her friends, Jenna spoke English. Why did she speak English? It was the custom where she lived, just as it is where you live. Everyone in her town spoke English.

If you do not remember what a **custom** is, look up the word in your Social Science Dictionary.

At Jenna's school, though, all the children in the fourth grade began to study a second language. Some took French. Others took Spanish. Still others took German. Jenna took Spanish, but she hadn't really *decided* to learn it. She didn't see any need for the new language. She didn't work very hard at learning it. ●

One day, a family from Arizona moved into the house next door to Jenna's. Jenna and Lupe, one of the neighbor's children, soon became friends. Like the rest of her family, Lupe spoke both English and Spanish. She could choose which language to speak. She could say "How are you?" or she could say "¿Cómo estás?"

Why did Lupe know both these languages? You can probably guess why. In the community where Lupe lived, it was the custom for many people to speak both English and Spanish.

Recall some of the important acts of learning:

1 Deciding to try to learn
2 Practicing what is to be learned
3 Receiving a reward

Jenna really wanted to be able to talk to Lupe in Spanish. She decided to work a little harder. Each day, she practiced saying and writing what she had learned in class. Of course, she made many errors, but she kept on trying. Her teacher helped her, and so did Lupe. Most of all, practice helped. After a while, Jenna was able to talk to Lupe. ●

Jenna decided to try to learn. She practiced, too. What was her reward for learning Spanish?

Recall that **norms of behavior** are the ways that people in groups expect themselves and others to act.

LEARNING IN THE GROUP

Jenna decided to learn to speak Spanish because she wanted the reward: She wanted to be able to talk to her friend. She chose all by herself to learn Spanish. Nobody chose *for* her. In fact, nobody else in Jenna's family even spoke Spanish. Jenna chose her own goal and set out to reach it.

Both Jenna and Lupe learned some things for themselves. But they also learned in order to share what the people in their families and their communities knew. They learned how people expected them to behave. They learned the norms of behavior of their groups. They learned just as the Blackfoot boys and girls learned the norms of the Blackfoot groups.

Each girl had learned the customs of the groups of which she was a member. In Jenna's community, only English was spoken. In Lupe's community, it was the custom to speak both Spanish and English. The members of Lupe's family spoke both languages. That is why Lupe formed the habit of speaking both Spanish and English. So did the families in her community. Is there a community near you where it is the custom to speak two languages?

In some parts of Vermont and Louisiana, people speak both French and English. In New Mexico, California, and Texas, there are families and communities in which both Spanish and English are spoken. In the cities of New York and San Francisco, there are families and communities in which people speak both Chinese and English.

We often call acts which are learned and which we do over and over **habits**. Habits are not inborn. They are not like the heartbeat or breathing. Habits are learned. A custom is a habit which is shared by a whole group. A custom is a habit which is practiced by everyone. Lupe had formed the habit of speaking both English and Spanish. Jenna had formed the habit of speaking English.

What habits do you have that you learned from the groups to which you belong? Did you decide to learn them yourself? Who decides that you should learn a custom such as sleeping in a bed or wearing a dress?

From your earlier studies, you may remember that you learn customs from all the people in your environment—your family, your teachers, and many others. They do not always make a decision each time they teach you something. They teach you many things that they take for granted in your **social environment**. For example, they take for granted that you need to learn to speak correct English. Why do you need to do this in your environment?

Many of your ways of behaving come from the customs of the groups to which you belong. ● You learned to speak English because it is a custom of your groups, didn't you? This is also why you formed the habit of thinking of yourself as an American. Everyone who is a member of our society thinks of himself as an American. It is one of the meanings that we share.

What is the reward for learning the customs of the group? You can guess. It is the approval of the group. It is the feeling that you are a member. This is a feeling that all people need.

Recall that your **environment** is everything around you. What does **social environment** mean? If you don't know, look it up in your Social Science Dictionary.

=== **AT THIS POINT IN YOUR STUDY** ===

Do these statements seem correct?

1 People sometimes learn by trial and error.

What have you learned this way? Name at least three things. Did you try only once when you learned these things? How did practice help?

2 People are rewarded for learning customs.

What habits do most of the people in your family share? These are your family's customs. How are you rewarded for learning them?

List at least three customs that the people in your community have. How were you rewarded for learning them?

BEFORE YOU GO ON

Choose the ending for each of these sentences.

1 To do something well, a person must
   (a) practice
   (b) try once and give up

2 A boy your age was given a bicycle on his birthday. The first few times he rode it, he fell off. He was
   (a) not learning
   (b) learning by trial and error

3 When most people in a group have a habit, it is
   (a) a custom
   (b) inborn

USING WHAT YOU KNOW

Sid and Harry both wanted to join the Little League baseball team. Every day, Harry practiced catching and batting with an older boy. Sid sometimes joined them. Other times he did not. Which boy, Sid or Harry, had a better chance of improving his catching and batting. Why?

ON YOUR OWN

1 Here is a statement: Some customs you learn in your community are like the customs children learn across the United States. How would you test this statement? How would you get evidence?

2 When you were still very young, you learned to eat with a knife and fork. Why did you learn this? How were you rewarded?

In China and Japan, children learn to eat with chopsticks. It is the custom in their countries. Have you learned to eat with chopsticks? Why or why not?

IN TRANSIT

We learn habits, and we learn skills. ● We learn by trying to reach a goal. Sometimes we have a question we can't answer or a problem that bothers us. How do we learn then? To find out one way, turn the page.

3. "Seeing Into" a Problem

Sultan was a friendly young chimpanzee. A psychologist observed Sultan to find out more about learning. Chimpanzees can do a great many things that pigeons and rats can't do. In fact, they can learn to do some of the things people do. They can, for example, learn to roller-skate.

SULTAN LEARNS TO USE A TOOL

Sultan was given a problem. A banana was put outside his cage, and he had to get it for himself. ● That was his goal. Sultan had already learned how to use a stick to pull a banana into his cage. But now his stick wasn't long enough. ▲ He couldn't reach his goal.

In his cage was a second stick. By itself, this stick also was too short to reach the banana. ■ But the second stick had a hole into which the first stick could fit. When playing, Sultan had sometimes put the two sticks together. Would Sultan think of fitting the first stick into the second? If he did, he would have a stick long enough to reach the banana. He would have a tool.

Again and again, Sultan walked by the second stick. Then he walked across the cage and tried the first stick again. He made grumbling sounds and screamed in anger. ►◄ The first stick alone just wouldn't work.

Then, suddenly, Sultan went over to the second stick and fitted the first one into it. ● He walked quickly to the bars of his cage and pulled the banana in with the double stick. ▲ He had reached his goal and

had gotten his reward. From that time on, whenever a banana was out of reach, Sultan used his new tool, the long double stick. How had Sultan solved his problem?

The chimpanzee Mr. Giggs learned to roller-skate by trial and error. ● He practiced. Sultan tried and tried to reach the banana, too. Yet he didn't seem to be learning anything—except that the stick didn't reach! Trial and error did not help Sultan much.

At first, Sultan seemed to see each stick as something separate that he could use to try to reach a banana. He knew the two sticks could be fitted together. He had put one of them into the other when he was playing with them earlier. But he didn't use them together at first. He had to have the **insight** that the two sticks together could be used as a tool to reach his goal. He had to "see" them as one stick. He "saw the whole picture" at once. Psychologists call this way of learning **insight**.

SOME EXPLANATIONS

Some psychologists study learning. They observe how people learn. Some of them observe learning in animals, such as pigeons, dogs, rats, and chimpanzees. Like all scientists, psychologists try to explain what they observe. An explanation of what is observed is often called a **theory**.

The theory of conditioning is one way of explaining how animals learn simple acts. For example, dogs can be conditioned to come when they are called and to go to their own dishes to eat. The theory of conditioning also helps explain how you learn your first simple acts, too. For example, this is probably the way you learned to respond to your name. What else have you learned by conditioning?

Trial and error helps you learn. Do you remember running the maze? You had to try and try before you

could run it. Could you use a trial-and-error method to write a poem? How would you learn to make a new kind of paper airplane? To learn these things, you may need to see the whole picture at once. You need some kind of insight. So, one theory of learning is the insight theory.

OTHER EXPLANATIONS

We are using simple names for two of the theories of learning. As you go on in your study of the social sciences, you will learn more about the way people learn. So far you have begun to study:

> **conditioning**
> **insight**

Some psychologists have another theory of learning. They think that what you can learn depends partly on your growth. They don't mean that what you can learn depends on how old you are in years. Your age isn't important because each of you grows at your own rate. They are saying that as your body grows, learning becomes easier. For example, most toddlers can't learn to draw a triangle even if they have one to copy. ● But before they go to school, many children can copy a triangle. ▲ Probably you can draw one now, even if you don't have a picture to copy. ■

Also, psychologists have observed that all of us have certain needs. For example, we all need food. We learn very quickly to look for food when we are hungry. Another of our needs is the need for love. We learn to behave in certain ways so that we will be loved. We also need to give love. Is there a reward for being loved and giving love? What is it?

As you can see, psychologists don't always agree about the way people learn. There are many different theories. In the complicated things we learn to do, we may use some kind of conditioning and insight. We may use all the ways together.

How do we learn to work jigsaw puzzles? ● How do we learn to guess the right answer to a problem without actually doing it? Scientists are still learning about learning. But they do agree on one point: All of us learn. We learn all the time.

══════ AT THIS POINT IN YOUR STUDY ══════

Do these statements seem correct?

1 The insight theory is one of the theories that helps explain learning.

Describe at least one way you act that you learned by insight. What was your goal? What problem did you want to solve?

2 Although psychologists agree that we all learn, they do not always agree on how we learn.

How might you learn to unlock a door? Could it be by insight? by conditioning?

How might you learn to use a typewriter? Could it be by conditioning? by insight?

Choose the ending for each of these sentences.

1 A theory
   (a) is good guesswork
   (b) explains what has been observed

2 A dog learns to come to the door at six o'clock, just before he is fed. This is best explained by the theory of
   (a) conditioning
   (b) insight

3 John wondered how he might report to his class on a model airplane he was building. How could he explain how the different parts fit together? Then he thought of making a chart. John's actions are best explained by the theory of
   (a) conditioning
   (b) insight

USING WHAT YOU KNOW

1 A psychologist hung some food inside a cage. A cat was standing outside the cage. The psychologist wanted to see if the cat could figure out how to get the food out of the cage.

   The cat reached in between the bars with her paws. When she found that she couldn't get to the food, she sat down and looked at the string. Then she jumped on top of the cage and used her mouth and her paws to haul up the string which had the food on it. How had the cat solved the problem? By conditioning? By trial and error? By insight?

2 Which of the acts listed below are inborn? Which of the acts show learning by conditioning? Which show learning by insight?

   seeing what to write a poem about

   jumping if someone says "boo" in back of you

   getting up to an alarm clock

   Explain your answers.

ON YOUR OWN

Are people born with likes and dislikes? Or do they learn them? Name one of your likes and one of your dislikes. Were they inborn or did you learn them? Explain your answers.

IN TRANSIT

All your life, you will go on learning. All your life, you will depend on something important—something which helps you learn from other people. Turn to the next section to find out what this is.

4. Building on What You Learn

Long ago in Greece, so the story goes, a father and his son were held as prisoners on an island. In order to escape from the island, they melted wax from beehives. They used the wax to fasten together feathers from birds. ● With the giant wings, they soared off the island. But only the father escaped. Icarus (ik′ə·rəs), the son, flew too close to the sun. The wax melted, and he dropped into the sea.

Is this story true? No, it is not history. It is a myth—a story that people have told over a very long period of time. But it tells us something about life in Greece several thousand years ago. Why didn't Icarus and his father try to leave the island by airplane? The father was an architect who knew how to design houses and other buildings. Why didn't he build an airplane to carry them away?

PUTTING TWO AND TWO TOGETHER

At the time that Icarus lived, no one knew about human flight. No one knew about steel for making airplanes. No one knew about oil for fuel. Icarus's father didn't even know that airplane flight was possible. There was nothing in his social environment to teach him about airplane flight. He had learned all he knew about flying from watching birds. When he made feathered wings, he was using what he had learned. He was using his experience.

You learn many different things, and you learn them in many different ways. Perhaps we can say that you *build on what you know*. In a sense, you add up your learning experiences all the time.

One way in which you use your experiences is in building **concepts**. What is a concept? It is a way of putting together the ideas you already have about something. For example, we think that you already know something about the concept of "bird." What do you think when you see the word "bird"? You probably think of things like these. ●

Surely, you have seen many different birds. You have seen big birds and small birds. But you know that all birds are alike in some ways. You know, for example, that all birds have wings. The ways in which all birds are alike are their likenesses. A concept puts together all the likenesses of things.

You have, we are sure, some concept of "tree." You may think of different kinds of trees. But when you see the word "tree," you do not think of grass or an apple or a flower. You know the concept of "tree."

In your mind, you put together all the likenesses you have observed. You do not mistake a "fish" for a "dog," or a "dog" for a "cat," or a "cat" for a "bird." You know all the likenesses—feathers, beak, wings— which make up the concept "bird." These likenesses do not make up the concept "cat."

You also have begun to build the concept of "group." Look at these two groups. ● What are their likenesses?

Recall what you have learned about groups:

1 Each group is made up of members who share the same purpose, or goal.

2 The members of a group interact.

3 The members of a group depend on each other.

4 The members of a group share meanings.

All the groups you see in the picture are alike in these ways. Their likenesses make up the concept of "group." In your study of the social sciences, you will build concepts. You will be searching into the way people behave. Of course, as you search out likenesses, you will find differences, too.

MAKING LEARNING EASIER

You learn from your own experiences. But you also learn from the experiences of others because people can tell you what they have learned. They add what they know to the concepts you have.

Even the people who lived long ago can teach you because you have learned to use written **symbols** (sim′bəlz). Such symbols are important to people. Because of symbols, people can learn more than any other kind of living thing. People can build concepts. They can also read. ▲

The language we write is made up of symbols. Write the word "table" on a piece of paper. If you show it to anyone who can read English, he'll know what it means. You don't need to show him a *real* table. You can use the symbol for table. That is, you can use the word "table."

Communicate means to exchange thoughts and ideas with other people.

By using symbols, you can **communicate**. You can describe what has happened to you. You can even describe concepts like "beauty" and "freedom." "Beauty" and "freedom" cannot be touched and cannot be seen. "Beauty" means *all* the things you've

Here are different kinds of written symbols. Point to the symbols that you know. Some symbols have been used at other times and in other places. Can you point to the picture symbols that were used thousands of years ago in Egypt? Can you point to the symbols that are used in Japan?

ever seen that you thought were beautiful. "Freedom" means *all* the ways you know of being free. You use these words as symbols. The words stand for all the meanings of "beauty" and "freedom."

Using symbols, you can learn about experiences without having them yourself. ● You can read about people who live in other countries or learn about the lives of well-known people in history. Symbols help you learn many things.

To learn more about the importance of symbols, try the investigation on the opposite page.

LEARNING TO BUILD A BETTER WORLD

Do you remember Jenna? You read about her earlier in this unit (page 45). She learned to speak Spanish because she wanted to be able to talk to her friend Lupe. Jenna *decided* to learn. She made that choice herself.

AN INVESTIGATION into symbols

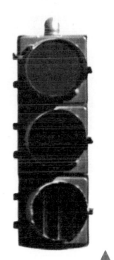

Study the map on pages 292-293. Make a list of the symbols which are used on the map. Then answer these questions:

1 Are all the symbols language?

2 What does each symbol mean?

3 Did you learn the meanings of each symbol by yourself?

4 Who gave each symbol its meaning?

5 Would each symbol mean the same thing to a person in China or Egypt?

6 Write down the things you had to know *before* you could use the map. List such things as what a country is and what a globe is. How did you learn the concept of "country"? How did you learn the concept of "globe"? ● How did symbols help?

A Problem on Your Own

You know that language is made up of symbols. But there are many kinds of symbols that are not language. Look at the pictures. A red light is a symbol, isn't it? ▲ The Statue of Liberty is another kind of symbol. ■ What does it stand for? Why is a fireman's badge a symbol? ▻◅

Name three other symbols that are not language. Tell what each symbol stands for.

61

Name some things that must be learned before a factory can be built.

All over the world, people learn to act in new ways. They choose goals for themselves. They learn because they want to learn. Sometimes the people in communities decide to learn how to change their environment. For example, for many years, the water supply for a town in New Mexico came from pumps in the yard of each house. ● A few years ago, the people of the town decided to learn how to put in a village water supply. They wanted to bring water to the whole town through pipes. The water was stored in huge tanks on a hilltop outside of town. The tanks looked like this one. ▲

The people of Puerto Rico also decided to learn new ways. Have you ever heard anyone say, "He pulled himself up by his bootstraps"? You can guess that it means "He did it by himself." Over twenty years ago, the people of Puerto Rico started Operation Bootstrap. They wanted a better life. Since that time, they have built roads and tourist hotels. They have built factories, too. There are many new jobs. Because Puerto Ricans chose to learn, people all over the island live better lives. The children go to new schools. Many adults also go to school to learn new ways.

People of all ages go to school throughout the United States. They want to learn more. Their goal is to learn ways to change their environment so that they can build a better future. Your teacher may go back to college to learn more to teach you. Your mother may go to a school of nursing because she wants to be a nurse. Your father may go to a special school if he wants to learn a new job. ■ Many people who come to the United States from other countries go to school to learn English.

In the public schools throughout our country, adults go to school. They may want to learn something new just for fun, like painting or pottery. ◄ They may want to learn the skills that are needed to make their community a better place in which to live.

LEARNING—IN THE HUMAN WAY

To help you understand how a scientist studies learning, we looked at some of the ways in which rats learn. But human learning is different, isn't it? Rats and pigeons can learn, but they can't use concepts and language. They can use only very simple symbols. A rat can't add up all he has learned and change the future. But *you* can!

AT THIS POINT IN YOUR STUDY

Do these statements seem correct?

1   Symbols help us learn from each other.

What set of symbols do you use every day? How do they help you learn?

2   People can change their environment by learning.

What would our environment be like if no one had learned how to be a carpenter? What would our environment be like if no one had learned how to grow food?

What can you learn that will help you change your environment?

BEFORE YOU GO ON

Choose the ending for each of these sentences.

1 People learn from experiences
   (a) of their own
   (b) of their own and others
2 People use symbols
   (a) to communicate
   (b) to put milk in
3 Concepts help us
   (a) learn only about groups
   (b) to put likenesses together

USING WHAT YOU KNOW

1 The American flag is a symbol. It stands for our land, our people, and our government. What else does it stand for?
2 In *Through the Looking-Glass*, Humpty Dumpty says, "When *I* use a word, it means just what I choose it to mean—neither more nor less." Do you think Humpty Dumpty had trouble communicating?

ON YOUR OWN

1 Psychologists try to find out how people behave. B. F. Skinner is a psychologist who studies learning. ● Dr. Skinner has tried to find out how all people learn. He has tried to find out how people learn in any kind of environment. Among other things, Skinner has taught rats to run mazes.

Why do psychologists like Skinner study how people learn? How do you think Skinner tests his theories?

2 Kenneth B. Clark is a social psychologist. ▲ He has studied children who grow up in large cities. In crowded areas of some cities, there are not enough teachers and schools, and children do not have much room to play. Clark has studied how this kind of environment can change or form behavior.

Why is Clark called a social psychologist? (Look up the word **social** in your Social Science Dictionary.) How is Clark's work different from that of Skinner? How is it the same?

3 Edna Heidbreder has studied how people learn concepts. ■ In her studies, she found that people learn some kinds of concepts more easily than others. For example, it may be easy for people to learn concepts of things which can be seen or touched. It may be harder to learn other kinds of concepts.

Would Dr. Heidbreder say that a very young child could learn the concept of "tools" more easily than the concept of "justice"? Why or why not?

Some of the things you do were not learned at all. You were born already doing them. You do them without thinking. When you were a baby, you closed your hand around a finger in your palm. If you touch a hot pan, your hand jumps away. You do not think about pulling your hand back. If the weather turns cold, you shiver.  You didn't learn to do any of these things.

Perhaps now we can make this statement about the concept of **behavior: People are born with some ways of responding to their environment.** That is, people do not have to learn everything they do.

Changing the Way We Behave

A young baby cries. He soon learns to make other noises. He learns to know sounds, such as his mother's voice. At first, when his mother says his name, the baby does not respond. But soon he may learn to smile or to turn his head. When he responds, he is rewarded by a hug or a kiss. He becomes conditioned to respond to the sound of his name.

As the child grows, he learns other things. He learns how to dress himself. He learns how to find his way to school. He learns by trying to do these things. He makes mistakes and tries again. He practices what he has learned in order to do it well.

Can conditioning explain how we learn to read or to solve problems in arithmetic or map reading? Psychologists have theories which try to explain how we learn these things. One of them is the theory of insight. Somehow, as we learn, we "see into" the problem. We may see the whole answer at once.

When people learn, they change the way they

About five thousand years ago, the Egyptians used this symbol for the first letter of their alphabet.

In another country, the people changed the Egyptian symbol so that it looked like this.

About three thousand years ago, the first letter of the alphabet was again changed.

In about 600 B.C., the Greeks changed the symbol so that it had this shape.

In about A.D. 114, the Romans gave the letter "A" the shape we use today.

behave. At this point in your studies, you can, then, understand this statement about the concept of **behavior: People learn to respond to their environment.** They learn how to act by conditioning and by insight. They learn in other ways, too.

Learning from Each Other

You learn from your own experience. But you can also learn from the experience of others. How would you learn if you couldn't read or if you couldn't speak to other people? Symbols help us to communicate with each other. Language is one set of symbols. • Symbols also help us to think in complicated ways. They help us to think and talk about ideas and concepts, as well as things we can see and touch. Symbols can tell us what people who lived in the past learned. With symbols, we can make records of what we have learned.

Now we can add this statement to what you already know about the concept of **behavior: Using symbols, people learn from the past experience of others.** Through symbols, people learn how others have acted. They learn what others have already learned.

Learning How to Change

You have studied some of the ways that animals and people learn. Some of these ways are alike, and some are different. Animals can't use language symbols or build concepts. Animals can't choose to change their environment. They can't choose how they will behave or what they will learn. Only people can decide these things for themselves.

You have, then, learned this about the concept of **behavior: People are born with some of their ways of behaving. But people learn most of their ways of behaving.** Unlike animals, people can choose to learn new ways of behaving.

Focus on the Concept

A   In the early 1900's, Dr. Ivan Pavlov (päv'lôf) did the first important experiment on conditioning. ● He observed the responses that a dog makes.

Whenever a dog eats, his mouth waters. This is an inborn response. Dr. Pavlov began to ring a bell just before he fed the dog. He did this again and again. After a while, the dog's mouth began to water as soon as the bell rang, even before any food had appeared! Soon, the dog's mouth watered each time he heard a bell ring. This happened even when he wasn't given any food afterward.

1   The first stimulus was the food. What was the inborn response?

2   The new stimulus was the bell. What was the learned response?

3   Predict whether, for the rest of his life, the dog's mouth would water every time he heard a bell. What might help him to keep what he had learned?

4   How is the dog in this picture responding? ▲

B Analyze these three figures. ● What do you "see" here?

Insight will help you. Some people call insight the "Aha!" experience. Is that what you felt when you recognized each figure?

What did you need to know before you could solve this problem? How did your earlier learning help you?

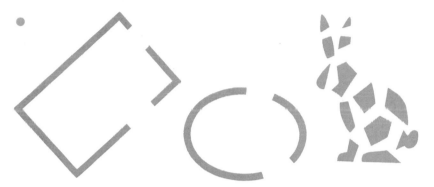

B. AN ANALYSIS OF VALUES

When the United States began, not everyone felt that every child needed to have the right to go to school. But even the pioneers built one-room schoolhouses like these. ▲ Over the years, Americans have decided to give each child the right to more and more education.

Why is learning so important? Why have Americans come to value education so highly?

▲

Focus on the Social Scientist

Some of our ways of behaving are inborn. But almost all of our behavior is learned. We learn in many different ways. Because this is so, it is not always easy to study learning. How do people learn? Why do they learn? Many social scientists are trying to find the answers to these questions.

One psychologist, Dr. N. K. Ach, wanted to find out more about the way young children learn the meanings of words. He taught a group of children nonsense words like "gatsun" and "fal."

Do these words have any meaning to you? Probably not. After a while, they began to have meaning for the children Dr. Ach taught. For example, Dr. Ach might have said to the children, "That toy truck is so gatsun that you can hardly lift it." So, "gatsun" began to mean "large and heavy." "Fal" began to mean "small and light." Can you think of a sentence using "fal" in this way? Now, do the words "gatsun" and "fal" mean something to you?

The nonsense words became real words to the children in Dr. Ach's group. The words began to mean certain ideas. That is, they became language symbols to the children.

Dr. Ach was trying to find out how much children had to grow up before they could learn to use language symbols. He was also trying to find out how children learn to use these symbols. From his observations, he was building an explanation, or theory, of how children learn.

How does a scientist like Dr. Ach test his theories? What are some of the methods he might use? What happens if, later in his work, he discovers some facts that don't fit the theory?

A NEW VIEW OF BEHAVIOR

Are you behaving when you wash your hands before dinner? "Yes," you will probably say, "I am behaving myself." Are you behaving when you talk with your friends on the way to school? Perhaps you will answer that you're not being either good or bad and the question doesn't make sense. But it does make sense. In your studies, you have learned a new meaning for **behave**. You have learned the scientist's meaning. To him, **behavior** means all the actions you make throughout your life. It does not mean only doing as you are told.

Social scientists, such as psychologists, say that people all over the Earth share certain kinds of behavior. All people have ways of behaving to fill needs like these:

> food
> shelter
> clothing
> companionship
> child care

How each person behaves depends on his needs. Behavior also depends on values and goals. Sometimes it depends on feelings, too.

JAPAN

Study each of the pictures. ● Then try to answer these questions:

1 Why are the people behaving the way they are?
2 What needs are they trying to fill? How do you know?
3 Did they learn to do what you observe in the pictures? How might they have learned?
4 Did they choose how to behave?
5 Are they showing their feelings? How?
6 To what groups do these people belong?

The people in these pictures live in Japan. ▲ Find pictures of people in other lands who act like this in order to fill like needs. Write down in your notebook how their behavior is like that of Japanese people. Write down how it is different, too.

ACTING TO USE RESOURCES

Introduction

You have looked into the ways rats and pigeons behave—and the ways you behave. You have begun to learn how you learn. You have begun to learn why you behave the way you do.

As you go on in your study of the social sciences, you will learn more and more about the ways people behave. In this unit, you will look at the way people used the environment of this country. You will see how, at first, their actions were not very wise. The people of this country were destroying an important part of the environment.

Then men and women learned new ways of acting. They adapted. That is, they changed their behavior. Why? Their behavior had to change. If they could not use this important part of their environment, they could not live.

Psychologists, pigeons, Blackfoot Indians—none of us live without this part of our environment. It is in all the pictures. ● What is this great treasure in our environment? To find out, begin reading the next section.

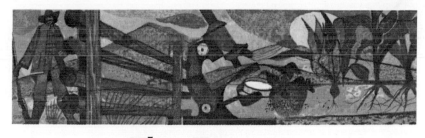

1. The Treasure

On this page, you will find a boy and a girl. ● The boy is wearing a jacket made of a material that does not come from a plant or an animal. His shirt and the girl's sweater are both made of wool. Her skirt is made of wool, too. Her blouse and his blue jeans are made of cotton. So are their socks. Both are wearing shoes made of leather.

Both the boy and the girl have had breakfast. One had fruit juice and cereal and milk. The other had juice and eggs.

Almost everything they are wearing has something in common. Everything they have eaten has something in common, too. If you know what this thing is, you will know what the treasure in our environment is.

THE RUSH FOR TREASURE

In 1889, settlers were told that they could make claims on land in Oklahoma at noon on a certain day. On the northern border of Oklahoma, men, women, and children waited. Some waited on horseback. Many waited in wagons of all kinds. Still others just stood and waited. They were waiting for a signal that would tell them it was noon. When the guns went off, they would rush to get land. The fastest would get the best land.

In later years, there were more rushes into Oklahoma. To the people who took part in the rushes, land was a treasure. It is still a treasure all over the world. Why is this so?

FOR LIVING THINGS

Without soil, you cannot live. You know that most of the food you eat comes from the soil. Fruit and vegetables, milk and meat, bread and butter—all come from plants and animals that depend on the soil for life.

Where do cotton, wool, and leather come from? These, too, come from the soil. At least part of your home is built of wood that comes from trees. To fill the basic needs of food, clothing, and shelter, you depend on soil.

Name one land plant or land animal that does not depend on soil. The eagle? What does it need for life? The eagle hunts rabbits. Rabbits eat plants. Plants grow in soil. The tiger? What does it need for life? Where does the tiger get its food?

All the food that you need to keep alive can be traced back to the soil. The plants on which all living things depend grow in the **topsoil**. Topsoil is a thin layer of soil on top of the ground. Suppose that all the topsoil in the United States were spread evenly over the land. All this topsoil would make a layer only about seven inches deep.

Of course, topsoil is not spread evenly over the land. Suppose that a Kansas farmer let you dig a hole in his wheatfield. You might have to dig down through several feet of topsoil before reaching the next layer of soil.

However, if you were to dig only an inch or two into a rocky hillside in Vermont, you would reach the **subsoil**. The subsoil is the layer below the topsoil. You might even reach solid rock. Subsoil is made up of gravel, clay, and sand. In some places, it is only hard-packed clay. The plants needed for life cannot grow in subsoil alone.

What is the difference between the layers of soil? What is topsoil made of? To find out, try the investigation on the opposite page.

AN INVESTIGATION into topsoil

Into a quart jar, put one measuring cup of soil from the surface of a field, your backyard, or any place where plants are growing. ● Then add enough water to fill the jar. Stir the soil and water for about two minutes with a long spoon. ▲ Let the jar stand for about twenty minutes.

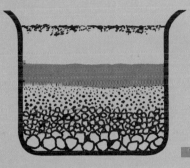

Notice that the soil separates into layers. ■ On the bottom of the jar, there will be particles of sand and perhaps gravel. Next will be a layer of very fine particles. These are called **silt**. On top of the silt, making the water cloudy, are clay particles even finer than silt. The dark-colored matter floating on the surface is called **humus**. Humus comes mainly from the rotting, or decay, of plants and animals. What does topsoil have that subsoil doesn't have?

Keep the jar standing for at least a week. You will use it later.

A Problem on Your Own

Does soil everywhere have the same amounts of humus, silt, clay, sand, and gravel? Take some soil from a roadside or any patch of earth where few or no plants are growing. Repeat your investigation.

What are the differences between your two samples of soil? What can you now say about the parts of soil that help plants grow?

GROWTH OF SOIL

Topsoil that is made up of sand, silt, clay, and humus is called **loam**. ● Loam is not the same everywhere. Have you ever seen loam of different colors in different places? Light-brown loam may have more sand in it. Gray-brown loam may have more clay. Red loam may be colored by iron oxide. Brownish-black loam may have more humus.

Sand, silt, and clay come from rocks as a result of **weathering**. Weather breaks down rocks. ▲ Sun, wind, rain, and frost work on them. The sun warms the rocks during the day, and they expand. At night, the rocks cool and contract. Different materials in the rocks cool at different rates. Parts of a rock that cool quickly contract and pull away from parts that are still warm. Tiny cracks are formed. Pieces of the rocks may chip off. Rain that freezes in the cracks of the rocks also breaks up the rocks. The weather keeps on destroying rocks and, thus, builds soil. Have you ever observed how streets and roads are changed by weather? Sometimes, these changes are easy to see.

Weathering is a long, slow process. Geologists (jē·ol′ə·jists) are scientists who study the physical make-up of the earth. They study how the soil is built. From their investigations, they believe that it can take many hundreds of years to build an inch of topsoil.

As you learned in the investigation, **humus** comes from the decay of plants and animals. Grass from lawn cuttings and plants that die in a field decay. Petals that fall in a flower garden decay, too. As these parts of plants decay, they become humus. Decay of any living thing in the soil adds humus to the soil.

Have you ever kicked over leaves under trees in the woods and found the remains of rotten leaves underneath? Below these leaves, there may be pure humus that was formed from leaves of earlier years. Many millions of years ago, when plants first appeared on the earth, humus became part of the soil.

MINERALS IN SOIL

In your investigation, you stirred soil and water in a jar. What would you expect to find in the water? Without stirring the soil, carefully pour or ladle some water from the jar into a saucer. Set the saucer in the sun. What will happen to the water? What do you expect to find left in the dish?

How do you know that what is left in the dish was not in the water in the first place? How do you know it came from the soil? Try to think of a way to test your answer.

The part of the soil that results from the weathering of rocks contains minerals. Minerals are substances found in the earth. Soil minerals are, of course, found in the soil. Many minerals **dissolve**. That is, they mix completely in water. To grow, plants need certain minerals. The minerals must be dissolved in water, because only liquids can be taken in by the roots of the plants.

Do you remember what **environment** means? If you don't, look up the word in your Social Science Dictionary.

When you saw something left in the saucer, you were seeing some of the minerals that plants take from the soil. The kind of environment that plants live in is very important to them, just as your environment is important to you. Is soil part of a plant's environment?

Humus (decayed plants and animals) helps return minerals to the soil. Rain dissolves the minerals in humus and washes them back into the soil. Fertilizer also returns minerals to the soil. All over the world, farmers use fertilizers. They may use the manure of farm animals. But today's modern farmer is more likely to use chemical fertilizers.

Study the two pictures. ● One shows a field without certain minerals. The other shows a field on which fertilizer has been used. Can you tell which field has been fertilized?

Without minerals dissolved in water, plants could not grow. Without plants, there could be no animals. Without plants and animals, you could not live.

AGRICULTURE AND SOIL

Plants and animals that live on land cannot live without topsoil. Roots of plants grow in the topsoil. Topsoil has minerals in a form in which plants can use them. Farmers know how important topsoil is. The wheat farmer in Kansas knows. So does the dairy farmer in Wisconsin or New York. The fruit grower in Florida or California, the rice farmer in Texas, the vegetable farmer in New Jersey—all know the importance of good topsoil. There would be no **agriculture** (ag′rə·kul′chər) without topsoil. Agriculture is the raising of plants and animals.

A soil scientist can help the farmer use the soil in the best possible way. A soil scientist studies soil. Observe how he takes a sample of soil for study. He digs into the soil with a soil borer. ● (A soil borer is shaped like a tool that bores holes in wood.) Then he pulls the tool out of the soil. He puts the soil held on the end of a soil borer into a container. This sample is then sent to the state agricultural department. There, the soil sample is carefully studied.

What do you think a sample will tell a soil scientist about the soil? ● Will it tell him how deep the topsoil is? Will it tell him about the subsoil? It will. A sample will also tell him how much humus and how many minerals there are in the soil. How do you think a study of a soil sample will help the farmer?

The people who made land rushes into Oklahoma did not know about studying soil samples. But they did know the importance of good soil. They wanted to farm the land. To them, soil was a treasure.

▰▰▰▰▰▰ AT THIS POINT IN YOUR STUDY ▰▰▰▰▰▰

Does this statement seem correct?
Life on land depends on topsoil.
Name one plant that lives on land and does not need topsoil.
Name one animal that can live without minerals in its food.
Could we grow food without topsoil?

Choose the ending for each of these sentences.

1   Topsoil gives life
    (a) to plants only
    (b) to plants and animals
2   To the topsoil, humus returns
    (a) minerals
    (b) clay and silt
3   Without soil, there would be
    (a) life as we know it
    (b) no life on land

USING WHAT YOU KNOW

1   President Theodore Roosevelt once said, "When the soil is gone, man must go." What did he mean? Do you agree? Why or why not?
2   Building topsoil takes a long time. What is needed to build it? Destroying topsoil can take a very short time. What is needed to destroy it?

ON YOUR OWN

1   Can food be grown without any soil at all? Look up the meaning of "hydroponics." When food is grown this way, how do plants get the minerals they need?
2   Are there any plants and animals that do not depend on soil? Where do they live? Scientists are trying to find ways that plants like these can be used for food. Try to find out something about the work of these scientists. Where will you look?

IN TRANSIT

You know now that plants and animals that live on land depend on topsoil to live and grow. ● You know that, without topsoil, there would be no agriculture, or farming, as we know it. But is soil the only thing that growing life needs?

Can soil be useful if it has no water? Is there anything we can use instead of water? To find out, turn to the next section.

2. Water

What do you need to stay alive? You know that you could not stay alive without air. You must breathe in air to live. If you try, you can stop breathing for a short time, but not for long.

You must eat, too. You could live for a short time without food—a week, or perhaps more—but not for much longer. Long before a week passed, you would feel a great need for something else—something more necessary to life than food. As you probably have guessed, it is water.

You need to drink water many times a day. Some doctors say you should have six to eight glasses during the day, because your body loses water steadily. Ballplayers can lose as much as four to five quarts of water in a single hot afternoon!

When you are thirsty, you find it hard to wait very long for a drink. Thirst is a sign that your body needs water. The water you have lost must be replaced, so you act. You hurry to get a drink.

Plants and animals get thirsty, too. All living things depend on water. But where does the water that living things use come from?

WHERE IS THE WATER?

What does **analysis** mean? If you don't know, look up the word in your Social Science Dictionary.

Let us begin our study of water with an **analysis** of the map on pages 296-297. Find the following:

1   The Mississippi, Ohio, Missouri, Columbia, Delaware, Colorado, and Snake rivers

2 The Great Lakes

3 The river nearest your home. What is it called?

4 Turn to the map on pages 294-295. Find the states through which the Mississippi River flows. What are their names?

Do you think the map shows *all* the water in the United States? Of course, you know that it doesn't. It doesn't show all the streams, creeks, springs, wells, and ponds. A very large map would be needed to show all the places with water! And such a map couldn't show underground water.

FROM THE CLOUDS

Rivers and lakes begin in the clouds. ● Remember the saucer of water you put in the sun (page 81)? Think of the United States as a giant saucer. True, some of the water is below the surface. But great amounts of water are **evaporating** (i·vap′ə·rāt·ing) from the giant saucer all the time. That is, water is rising as vapor, or moisture, into the air. The hotter the air is, the greater the amount of evaporation.

Great amounts of water evaporate from the land, from bodies of water on the land, and from all living things. This water forms clouds above the Earth. It returns to the oceans and land in the form of rain and snow. The lakes and ponds are filled. The dry land soaks up the water.

Water, then, moves from clouds to the Earth. It then makes clouds again. A hydrologist (hī·drol′ə·jist) is a scientist who studies water. He studies the ways water moves from the land to the air and back again. He calls this circular movement the hydrologic cycle (hī′drə·loj′ik sī′kəl). As this cycle goes on and on, water is used over and over again.

Does all land get the same amount of water from the clouds? Of course, you know that it doesn't. On the next two pages, analyze the rainfall map, and try to answer the questions.

Before you study rainfall, you should know something that will help you read maps. Point to these states on the rainfall map: Delaware, New Jersey, Maryland. Are the names spelled out? On maps, words are often abbreviated (ə·brē′vē·āt·id), or shortened. The list on the right will help you read maps in this and other books.

Now you should be ready to study the rainfall map. Try to answer these questions:

1 What areas get the most rain? ● What areas get the least? ▲

2 Find the twenty-inch rainfall line. What area of the United States does it go through?

3 How much rain falls in your area?

4 How do the people who live in dry areas get water?

5 If you knew the rainfall in an area, could you predict next year's rainfall? Would you ever be wrong?

STATES	ABBREVIATIONS	STATES	ABBREVIATIONS
Alabama	Ala.	Montana	Mont.
Alaska	Alaska	Nebraska	Neb.
Arizona	Ariz.	Nevada	Nev.
Arkansas	Ark.	New Hampshire	N.H.
California	Calif.	New Jersey	N.J.
Colorado	Colo.	New Mexico	N.M.
Connecticut	Conn.	New York	N.Y.
Delaware	Del.	North Carolina	N.C.
Florida	Fla.	North Dakota	N.D.
Georgia	Ga.	Ohio	Ohio
Hawaii	Hawaii	Oklahoma	Okla.
Idaho	Idaho	Oregon	Ore.
Illinois	Ill.	Pennsylvania	Pa.
Indiana	Ind.	Rhode Island	R.I.
Iowa	Iowa	South Carolina	S.C.
Kansas	Kan.	South Dakota	S.D.
Kentucky	Ky.	Tennessee	Tenn.
Louisiana	La.	Texas	Tex.
Maine	Me.	Utah	Utah
Maryland	Md.	Vermont	Vt.
Massachusetts	Mass.	Virginia	Va.
Michigan	Mich.	Washington	Wash.
Minnesota	Minn.	West Virginia	W. Va.
Mississippi	Miss.	Wisconsin	Wis.
Missouri	Mo.	Wyoming	Wyo.

AVERAGE YEARLY RAINFALL IN THE UNITED STATES

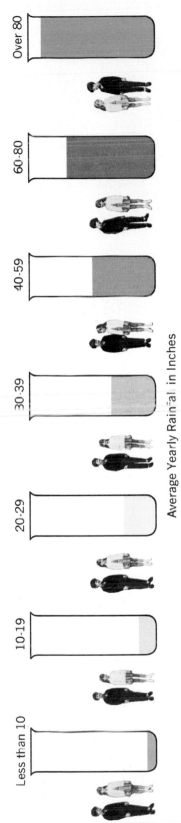

Average Yearly Rainfall in Inches

| Less than 10 | 10-19 | 20-29 | 30-39 | 40-59 | 60-80 | Over 80 |

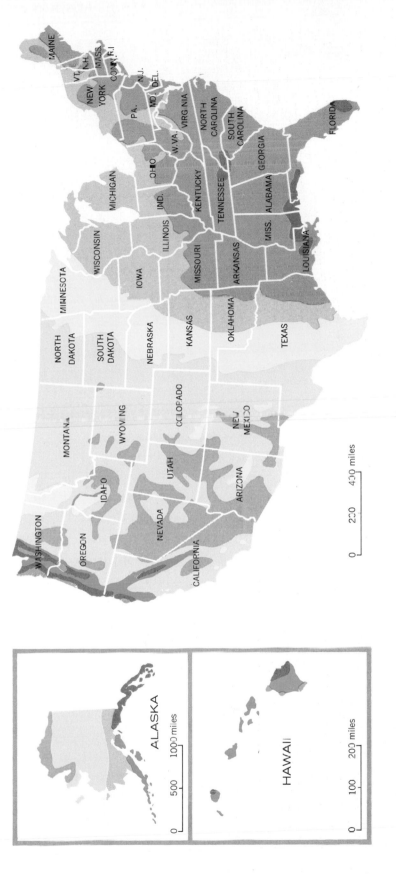

RUNNING WATER

Perhaps you have noticed places where rain has washed away the soil. Rain will move loose soil. Where there are no trees or plants to hold it, soil often moves away with the flowing rainwater.

Study the picture. ● This deep gully began with rain dripping off a barn roof. It grew and grew as the water ran downhill. Rainwater can carry away forty thousand tons of soil to make a gully! When rainwater washes or carries the soil away, the result is a form of **erosion** (i·rō′zhən).

To study how erosion takes place, try the investigation on the opposite page.

What is the difference between **weathering** (page 80) and **erosion**?

SOIL IN WATER

Soil moved by erosion often takes a long journey. Rainwater moves soil into streams. The streams carry the soil into rivers. Kentucky soil may be carried by the Ohio and the Mississippi rivers all the way to the

Is washing the dirt off your face an example of erosion?

AN INVESTIGATION into soil erosion

Scientists often make models of what they wish to study. A model is not the real thing, but it takes in everything the scientist wants to study. It helps the scientist analyze what really happens. In this investigation, you will make a model of erosion. You will need a hammer, a small nail, a tin can, a flowerpot or another tin can, and some coins or bottle tops.

Make a sprinkling can by using the hammer and nail to punch small holes in the bottom of the tin can. Fill the flowerpot with loose soil and press the soil down lightly until it is even with the top of the pot. ● Place the coins or bottle tops on the surface of the soil. ▲ Set the pot in a basin, and sprinkle the soil with water. ■ The sprinkling should be like rain. First sprinkle lightly for light rain. Keep on sprinkling for heavy rain. What happens to the soil?

The trees are here for a reason. What is it?

A Problem on Your Own

What is a gully? Try to find one in your own neighborhood. Photograph it or draw it. Measure how deep it is. Perhaps you and your classmates can find several gullies. Measure and bring in pictures of them. Analyze your pictures.

What caused the gullies? How could they have been prevented? Predict what may happen if land with gullies is not improved.

91

mouth of the Mississippi below New Orleans. Trace the journey of the soil on the map on pages 296-297.

When soil is set down at the mouth of a river, it often forms new land. This land is called a delta because it is often shaped like the Greek letter "delta." The letter "delta" is written Δ.

Was the Mississippi delta formed in this way? Was this delta in Alaska always there? ● No, a delta is new land built from the soil carried by a river. Is the delta at the mouth of this river in Alaska shaped like the Greek symbol Δ?

Soil that is not properly cared for will erode— especially if it is on sloping or hilly land. Can a delta be formed without erosion?

What is a **hypothesis**? If you don't know, turn to your Social Science Dictionary or to page 27.

Perhaps you will want to form a **hypothesis**. Is the new land formed in a delta good soil? What is your reasoning? What facts do you have?

WATER IN THE SOIL

Not all rainwater runs off into streams. Much of it sinks into the ground. At different depths, the earth is full of water. The surface of the underground water is called the **water table**. Sometimes men dig into the ground. They hope to strike underground water in order to make a well. Many families on farms and in small towns depend on wells for water.

Recall that good soil is needed for plants and animals. But plants and animals must also have water. On a warm day, one tree may absorb eighty gallons of water through the roots! True, the water doesn't stay long in the tree. It comes out of the leaves as water vapor.

Water dissolves the minerals in the soil. Then the water carries the minerals into the roots of the tree. It rises in the trunk of the tree and finally evaporates from the leaves.

All living things take in water and lose it again. Even the cactus that lives in the dry, hot desert must have water to stay alive. ● A cactus plant needs less water in a week than you need each day, but it must have some.

Which states are part of the Southwest?

NOT ENOUGH WATER

Study once again the map of rainfall in the United States (page 89). Find the twenty-inch rainfall line. To the west of this line, water is badly needed. This is the reason that there has been conflict over water rights in the Southwest. Water, like good soil, is a treasure.

In some places the soil is good, but because there is no water, plants will not grow. Thousands of years ago, man began to learn how to live in such places. He had to **adapt**—to learn patterns of behavior which would keep him alive. He adapted by learning how to **irrigate** (ir′ə·gāt) his fields.

LARGE IRRIGATED AREAS

0   300   600 miles

In the United States today, much farmland is irrigated. Dams across streams and rivers hold water in lakes. Then pipes carry the necessary amount of water to crops. When there is not enough water, **irrigation** helps to make up the difference. Then farmers need not depend so much on rain. Study the map. ● Point out the irrigated areas. Where might this irrigation canal be? ▲

━━━━ **AT THIS POINT IN YOUR STUDY** ━━━━

Do these statements seem correct?

1   Without water, we could not live.

Why don't great numbers of people live in the desert?

People who live in the desert are often careful of the amount of water they use for bathing. Why?

2   Without water, soil cannot grow food.

Can food be grown anywhere without water? Can poor soil with water grow food?

94

BEFORE YOU GO ON

Choose the ending for each of these sentences.

1 Water, like soil, is necessary for the growth of
   (a) most plants
   (b) all living things

2 The supply of water is spread throughout the Earth
   (a) unevenly
   (b) evenly

3 Soil is necessary for plants. But sometimes water
   (a) erodes soil
   (b) turns into soil

USING WHAT YOU KNOW

1 Along the banks of the Brandywine River, the soil was washing from the fields into the water. Each rainfall caused more erosion. One Saturday morning, some Boy Scouts began to plant willow shoots firmly into the eroding soil on the banks of the river. The Scouts wanted the shoots to grow into willow trees. Why did they want trees to grow along the banks of the Brandywine?

2 How do gullies change the way people behave? Give one example of how they might change the behavior of people in a farm community.

Suppose that people did not work to stop erosion of the land. How might erosion change your whole society?

ON YOUR OWN

Look at the map on page 89. Point to Texas. Then point to Alaska. Texas looks larger than Alaska, doesn't it? Yet Texas is only about one-half the size of Alaska.

Texas seems to be larger, because the states are drawn to different scales. On the scale for Alaska, about one and one-quarter inches are equal to 1000 miles. What is the scale for Texas? Using the correct scale for each of the states, measure how wide and how long each state is.

Now, can you see that Texas is not really larger than Alaska? If you want to understand more about scale, try the special investigation on page 96.

IN TRANSIT

We have seen how important soil and water are for growing things. Without them, there could be no agriculture.

What part did agriculture play in settling the land which is now the United States? How has the American farmer used the soil? To find out, turn to the next section.

Look at the pictures of the city block.  What is shown in each picture? One picture is much larger than the other. Is one block larger than the other? The block is one size, but the pictures are different sizes. We call this difference scale.

Now look at the two maps of Hawaii. ▲ One map is much smaller than the other. Each map has the same number of islands and the same islands. Do the maps have different scales?

Look at these pictures. ■ One picture shows a mountain. The other picture shows a boy measuring mountains on a map. The boy is using the mile scale on the map. On his map, one inch is equal to 100 miles. About how many miles wide are the mountains that the boy is measuring?

Now turn back to the map on page 152. Look at the scale for this map. Then, using the scale, measure the distance between New York and San Francisco. Turn to pages 293-294. Is the map

a different size? Does it have a different scale? On this map, measure the distance between New York and San Francisco. Do you find that the distance is the same on both maps?

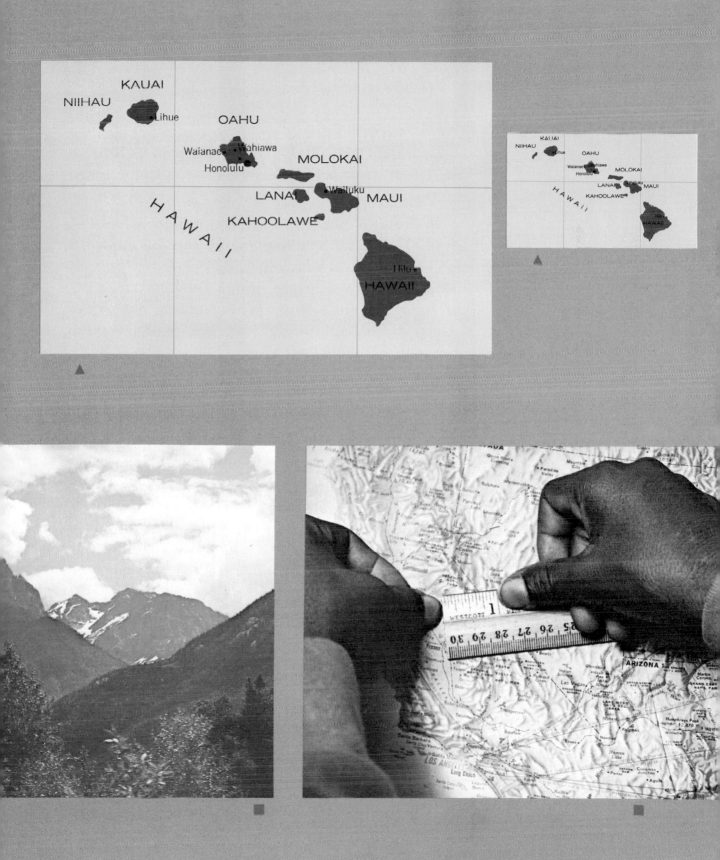

3. The Farmer and His Work

A handful of dark, rich soil smells good to a farmer. He knows how important it is to his crops. He watches the sky, for he knows that he also needs rain so that his crops will have water. He knows, too, that the warm sun must shine on his crops for many days. Good soil, enough water, and sun—without these, crops will not grow well.

The farmer knows that weather can play tricks on him. A sudden cold spell with frost, a bad storm with high winds, a long dry spell, or drought (drout), too many rainy days—any of these could harm his crops. He knows, too, how insects and plant diseases can cause harm.

In the growing season, there are many things for the farmer to think about. Between the planting of seeds and the harvest, many things can happen. The farmer must be able to adapt.

A LAND OF FARMERS

Let us make this statement: Most of you are probably part of family groups that don't grow food. Your families buy most of the food you eat. Let us make another statement: Those of you who live on a farm don't grow *all* the food you need. Are we right?

Suppose that you had lived in one of the thirteen colonies in 1750—perhaps in Connecticut or Maryland or Georgia. Could we make the same statements about you? Probably not.

Not all the people who came to the eastern colonies were farmers. Recall the Pilgrims. Few of them had been farmers in Holland or England. Many did not live through the first cold winter after they landed at Plymouth Rock.

Those who did live had to learn new ways of acting in order to survive. They needed more food than they could find in their environment, so in the spring, they learned how to farm. The Indians taught them how to plant corn and how to work with the soil.

The English colonists in Jamestown also learned to be farmers. To William Penn's Pennsylvania came men who had already learned farming in Germany. These were the "Pennsylvania Dutch." ● To Delaware came the Swedish. They, too, were good farmers.

Throughout the thirteen colonies, most of the colonists learned to till the rich soil of the new land. At that time, there was enough good land for everyone. The colonists used wooden plows to turn over the soil. They planted corn and wheat. In the South, tobacco and rice fields gave good harvests.

Why were these farmers called the "Pennsylvania Dutch"?

●

The first **census**, or counting of people, in the United States was made in 1790. When it was taken, nineteen out of twenty people either were farmers or lived with a farm family. As you can see, the United States was a land of farmers at this time.

Would farmers value the land more than people who lived in cities? Why or why not?

THE CLEARING OF THE LAND

In 1790, the United States was also a land of trees. Great forests stretched from Maine south to Georgia and from the east coast west to the Mississippi River. Clearing land was hard work. With fire and ax, farmers removed most of the trees. The land was cleared by slashing and burning. ● Little thought was given to the trees, because there were so many of them. People thought there would always be enough wood.

The farmer built his home in a clearing—land from which he had removed the trees. His home was built from trees he had cut down. The farmer also cleared land for his crops. He needed the help of his family group to clear the land. Often he needed the help of his neighbors, too. Even in pioneer days, people depended on each other. They needed each other's strength to clear the land.

POOR FARMERS, POOR SOIL

Land can wear out. Crops such as corn and cotton and tobacco take minerals from the soil and leave it poorer. If these crops are planted in the same fields year after year, the soil will have less and less of the minerals the crops use. Then the yield, or harvest, will grow smaller.

The soil can be helped to keep its fertility, or richness. Fertilizer helps by adding minerals. Planting a different crop may help, too. If the crop does not use the same minerals, the soil will have a chance to build up minerals. Letting the field lie fallow, or free of any crop, for a year will help, too.

Thomas Jefferson was a farmer who lived in Virginia. He knew the value of good soil. He knew how to plow so that soil would not wash away. He told his farm workers to follow the **contour** (kon′tŏŏr), or the shape, of the earth. Instead of plowing straight up and down a hill, they plowed around it. That way, water would be caught in each furrow, instead of rushing down the hill and carrying away soil. Study the picture of contour plowing on page 118.

Jefferson also knew that soil must be given care. He knew that it was one of man's most important resources. If man did not choose to use the soil wisely, it would become less and less useful.

Many early American farmers did not know how to take good care of the soil. The soil didn't matter to them. When the land wore out, the farmer could always get more land for his crops. More good soil could always be found just to the west.

If you do not know what a **resource** is, look up the word in your Social Science Dictionary.

FARMERS MOVE WESTWARD

Farmers from North Carolina and Georgia moved to Alabama, Mississippi, and Texas. ● Farmers from Virginia moved to Kentucky and Tennessee. Farmers from New England went to Ohio and Illinois. You will study more about this westward movement. The farmers moved from the eastern seaboard to lands west of the Appalachian (əp′ə·lā′chē·ən) Mountains and from the Mississippi River valley to the prairie country of Missouri, Kansas, and Nebraska.

Once the farmers crossed the Mississippi, they did not have to clear many trees. On the prairies, the grass grew "as high as a horse's belly." The tough roots of the grass made plowing difficult. ▲ Until the invention of the steel plow, which could easily break these roots, plowing was a hard and endless job. But the soil was deep and rich.

Trails led through the Rocky Mountains to good farming land in California and Oregon. Therefore, farmers and their families joined wagon trains and made long journeys. ■ The journeys were full of hardship, but good land was at the end of them.

In their search for better land, the farmers moved from the Atlantic coast farther and still farther west, until they reached the Pacific Ocean. As they moved, they changed the face of the land. They changed the forests and plains into farmland. They changed their environment so that they could grow food from their basic resource, the land. In order to get what they needed to live, they learned new ways of acting in new environments. ◄ But, early in the westward movement, the farmers did not always use the land wisely.

The last part of the country to be settled was the Great Plains, where the Blackfeet had hunted buffalo. Farmers found that the grass which made plowing hard was good for grazing, or feeding, animals. They became cattlemen and sheepmen. Soon great numbers of cattle and sheep were grazing on the plains.

Recall that your **environment** is everything around you.

Recall how quickly Oklahoma was settled during the land rushes. ● The United States was settled in less than three hundred years, from the time the colonists arrived in Jamestown in 1607. The 1890 census said that there was no more **frontier** (frun·tir′). A frontier is unsettled land at the edge of lands where people live. The West had been settled. Farms were spread across the nation, from coast to coast.

Where is "the West"? What does this mean? Has it always meant the same thing? To find out, try the investigation on the opposite page.

━━━━━━━ **AT THIS POINT IN YOUR STUDY** ━━━━━━━

Do these statements seem correct?

1 The early colonists moved west to find new land.

The early colonists moved west when their land was worn-out. Why didn't they stay where they were and use the land they had wisely?

2 The early farmers changed the environment.

Did the farmers *plan* to change the environment? Why did they change it?

AN INVESTIGATION into meaning: where is "the West"?

To the farmer in Plymouth or Jamestown, "the West" meant the land in western Massachusetts or Virginia. To George Washington, "the West" meant Fort Pitt, in western Pennsylvania. What did or does "the West" mean to each of these people?

1 Thomas Jefferson
2 a cotton farmer with worn-out land in Georgia
3 a Blackfoot Indian
4 a farmer and his family on one of the trails through the Rocky Mountains
5 a wheat farmer in Kansas today
6 a fruit grower in California today
7 an astronaut
8 a Hawaiian pineapple grower
9 you

A Problem on Your Own

In 1800, part of the United States was called the Northwest Territory. Look at the map on page 197 to find out where it was. Is this part of the country now called "the Northwest"? What is called "the Northwest" today?

Choose the ending for each of these sentences.

1   When the English first settled in Jamestown, it was said that a squirrel could go from the Atlantic Ocean to the Mississippi River and never touch the ground. This saying means that

(a) the Jamestown colonists had flying squirrels

(b) the land was covered with trees

2   The first colonists were able to use the land because

(a) they adapted to the new environment

(b) they behaved exactly as they had in their old environment

3   One way many farmers solved the problem of worn-out land was

(a) to plant a new crop on it

(b) to move to new land and clear it

USING WHAT YOU KNOW

The roots of the grass on the prairies helped to hold the soil so that it wouldn't be washed away by the rain or blown away by the wind. One day, in South Dakota, an old Sioux (soo) Indian watched a farmer plowing.

With his plow, the farmer dug into the tough grass. The grass was turned over with the roots up. For a long while, the old Sioux watched. Finally, the farmer asked him if he wanted something. The Indian said only three words, "Wrong side up," and walked away. What did he mean by "Wrong side up"?

ON YOUR OWN

One kind of crop that farmers usually plant every few years in a field is a leguminous (lə·gyoo′mə·nəs) crop, peas or beans. Find out what these plants do that other plants cannot do. Try to find out about the nitrogen cycle. How are leguminous plants part of this cycle?

IN TRANSIT

The corn, the tobacco, the cotton, and the potatoes that farmers grow must be harvested. For a long time, man had only his own muscle to use. Today, machines do much of the harvesting. However, not all crops are picked by machines. Fruit, beans, potatoes, and tomatoes are still usually harvested by men, women, and children.

Where do these men, women, and children come from? Begin reading the next section.

4. Two Families—East and West

Part of the farm environment is soil and water. Part of it is weather—rain, snow, wind, sun, heat, and cold. Part of it is crops that the farmer plants and animals that he raises. Another part is people who work in the fields with machines or with their hands. One of the people who work with their hands is a boy. We'll call him George Hunter. ●

A MOVING LIFE

One spring morning, George was listening to his father and the crew leader, Big Tom. They were saying that it was the middle of April and time to start north. George was not surprised. From October to April, the Hunter family lived in Florida. They worked in the orange groves there. In April, when there was not enough work for them, they moved.

George knew that, in another week, they and the other families would go to pick beans. They would pick beans in South Carolina in May, and in North Carolina and Virginia in June. Later, they would dig potatoes in Pennsylvania. By late summer, they would have traveled through Pennsylvania and into New Jersey and New York. By October, there would be no more field work in the North. They would return to Florida.

George was ten years old. As long as he could remember, his family had spent the winter months in Florida. In the spring and summer, they traveled from field to field on the long trip north. Big Tom's crew,

or group, was known as the "Bean Pickers." They followed almost the same route each year. Look at the map on page 110. The routes of the "Bean Pickers" are in red. Follow one route with them. Which states did they go through? Is one of them yours?

George had a brother and two sisters. They were younger than he was. His sister Faith, who was nine, loved to go to school. But there wasn't much chance for her to do that when they were traveling. The family never stayed long enough in one place. One summer, George and his brother and sisters had gone to school in the camp where they were living. But they had stayed in that camp for only a month.

Another summer, George had gotten sick. His father had said George was sick from the water he drank. George didn't like some of the places where they stayed. Sometimes there wasn't enough room. Often there wasn't any place to keep anything. Sometimes there wasn't even an icebox where they could keep food.

When his father finished talking to Big Tom, he came over to George. "Next Monday," he said, "we'll be leaving. We're stopping in Delaware this summer." He pointed to an old school bus. "That's how we're traveling."

THE FRUIT PICKERS

The Roberts family are farm workers, too. They live in a small town in the San Joaquin Valley. ● In the town where the Robertses live, most families are farm workers who spend part of the year working in the orchards and fields of Oregon and Washington.

For nine months of the year, the Roberts family work in the orchards near their home. Every year, in the late summer and early fall, they go to Oregon to pick cherries and apples. Because they spend most of the year in one place, the Roberts children are able to go to school.

Many farmers all over the United States depend on farm workers like the Hunters and the Robertses. Who are these farm workers?

THE MIGRANT STORY

People move into your neighborhood and move out. Perhaps you have moved with your family to a house in a different town. People move to new homes all the time. That doesn't surprise us. But the kind of moving done by the Hunters and the Robertses is different.

The people who move about the United States to work on the crops make up a group called **migrant laborers**. They are **migrant** because they move about. They are **laborers** because they work—in cotton and tobacco fields, in bean and potato fields, and in orchards. Migrant workers are needed to harvest—to pick the crops. They go wherever crops are ready to be harvested. Migrant workers are sometimes called traveling harvesters.

Where do migrant workers come from? Most of them come from worn-out farms or farms too poor to give a living. Some are flown in from Puerto Rico, the British West Indies, and Japan. Some come across the border from Mexico into Texas, California, Arizona, and New Mexico. Still others come from Canada.

No one knows exactly how many workers there are. Because they move about so much, they are hard to count. One guess is that there are about 2 million migrant workers—enough people to fill a big city.

How is a crew leader like the leader of a Blackfoot band?

Recall the story of George. Usually, a number of families move together. One man is in charge of the group. He is the crew leader. He gets the buses and trucks in which the crew travels. He finds the fields in which the crew works. The crew leader agrees with the farmer or grower on the wages his crew will receive. He then pays the workers.

**MAIN ROUTES OF
MIGRANT WORKERS**

The migrant workers find jobs in most of the states. One of the groups moves up the east coast from Florida to Maine. The largest group moves out of southern Texas. Parts of this group work in North Dakota, Utah, the Southwest, and California. A third group travels through California and moves along the Pacific coast into Oregon and Washington.

To learn more about the routes of the migrant workers, try the investigation on the opposite page.

THE HANDS OF PEOPLE

Farmers and growers depend on migrant farm laborers. Even though machines do more of the harvesting all the time, much still has to be done by the hands of people.

Perhaps you can guess some of the problems faced by the migrant workers. Recall George's sister who liked to go to school. Can you see why going to school might be hard for these children? Even if their families didn't move so much, the children are often needed to

AN INVESTIGATION into migrant labor

Study the map carefully. ●

1 Can you find states which are not touched by any of the routes? Which states?

2 Where do most of the routes start? Why do you think the migrant workers work their way northward? Why couldn't they start in the North and work their way to the South?

3 Some of the migrant workers come from Puerto Rico. Which route do you think they take? Some come from Japan. Where do you think they work?

4 Name at least five crops that are harvested by migrant workers. ▲

5 How does the behavior of migrant workers differ from that of people who work in only one place? Describe at least one way.

A Problem on Your Own

Imagine that you belonged to a migrant family. What would your social environment be? What would your physical environment be? Explain how your environment would be different from your environment now.

work in the fields. Without the children's help, their families sometimes cannot make enough money to live.

Many of the camps do not have good housing. Many camps do not have good food. Even drinking water may be hard to get. There is often sickness. Migrant labor families do not have enough money to buy many of the things they need.

There is another problem that migrant workers face. More and more harvesting is being done by machines. Peaches that will not bruise easily have now been grown. This means that it is no longer necessary for someone to climb a tree and pick each peach. A machine can shake the whole tree hard enough to knock all the ripe peaches into a net below.

Tomato plants on which all the tomatoes become ripe at the same time have now been grown. When the tomatoes are ripe, a machine can go up and down a field pulling up the plants. ● The machine shakes the tomatoes loose and catches them in a bin.

It is no longer necessary for human hands to pick fruit gently or for human eyes and brains to decide whether it is ripe enough. Machine harvesting is a help to the farmers. But to the migrant workers, it means that they must change their way of making a living. They must learn new skills and perhaps even a new way of life. They must adapt—they must learn new ways of behaving.

▰▰▰▰ AT THIS POINT IN YOUR STUDY ▰▰▰▰

Do these statements seem correct?

1 People are resources.

How are the migrant workers a resource? How do they help us use another resource?

2 People sometimes have to change their behavior.

How is the role of the migrant workers changing? Why might many of them have to learn new ways of acting?

Choose the ending for each of these sentences.

1 Migrant laborers are workers who
  (a) travel
  (b) stay in one place

2 Farmers in the United States depend on migrant farm laborers mainly to
  (a) plant crops
  (b) harvest crops

3 Migrant workers can be found in
  (a) almost every state
  (b) only a few states

USING WHAT YOU KNOW

1 Recall how people moved from their farms in the East to lands in the West. Would you say that farmers who moved from New England to Ohio were migrant laborers? How were they different from migrant laborers?

2 Many Puerto Ricans are flown to Pennsylvania to help harvest mushrooms. Some of them stay in Pennsylvania and work all year with the mushrooms. These people are sometimes called **staygrants**, instead of migrants. Why do you think they are called this?

ON YOUR OWN

1 Some farmers and growers believe that, in a few years, all harvesting will be done by machines. What do you think will happen to migrant laborers? What new ways of acting might they have to learn?

2 Migrant children often do not have the chance to go to school. Do you think that this will have anything to do with the way they will live when they are adults? Explain your answer.

IN TRANSIT

The United States is a country rich in land resources. There is good soil on much of the land. The land produces a great many different crops. Migrant laborers help to bring in great harvests.

Recall, however, that land wears out. Soil erodes. Minerals are taken from it by crops. Is there enough good soil and water to give us all the food we will ever need?

The land must be used well if it is to give us food. Have the people of the United States used the land wisely? Are they using it wisely now? To find out about how Americans use the land, turn to the next section.

5.　　Saving the Land

You know that soil can be moved from one place to another. Recall how a delta is formed. Can all the topsoil in one place be lost so that it can never be used again? Perhaps you think that farmers would not let this happen. But many farmers did. They let the rich soil that covered thousands of acres be carried away by wind.

DUST BOWL AREA OF THE 1930'S

THE DUST BOWL

Suppose that you had a plant growing in a pot. What would happen if you stopped watering it? It would die. Then the soil around it would become very dry and hard. Suppose that you broke up the dry, hard soil. It would become almost like powder, and you could blow it away.

In the 1930's, parts of Oklahoma, Texas, and Kansas became a "bowl of dust." ● The dust was carried by the wind, and topsoil was blown away. In fact, in some places, *all* the topsoil was blown away.

Think of the Dust Bowl as a large flowerpot filled with thousands of acres of soil. Much of the soil was worn-out from too much planting. Years of drought had dried out the soil. The hot sun had baked it hard. But many farmers still plowed and planted in the dry soil. Like the soil in your flowerpot, the prairie soil turned powdery. When the winds blew, the soil was swept up and blown high and far away. Sometimes it was blown hundreds of miles.

Recall how many years are needed to make just one inch of topsoil. In two or three dust storms, the work of hundreds of years was blown away. Like water, wind wears away and erodes land that is not cared for.

For over two hundred years, many farmers moved when their land was worn-out and badly eroded. It seemed to them that there would always be more land. But finally there was not new land when farmers wanted to move. And some land was worn-out. It had not been used wisely.

What happened to the farmers who lived in the Dust Bowl? When their land wore out, they could not move to new land. The land they had made poor had blown away, and there was not enough new land for them. ● In order to live, they had to change their way of life. They had to adapt—to learn new ways of behaving. Many gave up farming. ▲ Some worked on other people's farms. Some joined the migrant groups.

WISE USE

If only the wind could be stopped from blowing or the right amount of rain could be made to fall! But farmers could not stop the wind or bring the rain. They had to learn what they could do. They could value the soil. They could use it wisely. That is, they could learn to **conserve** (kən·sûrv′) it. To conserve means to "save" or "protect." When you take good care of something so that it can be used again and again, you are practicing **conservation**. Conservation means wise use. Conserving soil means using the soil wisely, so that it does not wear out.

A TRUE STORY OF A CONSERVATIONIST

When Hugh Bennett was ten years old, his father let him help with a special job. Topsoil was washing off the Bennetts' North Carolina farm. Hugh's father

Do you recall the reason for dust storms?

decided to try **terracing**. Terracing means making steps on steep, sloping land. ● Each flat step holds rain that would run straight down a steep slope. Terracing was hard work. When he was older, Hugh remembered his father telling him why they had to work so hard: "To keep the land from washing away."

Hugh never forgot. He spent his life studying soil erosion. He became a **soil conservationist**, someone who works to conserve soil. He worked hard to get the government to set up a soil conservation service that would teach farmers how to take care of the soil.

One day, Hugh Bennett was in Washington, D.C., talking to members of the United States Senate. As he talked, the room became dark. Somebody said it looked like rain. But Hugh Bennett knew the real reason. In Oklahoma City, there was a great dust storm. There was so much dust that it was making the sky dark all the way to Washington, D.C.!

After that happened, it was easier to get Congress to act on the problem of soil erosion. Hugh Bennett helped found the Soil Conservation Service in 1935. Along with a number of soil scientists, he taught farmers in the Dust Bowl and in the rest of the Great Plains. He taught them to value the soil. ▲ True, they couldn't control the wind or make rain. But perhaps they could copy nature in other ways.

In order to conserve the soil, the farmers had to learn first to hold the soil in place. They did this by planting tough Sudan grass and broom corn. After the harvest, they left the stubble, rather than plowing it under. The stubble is what remains of the cut stalks and their roots. The stubble gave cover to the soil. It protected the soil from hard rain and winds. The roots of the stubble held the soil in place.

People in the Soil Conservation Service have worked with farmers and helped them save the soil. ■ They have taught the farmers, among other things, **contour plowing**, **terracing**, and **strip cropping**.

CONTOUR PLOWING

Contour plowing was not new. Recall that Thomas Jefferson used it. In a sense, Jefferson was one of the earliest American conservationists. But in the 1930's, the idea that contour plowing would help keep water in the soil was new to some American farmers. Study the picture of contour plowing today. ●

You can see how this method helped farmers. Try to make a model of contour plowing like the one in the investigation on the opposite page.

TERRACING

You have walked down steps. Imagine each flat part of a step where you put your foot to be flat land. That part of the step, or terrace, is planted. Then there is a drop to the next level, which is also planted, and so on. ▲ A heavy rain does not rush down a steep hill that has been terraced. It does not wash away the soil. The water is held by each terrace and can sink into the earth. Recall that this was the first conservation method Hugh Bennett learned. At that time, many farmers did not practice it. However, men had been terracing the earth for thousands of years.

STRIP CROPPING

Suppose that you wanted to plant a corn crop. Corn plants must stand apart from each other. There is space between the plants, and rain can wash away the soil.

Suppose that you planted the corn in a long strip of a few rows, instead of a square field of many rows. Then the soil would not be washed far. Next to the corn, you could plant a strip with thick, low alfalfa, which would catch all the soil that the rain washed from around the corn. By planting different crops in strips next to each other, the farmer keeps the soil from washing away. ■

CONTOUR PLOWING

Contour plowing was not new. Recall that Thomas Jefferson used it. In a sense, Jefferson was one of the earliest American conservationists. But in the 1930's, the idea that contour plowing would help keep water in the soil was new to some American farmers. Study the picture of contour plowing today. ●

You can see how this method helped farmers. Try to make a model of contour plowing like the one in the investigation on the opposite page.

TERRACING

You have walked down steps. Imagine each flat part of a step where you put your foot to be flat land. That part of the step, or terrace, is planted. Then there is a drop to the next level, which is also planted, and so on. ▲ A heavy rain does not rush down a steep hill that has been terraced. It does not wash away the soil. The water is held by each terrace and can sink into the earth. Recall that this was the first conservation method Hugh Bennett learned. At that time, many farmers did not practice it. However, men had been terracing the earth for thousands of years.

STRIP CROPPING

Suppose that you wanted to plant a corn crop. Corn plants must stand apart from each other. There is space between the plants, and rain can wash away the soil.

Suppose that you planted the corn in a long strip of a few rows, instead of a square field of many rows. Then the soil would not be washed far. Next to the corn, you could plant a strip with thick, low alfalfa, which would catch all the soil that the rain washed from around the corn. By planting different crops in strips next to each other, the farmer keeps the soil from washing away. ■

AN INVESTIGATION into contour plowing

Take two small boxes about sixteen inches long, twelve inches wide, and four inches deep. Make them watertight by lining them with plastic material, aluminum foil, or tarpaper. At one end of each box, cut a V-notch one to one and one-half inches deep, and fit it with a spout to let runoff water out.

Take two flower sprinklers, each at least a quart in size, two half-gallon wide-mouthed fruit jars, and two sticks of wood about one-inch thick.

Fill both boxes with soil taken from the same place. ● Set them on a table, and place a stick under one end of each box to make a slope. Place the fruit jars below the spouts. Using your finger, make furrows across the soil in one box, and up and down in the other. ▲ Which soil has now been contour plowed?

Fill the sprinklers with water, and *slowly* sprinkle the two boxes at the same time. Hold the sprinklers at the same height above the soil, and pour at the same rate. Which jar fills up faster? ■ Which jar receives more water? more soil?

A Problem on Your Own

Contour plowing is only one of many ways to conserve soil. ◄ After the dust storms, a great belt of trees was planted from the northern part of North Dakota all the way to Texas. Why was this done? What were the trees supposed to do?

CONSERVATION IN PRACTICE

If you do not remember what a **norm** is, look up the word in your Social Science Dictionary.

Not all farmers were willing to learn new ways of behaving. Not all were willing to change their customs. Yet, they knew that, unless almost everyone changed, the soil would keep on blowing away. One man alone couldn't save the land if his neighbors didn't care. The farmers depended on each other. Slowly, wise use of the soil became everybody's work. Conservation became everybody's goal. Today, many farmers practice conservation. Using the soil wisely is becoming a norm of behavior for American farmers.

Another drought came to the Great Plains. It lasted for almost six years. But this time, the farmers did not suffer as badly as they had in the 1930's. The farmers who had adapted were rewarded.

If a resource becomes scarce, people must conserve it or lose it. In this case, the resource was land. Today, other resources are not being used wisely. For instance, we fill the air with smoke and with exhaust fumes from cars. ● We poison the rivers and oceans with sewage. ▲

Man learned to conserve the soil. Will he learn to conserve water and air? Will he learn to conserve all parts of the environment in which he must live? Someday, perhaps conservation will become the behavior of all Americans.

AT THIS POINT IN YOUR STUDY

Does this statement seem correct?
American farmers learned new ways of acting.
What evidence do you have that farmers did this? What reasons can you give for this change in behavior?
Why should all Americans learn to conserve resources? Which resources need to be conserved?

BEFORE YOU GO ON

Choose the ending for each of these sentences.

1 Many farmers had not practiced conservation because
(a) there were no ways to preserve the soil
(b) they had not thought it was necessary

2 When farmers practice soil conservation, they
(a) keep the soil from blowing or washing away
(b) leave the land bare of crops

3 In order to conserve their resources, people must
(a) stop trying
(b) work with each other

USING WHAT YOU KNOW

1 The Dust Bowl area has been called "a man-made desert." Do you think this is a good name for the Dust Bowl? Why?

2 Some states have laws about conservation. For example, one law says that, when trees are cut down, others must be planted in their place. A man in the state of Washington said that the law could not tell him what to do with his trees. He went to court. Finally, the Supreme Court of the United States said that the state law must be obeyed. (If you don't know what the Supreme Court is, look it up in your Social Science Dictionary.)

Do you agree with the man or with the Court? Why?

ON YOUR OWN

1 Patrick Henry is well known for the expression, "Give me liberty or give me death." He also said, "He is the greatest patriot who stops up the most gullies." What did he mean?

2 Find out something that people in your community do to conserve one of these resources: people, air, water, soil, minerals, or forests. Find out something that the national government is doing. ●

Focus on the Concept

Think about some foods you eat. Orange juice, peanut butter sandwiches, ice cream, and cake all begin as seeds in soil. Eggs come from chickens. ● Chickens depend on seeds. Milk comes from cows. The basic food of the cow is grass, and grass begins as a seed. One way or another, almost all of the food you eat depends on soil.

Look at the map. ▲ It shows where the plants and animals we use for food are grown.

Study the map. Try to answer these questions:

1 Which area or areas of the country produce milk?
2 Which areas produce meat? ■
3 Which areas produce the grains for cereal and bread?
4 Which areas produce fruit?
5 Which areas produce vegetables?

The map will help you to sum up some of the ideas in this unit. Perhaps this statement agrees with what you have learned about the concept of **environment: People depend on the land as a basic resource.**

The Farm Changes

You know now that farmland was not always used wisely. It was not always valued. Because the amount of good land seemed without end, farmers would move to new land, rather than take care of the old.

In the 1800's, the United States was growing in area and number of people. To get more food, people simply farmed new lands in old ways. Many believed there was no need to take care of worn-out soil. In the West, there was good, new land. Conservation was not yet a norm of behavior. That is, it was not yet behavior that was expected of farmers.

FARM PRODUCTS

ALASKA

HAWAII

FARM PRODUCTS OF THE UNITED STATES

| Barley | Cattle | Citrus Fruit | Corn | Cotton | Dairy | Flax | Fruit | Hogs | Oats |

| Peanuts | Potatoes | Rice | Sheep | Soy Beans | Sugar Beets | Sugar Cane | Tobacco | Vegetables | Wheat |

0   200   400   600
Miles

0   200   400
Miles

0   50   100
Miles

You learned that the people who moved west changed the environment. They cut forests, planted crops, and built homes. You have, then, begun to understand this about the concept of **environment: People change the environment when they use it.**

The Dangers of Poor Use

People sometimes change the environment so that plants and animals can no longer live on it. You have seen that the land in the Dust Bowl was changed so that plants could no longer live on it. ●

After the dust storms, farmers changed their behavior. They learned ways to conserve soil. They began to value the land. American farmers began to take on a new norm of behavior—caring for the land. ▲

Even now, all is not well with the land. People do not use the water wisely. They poison the air. Perhaps you can see that there is a great need: the need for us to use the environment well. You have, then, learned something else about the concept of **environment: People must take care of the environment if they are to get what they need from it.**

Today

Today, the United States is rich in farmland. Farmers can grow more than enough food for our needs. But will there always be enough food? Each year, there are more and more people. All of them need food.

There is only so much good land. If we take care of it, the land will take care of us. Your study of this unit has helped you understand this important statement about the concept of **environment: People use their environment to get what they need.**

Slowly, we are learning to value the air, the water, the land, and the life on it. Now we must act on our values.

Focus on the Concept

A. PROBLEMS IN ANALYSIS

Study the map. ● In this area, trees had been cut. When the trees were gone, so were the leaves which had once protected the soil from hard rains. Gone, too, were the roots which had kept the rich soil from washing away.

Heavy rains did not soak slowly into the ground. They washed the soil into the rivers. The rivers ran brown with the rich soil. The soil was lost from the land.

Rains swelled the rivers. Water rose above the river banks, and the floods came. And with the floods came ruined homes, ruined crops, and ruined lives.

In the 1930's, the national government set up the Tennessee Valley Authority, or TVA. The TVA used what was then known of conservation methods. ▲

TENNESSEE VALLEY AUTHORITY

▲

Map: Ohio River, KENTUCKY, Clinch River, Holston River, Cumberland River, Nashville, Oak Ridge, Knoxville, TENNESSEE, NORTH CAROLINA, Chattanooga, SOUTH CAROLINA, Tennessee River, GEORGIA, ALABAMA

❰ Some Important TVA Dams   0   50   100   ●

1   What conservation practices could the TVA have put into use? Name some. What is the purpose of each?
2   Like droughts, floods are a serious problem. What can be done to control the sudden swelling of rivers?

125

In this unit, you learned one way to solve the problem of not having enough water. How could this way also solve the problem of sometimes having too much water? ●

●

B. A PROBLEM IN PREDICTION

Once, man traveled over land on horses and mules. He traveled over oceans on sailing vessels. Trains and cars replaced horses. Steamships replaced sailing ships. The airplane is now beginning to replace most other ways of traveling.

Agriculture, or farming, is man's basic source of food. What might replace agriculture?

C. AN ANALYSIS OF VALUES

1 How might a conservationist act on his values? How might a farmer who is a conservationist behave if each of these things happened?

(a) Gullies began to show on his land.

(b) The land did not grow as much food as it did in the years before.

(c) He found cans and paper dumped on his land.

2 Has there been a change in the way people behave toward the land? Have their values changed? What evidence can you find that this is so?

Focus on the Social Scientist

The first soil conservationists looked at the ways in which men were using the land. They found that men were changing it so that it would no longer be a useful resource. They tried to teach wiser use of the land. Both conservationists and **human geographers** study man's ways of using the land.

In this unit, you began to study the ways in which people use the land to get their food. You also began to study movements of large groups of people (the farmers who went west and the migrant workers who travel from place to place). In other words, you began a study of human geography.

Human geographers are interested in how man has changed his environment. For example, the human geographer Emrys Jones has studied how people have moved from nation to nation and from the country to the city. He has tried to find out how such movements will change the environment.

Sometimes a human geographer puts what he has learned on a map. ● Maps can show where people move. They can show how the land is used. What maps did you study in this unit? Did they show either of these things?

Recall that **social** refers to people living and working in groups. Because human geographers are social scientists, they do not study the land alone. They observe people in their environment. They want to know how the physical environment changes the lives of people. They also want to know how groups of people use the environment.

A social scientist reasons from the evidence. He gets evidence from careful research into the way people behave. Do you see now why human geography is a social science?

UNIT FOUR

ACTING TO SHARE RESOURCES

Introduction

What would you do if you had earned some money? Would you spend it? Would you save it? Would you give it to a friend?

If you decided to spend the money, what would you buy? There are probably many things that you would like to have. Maybe you would not have quite enough money to buy something you wanted. Could you save your money until you had enough money to buy it?

Perhaps you would choose to buy a ball with your money. If you did, you would have to pay the price that the storekeeper set on it. How does the storekeeper decide how to set a fair price on his goods? How do goods get into the stores where you can buy them?

In this unit, you will learn how people share resources. You will learn how people depend on each other for their needs and wants. You will learn how people earned and spent money in the past. ● You will learn how they earn and spend money today. ▲

Let's begin our study by asking what you would do if you had fifty cents.

1. Some Money of Your Own

Suppose that somehow you had earned fifty cents. Suppose that you decided to spend the money. Could you buy everything you want?

If you saved your fifty cents and earned fifty cents more, you would have a dollar. Could you then buy everything you want?

Even with a dollar, you would still be **limited** in what you could buy, wouldn't you? You couldn't buy *all* the things you needed or wanted.

Perhaps you could do something to get more of the things you wanted. You could earn more dollars and increase your **income**. With more income, you would have more money to spend. Recall that people earn income by **producing goods** (making products). They may also earn income by **producing services** (doing things for people). Services and other goods are alike in an important way. Can you guess what it is? They both fill people's wants. That is why goods and services are produced.

People who produce goods or services are acting in the role of **producers**. People who use goods and services are acting in the role of **consumers**.

Recall the migrant workers (pages 107-112). They are human resources. You, too, are a human resource. Can you produce goods, such as kites or candy? Can you produce services, such as delivering newspapers or shining shoes? What resources do you have that you can use to produce services or goods? Your resources may also be other people who can do useful things.

Income is all the money that a person receives.

What are **resources**? If you don't remember, look up the word in your Social Science Dictionary.

To understand your resources better, try the investigation on the opposite page.

IS MORE MONEY ENOUGH?

Perhaps you are already using your resources to earn income. ● We don't know. Anyhow, let us suppose that you are. Now you may have five or even six dollars! Will you be as limited as you were with one dollar? No, five or six dollars can buy more things than one dollar, can't they?

Now that you have at least five dollars, perhaps you may see many more things that you would like to have. Perhaps you would like to have a baseball glove, a book, a doll house, or many, many other things. Or perhaps you might like to save this money, too.

Would you agree that there is a limit to what even five dollars can buy? Suppose you had a hundred or even five hundred dollars. Would you still be limited? Or could you get everything you wanted?

COULD THERE EVER BE ENOUGH MONEY?

You know now that you will always be limited in what you can buy. Everyone is limited in what he can have. Every person wants many, many things, but no one can have everything. Is this only because no one has enough money to buy everything?

No, indeed. The amount of money which you have will always be limited, but resources are limited, too. Earlier, you learned that resources must be conserved. You learned that they must be used wisely because they are limited, or **scarce**. No matter how many we have, we never have an unlimited supply.

Goods are made from the resources of our country. As you know, lumber comes from forests. Our food comes from farmlands. Automobiles and tools are made from minerals in the earth. What else is made

AN INVESTIGATION into your resources

What are your own resources? At the top of a piece of paper, write "My Resources." First, make a list of human resources. Write down what you *know how to do*. Then write down the names of *people you know* who may be helpful to you. They are human resources, too.

Second, make a list of the *things you have* that may help you produce services or goods.

When you make your lists, think about these things:

1 What skills do you have? For example, can you draw? Can you cook?

2 What skills do your friends or the members of your family have?

3 What tools do you have? A bicycle, a wagon, or a needle and thread? ●

4 What tools do the people who will help you have? ▲

How many more resources can you list? Can you use all the resources in the world? Or are your resources limited?

●

●

A Problem on Your Own

Goods and services both help to fill people's wants. ■ How many services can you name that are produced without using goods?

▲

from minerals? Perhaps you see that goods, too, are scarce, because resources are scarce.

Both goods and services depend on the human resources of our country. ● There are a great many human resources—people with skills and knowledge. But human resources are limited. No person can have all the services he wants. Services, too, are scarce.

IT'S A MATTER OF CHOICE

When you had fifty cents, you knew that you could not have everything you wanted. You had to make the kinds of choices that everyone must make. Sometimes, it is not hard to choose. On a hot afternoon in the summer, it is not hard to choose a cold drink instead of a hot drink. When you are hungry, it is not hard to choose a hamburger instead of a piece of bubble gum. But, when you have just enough money for skates or an airplane or a baseball glove, and your mother's birthday is coming, the choice is hard.

Who helps you make choices? When you are grown, you will make them for yourself. Sometimes other people may help you make them. Now, your parents or your teacher may help you choose. Perhaps your friends help you. Where you live may help you make choices, too. If you live in Texas or Florida, you might not choose to spend your money on skis or ice skates. Why not? What else might help you make choices?

We always seem to want more things than we can buy. Perhaps you can think of a way to buy everything that you want now. But you will certainly want more things later. You may have to choose between something you want now and something you know you will want later. Choices are always based on values. You choose what you value most. Of course, you do not have everything from which to choose. You must choose from what is available to you.

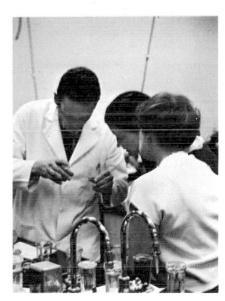

CHOICES—THEN AND NOW

Suppose that you had lived with the Blackfoot Indians on the Great Plains. What choices could you have made in food? in clothing? Recall that the Blackfeet used the resources in their environment—especially the buffalo—for most of the things they needed.

Suppose that you had lived with Daniel Boone in Boonesboro, Kentucky, in 1775. ● You would have had few foods to choose from—bear meat, deer meat, perhaps rabbit, and corn grown near the fort. Compare the limited choice then with the many different kinds of food in a supermarket today. ▲

In Boonesboro, what choice of clothing would you have had? Some woolens, perhaps, and leather clothes made from animal skins. How does this compare with the choice of clothing you have in a department store today? Of course, even in a department store, there are only a certain number of things from which to choose. You have to pick what you value most.

ANOTHER KIND OF SOCIAL SCIENTIST

There are social scientists who study *who* produces goods and *who* produces services. They study *how* goods and services are produced, too. They study the choices made by consumers, the people who use goods and services. They study how people earn income and how they spend it. They are interested in how many dollars are spent for fun. They are interested in how many dollars are saved.

These social scientists are called **economists** (i·kon′ə·mists). The subject that they study is called **economics** (ek′ə·nom′iks). Economists can, for example, tell us where income comes from and how it is used. When you study how people earn and spend money, you are studying some of the things an economist studies.

As you will learn later in this unit, economists are interested not only in money but in all of man's resources. They are interested in how people use the limited resources which are available.

◼◼◼◼◼◼ **AT THIS POINT IN YOUR STUDY** ◼◼◼◼◼◼

Do these statements seem correct?

1 Nobody can have everything he wants.

Suppose that you could buy everything you want today. Would you want something else tomorrow?

2 People must make choices about spending income.

When you have fifty cents to spend, what kinds of choices must you make? How do your choices depend on your values?

What kinds of choices must your family make? Ask your parents. How do your family's choices depend on their values?

BEFORE YOU GO ON

Choose the ending for each of these sentences.

1. If you had a large amount of money,
   (a) you could buy everything you want
   (b) you would have to choose what you need and want most

2. Nobody can have everything he wants because
   (a) goods and services are scarce
   (b) goods and services are not limited

3. Because resources are limited, people must
   (a) make a great deal of money
   (b) make choices

USING WHAT YOU KNOW

Imagine that you own some land near the edge of a town. It is wooded land with a stream running through it. Some people want to buy your land and build houses on it. Your town would like to buy it, too, to make a park for the town. The builders will pay more for your land than the town. You have to make a choice. Which of the following choices will you make?

sell to the builders
sell to the town
keep the land

Why did you make the choice you did? What else might you have wanted to know before you made your choice? What did your choice have to do with your values?

ON YOUR OWN

Suppose that you were the President of the United States. ● Whom might you ask for help in planning the use of our country's resources?

IN TRANSIT

We know that resources are limited. No person, town, or country can have everything. How do people decide how to use resources? How do they plan ahead? To find out, begin reading the next section.

2. Choosing and Planning

Recall that, when you had fifty cents, you had to make choices. Are families limited in what they can have? Are communities also limited in what they can have? All groups of people must make choices. All groups must plan how to spend their money and how to use their resources. Let's begin our study of the choices made by groups by looking at the family.

THE FAMILY MAKES CHOICES

What a family chooses to do with its money depends partly on how much income it has. But there are some things that every family must have. There are some things that a family cannot choose to do without. Most families spend money for food, shelter, and gas and electricity. Most of them spend money for clothing and for gasoline for a car. Some money may be set aside for taxes, and some for medicine and doctor bills.

Of course, the family may choose the *kinds* of food and clothing it will buy. It may choose the *kind* of car and the *kind* of house it will buy. What kinds of things it chooses to buy will depend on what it values most, won't it? Does your family value oranges more than bananas? Does it value wool or cotton clothing more than Dacron clothing? Does it value one kind of car more than another kind?

Sometimes, however, a family may have to make a choice between two very different things. A family might have to decide whether to spend money on a vacation or on a new car. Might a family have to choose between a color television set and braces for the children's teeth?

Families can make plans which are based on their choices. They can plan how much money to spend and how much to save. Let's look at one kind of plan which many families make.

THE FAMILY PLANS TO SPEND

Suppose that a family has a hundred dollars a week to spend. Of course, many families have a smaller income than this. Many families have a larger income. We are not saying that a family's income *should* be a hundred dollars a week. We are using this amount only because it is easy to work with.

What would the family's **monthly income** be?

If a family has a hundred dollars a week to spend, its weekly income is one hundred dollars. Weekly income is the amount of money which "comes in" each week of the year. Is there a limit to what this family can do? You know that no family can buy everything.

Families often make a plan for spending their income.● A plan for spending money is called a **budget**. Look at the budget for the family that has a weekly income of a hundred dollars. ▲

Try to answer these questions:

1   Do all families have an income of a hundred dollars a week?

2   Do all families with the same income spend their money in the same way?

3   What do you think "Other things" could be?

4   The budget shown is the same for every week. But would you expect the family to follow it *exactly* each week? Explain your answer.

5   Do some families need more, or less, money than other families? Why?

6   Does every family make a budget?

	Food	$25.00
	Rent	24.00
	Car	13.00
	Electricity and gas	2.00
	Clothing	9.00
	Doctor's bills and medicine	4.00
	Payment on a washing machine	3.00
	Savings	2.00
	Taxes	6.00
	Other things	12.00
		$100.00

Suppose that a family gets more income. How do you think the extra money will change the family's choices? What might happen if a family suddenly had less income?

THE COMMUNITY PLANS TO USE ITS INCOME

Planning is a way of deciding ahead of time how to act. Could you build a house without making some kind of plan? We doubt it. Does your family make plans? A family budget is one kind of plan for spending income.

Like families, communities have incomes. The income that a town or city receives comes from **taxes** that people pay. Some of the income of every family in the community is used for taxes. Businesses pay taxes, too.

Why are taxes collected? There are many things that each person cannot do alone. The people of a community elect leaders to do the things that cannot be done by each person alone. They expect their government to do things which all of them need done. Community taxes help pay for schools, a police force, garbage collection, playgrounds, public libraries, and care of the streets. ● Does any community have enough tax money to buy everything its members want?

Towns must choose what to do with their community income. They must decide on how much to spend on repairing roads and how much to spend on paying policemen. Because communities cannot have everything they want, they budget their tax money.

The leaders decide how much of each **tax dollar** will go for each of the community services. They plan to use some of it for police and firemen, some of it for schools, some for care of the streets, and some for each of the many other things that are needed. Study the way the tax dollar is spent in one community. ▲ For what is the biggest part of the tax dollar spent in this town? Why?

THE COMMUNITY PLANS TO USE ITS LAND

Land is an important resource in all communities. Most towns and cities make choices about the way land is to be used. Communities have to decide what they value most. They have to plan so that their town will become what the people want it to be. They choose to use some of the land for houses and some of it for stores and factories. They choose to use some land for schools and hospitals, some for roads and streets, and some for parks and playgrounds.

These choices are sometimes very hard to make. Perhaps you can guess why. Do you think that towns have as much land as they want? Can they have all the parks and playgrounds they want?

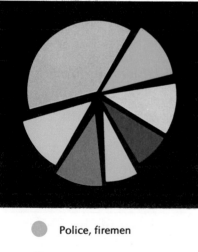

Police, firemen

Streets

Garbage

Playground, library

Help for old and sick

Town workers

Schools ▲

A few years ago, the city of New Haven, Connecticut, began to make some plans. Many of the houses in the city were old and needed repairing. Stores were old and unattractive. Streets were poorly laid out, and there were many traffic problems. ● People may have valued a beautiful city, but they had not acted on their values. They had not done what they should have to keep the city beautiful.

The city government carefully studied the many problems. They wanted people to live in good, attractive houses. They wanted nice stores for people to shop in. They wanted broad streets so that traffic could move smoothly.

When they had studied the problems, the city made a plan. Many people helped to make it. They knew it would take a long time to make their city beautiful again.

Most of the people who lived in the town agreed on the plan. Then work began. Old houses were repaired or torn down, along with old stores. New houses and stores began to appear. After two or three years, New Haven looked like a new city. ▲ There were signs of change everywhere. Most of the people were happy with the new city. Slowly but surely, the plan was being made to work.

People in many towns and cities in the United States are making plans. In San Francisco, for example, plans have been made for a subway that will help solve traffic problems. This subway is now being built. Plans have also been made to replace old, run-down buildings with new ones. Architects, like Jorge De Quesada, have designed big, new buildings. ■

People in many places are making choices and acting on their values. They know that careful planning will help them get what they want.

Communities plan in many ways. To learn about one kind of community planning, try the investigation on the opposite page.

AN INVESTIGATION into community planning

When a community decides how its land is to be used, it may divide the land into **zones**. ● Plans may be made to have different zones for different uses. For example, stores cannot be built in a zone that is planned for homes. Factories cannot be built in a zone for parks or playgrounds.

Find out whether your community is divided into zones. If it is, try to answer these questions:

1 What are the different zones? Are there zones for family housing? ▲ Are there zones for factories? ■ for offices or apartments? ►◄

2 When did the zoning begin? Who began it?

3 Is everybody pleased with the zoning? Why or why not?

A Problem on Your Own

Are all communities zoned the way yours is? If you live in a city, find out about a small town in a farming region. If you do not live in a city, find out about the zones of a city near you. (You may be able to get a zoning map by writing to a city chamber of commerce.)

Why is land zoned differently in different kinds of communities? How does zoning depend on the values of the community?

THE COUNTRY MAKES CHOICES

Study the map carefully. ● Observe that the United States is rich in many resources. Where is the land that is used for growing food? Where are trees that can be cut for lumber or made into paper?

Perhaps you have noticed something about the map. Only **natural resources** are shown on it. But men have built cities, towns, and highways in the United States. These **man-made resources** are not shown on the map.

What are **natural resources**? What are **man-made resources**?

▲

Where resources are found sometimes depends entirely on the environment. ▲ People cannot choose, for example, where oil is to be found in the earth. They cannot choose where the soil will be good for growing crops. But people do have to make choices about the way in which natural resources are used. For example, they must decide whether good soil is to be used for one kind of crop or another. They may have to decide whether land should be used for farmland or for homes.

All over the country, people make choices about man-made resources, too. Sometimes, where man-made resources are built depends on the environment. Can a harbor be built in the desert? But choices must often be made about where cities, towns, and highways should be built.

Across the nation, families and communities, businessmen and farmers, make choices about man-made and natural resources. How are these choices made? Choices depend on values. They depend on what people want and need most.

The people choose who will be the country's leaders. Leaders in the national government make choices about the way in which the country's resources are used. The leaders act for all the people—for the whole country. They act on the country's values.

Earlier, you saw that soil in the United States was not always used wisely. But Americans have now

NATURAL RESOURCES

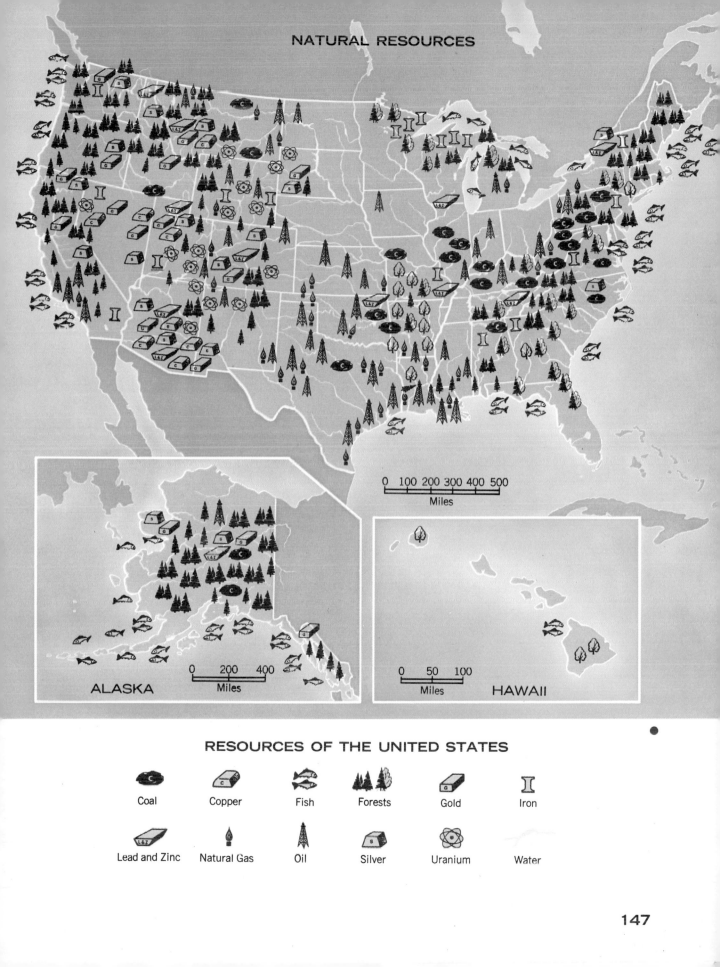

0 100 200 300 400 500
Miles

ALASKA
0   200   400
Miles

0   50   100
Miles
HAWAII

RESOURCES OF THE UNITED STATES

Coal

Copper

Fish

Forests

Gold

Iron

Lead and Zinc

Natural Gas

Oil

Silver

Uranium

Water

chosen to conserve the soil. They have begun to value it. Recall that the national government set up the Soil Conservation Service. This service teaches farmers how to use the land well—how to conserve it.

The government has chosen to set aside national parks, forests, and seashores. These resources belong to everyone—that is the choice that has been made. Why are some forests set aside and made into national parks? Why are some seashores set aside?

Economists study the choices you make. They study the economic choices made by your family and your community and your country. The way your family and your community use their resources is a matter of choice. The way a country uses its resources is a matter of choice, too.

PLANNING FOR THE FUTURE

Scientists predict that, by the year 2000, there will be twice as many people in the world as there are today. Some places, like Hong Kong, are already very crowded. ● It is hard to imagine so many people. Just suppose there were twice as many people living in your home. Would more food and clothing be needed? Would there be enough space for everybody?

Population means "number of people." The population of the world is the total number of people living in it.

Population scientists give us helpful information. They study how fast the **population** is growing. From **data** (information) about what is happening now, they try to predict the future. Careful predictions help us plan ahead. If we know what is going to happen, we can make better plans for the future.

What plans will have to be made to take care of everybody in the world in the year 2000? Think about plans for allowing enough space so that people will have places to live and work and play. Think, also, about plans for producing enough food and clothing.

Perhaps you are already making plans for your life. You are deciding how you will act in the future.

Of course, you don't know yet exactly what you will be doing in the year 2000. But you may have some good ideas. What are your plans?

========= AT THIS POINT IN YOUR STUDY =========

Do these statements seem correct?

1   Groups make choices which are based on their values.

Suppose that a family chooses to buy eyeglasses for one of the children instead of a new set of dishes. What would you say the family values more?

A community may choose not to allow many factories within the town. It may be zoned mostly for houses. What might one value of this community be?

2   Planning is choosing ahead of time.

What might happen if a family didn't plan for the future?

What might happen if a city didn't plan ahead? Does your community plan? Try to find out.

BEFORE YOU GO ON

Choose the ending for each of these sentences.

1 Choices are made by
   (a) some economists
   (b) everybody
2 Plans for spending income are made by
   (a) families
   (b) families, communities, and countries
3 Planning helps people make
   (a) wiser choices
   (b) a great deal of money

USING WHAT YOU KNOW

1 Before Garth goes to school, he delivers the morning newspaper. He uses his bicycle to deliver the paper. For his work, he earns five dollars a week.

   Garth saves two dollars a week for a new bicycle. He puts the money to be saved in the bank each week. The bank pays him **interest**. That means Garth receives an extra four cents from the bank for each dollar he leaves in the bank for a year. Do you think this is a good way for Garth to use his resources? Is a savings account a way of planning?
2 You saw that communities make budgets. They budget the money they spend for schools, parks, help to the old and sick, and street care. Do you think that the leaders of the United States government make a budget? What might be listed on the budget? Where does the national government get the money to pay for these things?

ON YOUR OWN

1 Does planning make you sure that things will work out the way you want them to? What else do you have to do?
2 Should a community spend more money for schools or for roads? for libraries or for snow removal? for parks or for bus drivers? How do your answers depend on your values?

IN TRANSIT

People plan in order to use their limited resources as wisely as possible. They choose what they need or want most. Then they decide the best way to go about getting it. People cannot always get what they want from the resources that are available.

How do people and regions use resources they do not own? What is trade, and how does it work? To find out, begin reading the next section.

3. A Fair Exchange

Sometimes boys collect cards that have pictures of baseball players on them. ● After a year, each boy may have a large collection of cards. But some of the boys may not have a complete set of cards for all players. Certain cards, such as those with pictures of stars like Carl Yastrzemski and Bob Gibson, may be very popular and hard to get. They may be especially limited, or scarce. If you collected baseball cards, how would you try to get the scarce cards you do not have?

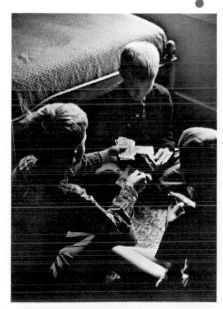

● Suppose that you had two Carl Yastrzemski cards. You still might want some other cards. Do you think you might be able to exchange the extra Carl Yastrzemski card for one that you don't have? Do you think you could find someone to trade with you? Perhaps one of your friends might not have a Carl Yastrzemski card. Perhaps he might have an extra Bob Gibson card which you don't have. Would you be able to trade the Carl Yastrzemski card for the Bob Gibson card? Would that be a fair trade?

TRADING

Of course, boys are not the only people who make trades. Different kinds of trading go on all the time. Some of you may collect and trade other kinds of cards. Some of you perhaps collect and trade stamps or coins. Some people collect and trade rocks or butterflies. Some parts of the national government trade land with

RAILROADS OF THE UNITED STATES TODAY

0   200   400   600 miles

Do you remember what **interact** means? If you do not, look up the word in your Social Science Dictionary.

other parts of the government. The land from this national park came from such a trade. ●

Do you ever make trades to get something you want? You have to find someone who wants what you have, don't you? Then you can agree on the kind of trade to make. **Trading,** or exchanging, is one way of interacting to get the things we need or want.

When you buy a loaf of bread, are you making a trade? What is different about this kind of trade? Recall Garth, who had a paper route (page 150). He traded the service of delivering newspapers for the money he was paid. Then he traded the money for the goods he wanted. Suppose that he had been paid in goods. Suppose that he had been paid in loaves of bread. Would it have been easier or harder to save enough of his pay to buy a new bicycle? Why?

You can see evidence of trading in the United States today. Try the investigation on the opposite page.

152

AN INVESTIGATION into transportation

Look at the map of the United States. ▲ It shows the railroads that run across the country. There are over 200,000 miles of railroad in this country. ■ Look back at the maps of resources and farm products on pages 123 and 147. How do railroads connect regions which depend on each other?

1 Find a steel-producing region which is connected by railroad with an orange-growing region.

2 Find a wheat-growing region which is connected with a lumber-producing region.

3 Find a mining region which is connected with a cattle-raising region.

4 Find the region in which you live on the map of resources and on the map of railroads. With what other regions does your region trade? Try to name some of the goods which are traded.

What do railroads show about trading in the United States? What other means of transportation make trading possible. ▶◀ Name three.

A Problem on Your Own

People in different parts of the world share each other's resources. Maybe you know which country produces over one-half of the world's coffee. How does transportation help when one country needs the resources of another country?

TRADING—EARLY AMERICAN STYLE

The early settlers in North America traded in much the same way as the boys who collect baseball cards. They traded goods for goods. Indians brought furs and skins of animals to the settlements. ● In exchange, the settlers gave them blankets, cloth, and guns. This kind of trading is called **barter,** or swapping. By bartering, both the settlers and the Indians got what they wanted. Each group traded something of which it had more than enough. It got something it didn't have but wanted. Does this remind you of trading baseball cards?

The settlers bartered among themselves, too. Farmers brought their grain and food to marketplaces in the settlements. ▲ There, the grain and food were put on display. In these marketplaces, there was trading from early morning until night. Today, many counties and states still have fairs, where the farmers' best foods and prize animals are displayed.

The farmer needed services, as well as goods. He needed his tools repaired and his horses shod. Sometimes the town blacksmith fixed the farmer's tools or shod his horses in exchange for a bag of grain. ■ The farmer sometimes paid his children's schoolteacher by letting him live at the farm for a month.

When a doctor was needed, the farmer may have paid him with a chicken or a pig. The doctor received goods for his services. Would you take a dozen eggs for delivering newspapers? Would you take a chicken for mowing a lawn?

TRADING RESOURCES TODAY

Do all countries use the same amount of oil? Why or why not?

Oil, or petroleum (pə·trō′lē·əm), is an important resource. For how many things is oil used? Study the map on pages 156-157 to see where oil is produced in the world. Look at the parts of the world that do not produce oil. What can they do if they need it?

WORLD OIL PRODUCTION

Which three countries are the world's biggest oil producers? In which regions of the world is a large amount of oil produced? Find a country which does not produce oil. How do you think it gets oil?

Countries which produce the most oil

Other countries which produce oil

Areas in which oil is found

Countries which do not produce oil

Wherever we live, our resources are limited. Nobody has everything. No one country has everything. Earlier in your studies, you learned that many different resources are found in each region of the United States. Every region has some resources, but no one region has all of them.

Regions are interdependent. In order to get what they want and need, people in one region depend on people in other regions. People in Montana may get their orange juice from Florida or Arizona or California. People all over the world use copper which comes from mines in Arizona. Steel beams produced in Gary, Indiana, are used in buildings all over the United States. In the United States, more than six out of every ten newspapers are printed on paper which comes from Canada's forests. ● The United States and Canada trade many things.

Where does your food and clothing come from? Study the resource map (page 147). As you can see, food is grown in many parts of the United States. It is prepared and shipped to the stores in which you buy it. ▲ Different parts of the clothes you wear may be made in different regions of the country. ■ All the parts may be put together in another region and then shipped to stores in many different places.

People in every region have some resources and do not have some other resources. People in regions that do not have oil depend on people in regions that produce it. (Look again at the oil map on pages 156-157.) People in regions that need oil may produce other goods—perhaps lumber or machinery or wheat. The people in these regions trade the goods that they produce for money. With the money, they, in turn, can buy the oil that they need.

Today, we do not barter to get the goods and services we need. Today, we use money when we trade. Either way, we get what we need by sharing what we have. Trade is one way in which we share.

People want to sell. Other people want to buy. Products and goods of all kinds are always moving across oceans, through pipe lines. ● They move over highways and railroads, and through the air between buyers and sellers. Trade goes on and on.

━━━━━━ AT THIS POINT IN YOUR STUDY ━━━━━━

Do these statements seem correct?

1 Trading helps people share what they have.

Suppose that you had to live for the rest of your life eating only what is grown in your region. What foods might you have to do without?

You will find it easier to answer this question and the questions below if you study the resource map (page 147).

2 Regions depend on other regions.

If you live in a region with cold winters, what do you get from regions that do not have cold winters? If you live in a region that is warm all year, what do you get from a cold region?

Choose the ending for each of these sentences.

1 Trading is a way of interacting to get
  (a) something you don't want
  (b) something you want or need more than what you have
2 Today, most people
  (a) barter for what they want
  (b) trade with money
3 Regions of the United States
  (a) each have all the resources they need
  (b) are interdependent

USING WHAT YOU KNOW

1 More cars are made in Detroit, Michigan, than in any other city in the world. Three airports and nine railroads serve

the city. Ships travel from its large port. Why do you think transportation is so important to Detroit?
2 Look at a globe. Try to find Panama, a country in Middle America. In the early 1900's, the Panama Canal was built. It is a waterway that connects the Pacific and Atlantic oceans. How does the Panama Canal help countries share resources?

ON YOUR OWN

1 Can feeling good inside be a fair exchange for producing a service? What are **volunteer workers**? Why do people become volunteers?
2 About five thousand years ago, man invented something very important. Almost all kinds of transportation depend on this invention. Without it, there would be no cars, airplanes, trains, wagons, or bicycles. What is the invention?

IN TRANSIT

Most of us do not barter for goods and services. We pay money for the things we get. How are prices set on the goods and services we buy? Why do prices change? To find out, begin reading the next section.

4.　What's It Worth to You?

Look at the pictures on this page. ● If you had a choice, which would you take to the store to buy food? You would probably take the twenty-dollar bill.

Why would you choose the twenty-dollar bill? That's easy, you say. The twenty-dollar bill is money. Of course, you could sell the cow or the horse and use the money to shop. Or you could lead either the cow or the horse to the store and try to use it to pay for your food. Perhaps you wouldn't like to do this. But at some time and in some place, each of the things pictured was money. In Massachusetts, the colonists paid their taxes with cows!

THE STORY OF MONEY

People have not always used the kind of money we use today. Sometimes they have not used money at all. They have depended on fair trades through barter. In barter, no money is needed. Recall the trading of baseball cards and the trading of animal furs for household goods.

At other times or in other places, some kinds of animals have been used as money. The prices of goods could be given in terms of the animals. That is, the price of a pair of sandals might be one pig. The price of a horse might be several pigs. The pigs were a **medium of exchange**, a tool for making trade easier. How much was a pig worth? It was worth whatever it could be traded for.

161

Recall that a **symbol** is something that stands for something else.

How much is a dollar worth today? It is worth as much as it will buy. A dollar is a **symbol**, isn't it? It is really only a piece of paper, but it means whatever it can buy.

In many places and at many times—even today—cattle have been used as a medium of exchange. So have horses, buffalo, reindeer, camels, sheep, goats, and pigs. But animals can get sick or be injured or just grow old and useless. A thin, sick pig is not worth as much as a fat, healthy one.

Some other things that have been used for money do not work well, either. Flour gets moldy, and salt isn't easy to use if it gets wet. In most places, people tried to find things which last a long time to use for money. For example, North American Indians who lived along the seashore used shells for money. They polished the shells and put them on a string. The strung shells were called wampum. ● Even the English and Dutch settlers used wampum as money.

Of course, many kinds of coins have been used for money. Iron, brass, gold, and silver coins have all been used, because these metals have been thought valuable by many peoples. ▲

The coins we use today are not pure gold or silver. But no matter what metals are used, each coin has the same value as another of the same kind. That is, a dime has the same value as any other dime. Of course, you know now that any kind of money is worth only what it can buy.

What kind of money is easy to carry and will last a long time? Coins are easier to use than animals and food. But all coins are heavy, especially when there are very many of them.

Paper is good to use for money. Can you see why? It is easy to carry and can be made so that it will last a long time. The paper used for money is much stronger than the paper you write on. It is stronger than the paper page of this book. You know that, when you decide to spend your dollar, you can buy something priced at a dollar with it. The **face value** of a dollar is the value it has marked on it. The face value will not change, even if you keep it for months and months.

Many people put their dollars in a checking account in a bank, where the money will be safe. Then, if they buy a television set, they can give the salesman a piece of paper called a check. ● The storekeeper takes the check as payment. Then he takes or sends the check to the bank. He knows that he can get the dollars that have been put in the bank by the buyer of the television set. The storekeeper can spend these dollars or can keep them in his own checking account.

Today, much trading and exchanging is done with checks. Why is a check a good way to trade for goods? Name one way in which a check might be more useful than dollar bills.

SETTING A PRICE

How much is a cow or a horse or a box of salt worth? How do you know how much to pay for a pair of shoes or a new coat or a baseball glove? When you go to the store, the prices are already marked on what you want to buy. The price tells you very clearly what you will have to pay for it. But how does a storekeeper know what price to charge consumers for shoes or a coat or the glove ?

Remember that the storekeeper, too, buys the goods he sells. The owner of the factory where the goods are made must pay for the materials, labor, and other resources used to make them. The factory owner must sell his products at a price which will repay him for the cost of making the goods. But the factory owner wants to do more than this. He also wants to have some money left over for himself.

The money that is left over is his **profit**. Why must the factory owner make a profit? He needs to buy food and clothing for himself and his family. He must pay rent. He has other expenses, too.

If you do not remember what a **consumer** is, turn to page 131 or to your Social Science Dictionary.

●

Why is he called a **middle-man**?

A factory owner usually sells his products to a **middleman**. A middleman often buys goods in large amounts from factories that make different kinds of products. He then sells the goods to department stores and storekeepers. The services of a middleman cost money. He wants to make a profit, too.

When the storekeeper buys the goods, he must pay a certain price for them. What other costs does the storekeeper have? Name some of them. How does the storekeeper decide the price that he will charge the consumer for goods?

Suppose that one warm day in the summer, a girl about your age went with her mother to a store. ● They bought a pair of sandals for five dollars. The girl liked the sandals very much and showed them to all her friends. Some of them wanted sandals, too. Suppose that, within a few days, twenty more consumers went to the same store. Each of them wanted to buy a pair of sandals. But there were only five pairs of sandals left in the store.

An economist would say that there was a **demand** from twenty people for a **supply** of five pairs of sandals. Twenty girls wanted sandals. There were only five pairs. As you can see, the demand was greater than the supply. ●

Of course, the storekeeper was very happy. His sandals were priced at five dollars each. He could make a reasonable profit and sell all that he had.

The next day, the storekeeper ordered more sandals for his store. But by the time they arrived, the summer was almost over. The storekeeper had a large supply of sandals, but nobody came into the store to buy them. There was no demand. ▲ Then the storekeeper put a sign in his window. The sign said, "Sale! Sandals at Greatly Reduced Prices! "Only $4.00 a Pair!"

He had lowered the price on the sandals. The storekeeper had made his profit smaller on each pair of sandals. Do you think there might have been more demand for the sandals at the lower price?

To learn more about supply and demand, try the investigation on the next page.

THE LAW OF SUPPLY AND DEMAND

Of course, the story you read about the storekeeper was just a story. It didn't happen exactly like that. But economists tell us that supply and demand do help to set the price on goods. The factory owner, the middleman, and the storekeeper must each be able to make a fair profit on their goods.

When there is enough of something for everyone who wants it, then the price is often low. When there is more than enough supply to meet the demand, the price tends to be low. When there is not enough of something for all who want it, then the price is often high. That is, when the supply is not large enough to meet the demand, the price tends to be high.

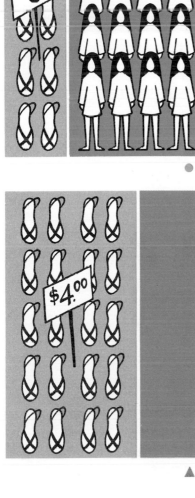

Supply   Demand

AN INVESTIGATION into supply and demand

One snowy Saturday, Steve and Larry asked Steve's father to let them use the shovel. First, they went next door. The lady who lived there paid them fifty cents to shovel the snow off her front walk. As they went along the street, they found more people who needed their driveways or walks cleared. ● By the time they went home for lunch, they had made three dollars.

At lunch, they planned the afternoon. I'll bet we could get people to pay sixty cents instead of fifty," said Steve. "Let's try."

The people at the next house wouldn't pay sixty cents. "There's another boy who is shoveling snow, and he'll do it for fifty cents," the man said. ▲ "Why should we pay sixty?"

"All right," said Steve. "We'll do it for fifty cents, won't we Larry? That seems to be a fair price." For the rest of the day, the children charged fifty cents.

Analyze the story, and answer these questions:

1 Why did Steve and Larry decide to raise the price of their services?

2 How did the higher price change the demand for their services?

3 How did the supply of the services change the price of their services?

4 What did Steve and Larry learn about the law of supply and demand?

5 Try to imagine an ending for the story. How did Steve and Larry spend their income? Did they help to make a demand for goods and services when they spent their money?

A Problem on Your Own

The price of rattlesnake meat is higher than the price of beef. In our culture, most people have not learned to eat rattlesnake. So, the demand for it is not great. Why is the price high?

Recall what you learned about trading. If you had a Carl Yastrzemski baseball card which was hard to get, would you want to trade it for a card which was easy to get? The demand for Carl Yastrzemski cards would be high and the supply low. You might ask your friend to give you two cards for your one card. You would be raising the price for your Carl Yastrzemski card, wouldn't you? On the other hand, suppose you had a baseball card which was easy to get. You might offer to trade it *and* another card for something you wanted. You might lower the price of the card.

We might write the **law of supply and demand** like this:

great supply + low demand   = low price
low supply   + great demand = high price

Watch for price changes in the stores where your family shops. Do the changes depend partly on supply and demand?

AT THIS POINT IN YOUR STUDY

Do these statements seem correct?

1 The price of goods and services depends partly on how much demand there is for them.

Suppose a modern two-story house is built on the desert. There are no people living near. Water must be brought in by truck. The house is beautiful, but the price is very low. What does the price have to do with the demand?

2 The price of goods and services depends partly on how large the supply is.

Suppose many people want the role of an airline pilot and learn how to be one. Suppose there are not many jobs open. Airline pilots produce services. Why might the income of airline pilots go down?

Choose the ending for each of these sentences.

1 A dollar is worth
   (a) what it will buy
   (b) as much as a pig used to be worth when pigs were used for money
2 If the price of a good or a service is high, it is likely that
   (a) the supply is great and the demand is low
   (b) the supply is low and the demand is great
3 If a cow or pig is used as a medium of exchange,
   (a) it is used as money
   (b) it is not as valuable as a dollar bill

USING WHAT YOU KNOW

In colonial Virginia, tobacco was used for money. There was a steady demand for it, so a barrel of it always had about the same price. A good tobacco crop meant that the grower had a lot of money.

One year, there was too much tobacco. The stores were full of it. Nobody wanted any more tobacco. With so much extra tobacco and no demand for it, the tobacco could not be exchanged for other goods. It was not good money. So, the people went into the tobacco fields and tore up the plants and destroyed the tobacco.

Did tearing up the plants solve the problem of the low price of tobacco? Why or why not?

ON YOUR OWN

1 Not long ago, a painting by the famous Dutch painter Rembrandt was sold for $2,300,000. What did supply and demand have to do with this price? What did the price have to do with how much Rembrandt's paintings are valued?
2 The United States government has some control over companies which produce electricity. It can keep these companies from raising their prices. Why do you think the government helps to control the price of electricity? Can you explain why the price of electricity does not depend on the law of supply and demand?

IN TRANSIT

The price of goods and services depends partly on supply and demand. People produce goods and services. How might a large supply of people with skills change prices? Is there always a supply of people with skills? What is the demand for people with skills?

To take a closer look at human resources, begin the next section.

5. Help Wanted

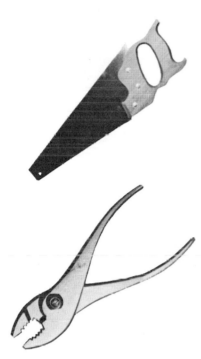

Imagine that you were taking a walk one day and saw these things: boards, a bucket of paint, a saw, and metal rods. Suppose that you also saw a wheelbarrow, sawhorses, and a large machine. Suppose that you saw all these things and nothing else. ● What would you guess was happening?

Many of the things needed for making or repairing a building were there. Something important was missing, though. Can you guess what that was? Was there anybody there to use all these things? Was there anybody there to do the work? Perhaps the building would repair itself. Perhaps a machine would do it. What do you think?

THE BUILDERS

People with special skills would be needed to use the things you saw. Carpenters would be needed to work with the lumber. Plumbers would be needed to work with the pipes, and painters with the paint. You can probably name some other kinds of workers who would be needed. The house would be built only if all the workers did their jobs. Without the work of these human resources—without their labor—how could the house be built?

Recall that **human resources** are people.

THE PEOPLE COME

Imagine that we are flying over the east coast of the United States. What do we see? Buildings, houses, stores, factories, schools? ● Highways, bridges? Fences, tractors, silos? ▲

English settlers came to Jamestown, Virginia, more than three hundred fifty years ago. Of course, there were no airplanes then. But imagine that a colonist had flown over the same area that we did. What would he have seen? What has changed the land to make it look the way it is?

In 1790, most of the people lived near the Atlantic coast between Boston, Massachusetts, and Charleston, South Carolina. They had come to America from many countries. At first, most of the colonists came from England, and settled in Massachusetts and Virginia. Some came from Spain, and settled in Florida and the Southwest. But then farmers came from Holland to New York, and from Germany to Pennsylvania. People came to Delaware from Sweden. The French came to the Carolinas. Negroes were brought from Africa to work as slaves in the rice and tobacco fields of the South. From the very beginning, human resources came to our country from many lands.

In colonial days, most of the people were farmers or worked on the land. In the South, Negro slaves did

much of the labor in the fields. In the other states, farmers and their families did most of their own work. A day on a farm was long and hard. Farmers who lived close together often helped each other.

In the 1800's, more and more people came to the United States. ● The Irish came to work in New England factories, such as Samuel Slater's textile mill in Rhode Island. ▲ More factories were built, and more help was needed. More people came. People from Poland came to work in the coal mines of Pennsylvania. Newly arrived Chinese helped to build the railroads. People came to the United States from all parts of the world. Human resources, as well as natural resources, were needed to build the country.

A NEW WAY TO SHARE HUMAN RESOURCES

As you know, colonial farmers worked together. They helped each other clear the land and build homes. But most farm families grew their own food and supplied most of their own wants. They had to

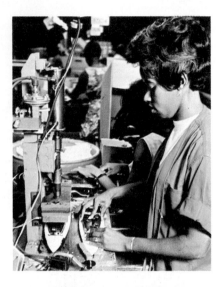

trade to get some of the things they needed but they were not as interdependent as people are today.

With the growth of factories, Americans began to make more goods. Machines in factories could weave cloth faster than a woman could at home. Machines also made it possible for fewer men to do the work on a farm. In time, there were fewer farmers. Farmers began to go to cities to work in factories. They took part in **manufacturing**, the making of goods.

Today, we are learning how to share our human resources **efficiently**. An economist often uses the word **efficient** (i·fish′ənt) to describe ways of doing things with the least amount of effort and time. In a dress factory, does one woman make a complete dress? In a factory that makes toy boats, does one person make a whole boat? ●

To share human resources in the most efficient way, factories **divide the labor**. This means that each worker does only part of the job. He may put only one part in cars traveling along an assembly line. Another man may fit the next part into the cars. An automobile is made by hundreds of workers, each doing one job.

This **division of labor** makes it possible for factories to make large numbers of a single product. Would there be many automobiles if each man in an automobile factory had to put a whole car together by himself? Perhaps each man working in a factory could make a whole automobile. But it would take him a very long time. Would consumers have to pay higher prices for automobiles if each one were handmade?

Do you remember your study of choices (page 136)? You found that you could choose from many more things than the Blackfoot Indians or the people in Boonesboro, Kentucky. Division of labor in factories is partly responsible for the many goods we now have.

To find out more about division of labor, try the investigation on the opposite page.

AN INVESTIGATION into division of labor

If you get the measles, a doctor will take care of you. If a water pipe breaks in your house, a plumber will repair it. The doctor knows his job. The plumber knows his job, too. Each one does the work of his role.

Look in the yellow pages of a telephone book.  List some of the services given under each letter of the alphabet. How many different kinds of services do you find listed under each letter? Here are some that you might find listed under *A*.

Accountants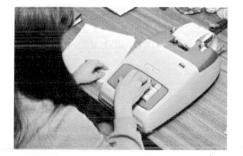
Advertising
Air Freight Service
Air Travel Ticket Agencies
Architects
Attorneys
Automobile Repairing
Automobile Road Service
Automobile Washing and Polishing

What does the list you make tell you about division of labor in your community?

A Problem on Your Own

How is labor divided when books, such as this one, are made? How is labor divided when movies are made?

ANOTHER WAY TO SHARE HUMAN RESOURCES

Like all resources, human resources are limited. One way in which we share them is by dividing our labor into different jobs. Another way to share human resources is by teaching. How do your parents and your teachers share their resources with you? Some Americans share the skills and knowledge they have learned by teaching people in other countries. ●

In the years to come, you will want to know how to do many things. Throughout their lifetimes, many people work at a number of different jobs. Job roles are changing all the time. For example, a farmer might learn the skills of a mechanic. More and more people are adapting to changing job roles. They are learning new ways of acting. They are learning from people who share their skills and knowledge.

What might happen if a person chose not to learn? What might happen if he could no longer find work at the job he knew? Could this happen? Earlier, you studied migrant workers. More and more, their jobs are being done by machines. You also studied the

What is a **role**? If you don't remember, look up the word in your Social Science Dictionary.

174

farmers who left the Dust Bowl. What happened to the job roles of these two groups?

Like all people, you will go on learning. No matter what kind of work you choose to do, you will use what you have learned from others. If you become an astronaut, you will use the knowledge of scientists and engineers. ● If you become a nurse, you will use what you have learned from many other people. Others will depend on your knowledge, too. Whatever your job, you will share your knowledge and skills. People will learn from you. What you have learned in the past will help you use and share your human resources wisely.

Are human resources always used wisely? Recall the story of the migrant farm workers (pages 107-112). Are human resources sometimes wasted? We are trying not to waste our natural resources, like soil and water. We are learning to use our natural resources wisely. That is, we are learning to conserve them. Must we learn to conserve our human resources, too?

AT THIS POINT IN YOUR STUDY

Do these statements seem correct?

1 Goods are produced by people who have learned skills. Services are produced by people who have learned skills.

What skills might be needed to build a chair? an airplane? an apartment house?

What skills are needed by a poet? a gardener? a doctor?

2 Human resources are shared by division of labor.

Suppose that each person today had to build his own house, grow his own food, and make his own clothes. How much time would he have for anything else?

3 Human resources are shared by teaching and learning.

How does sharing skills and knowledge make life easier for each person? Where does a doctor learn? From whom does he learn?

BEFORE YOU GO ON

Choose the ending for each of these sentences.

1 The resources of the United States include
   (a) iron, oil, soil, and water
   (b) iron, oil, soil, water, and people, too
2 Human resources are needed by
   (a) everyone
   (b) only a few people
3 Human resources
   (a) depend on learning
   (b) can't be changed

USING WHAT YOU KNOW

Economists tell us that, in 1800, machines did very little of the world's work. People did all the rest. Economists tell us that, today, machines do almost all the work.

What can people do that machines cannot do? Will machines ever be able to do it?

ON YOUR OWN

Elias Howe worked in a shop. ● One day, some visitors who came to the shop talked about how long it took to make clothes. When he went home, Elias Howe thought about the visitors. He had an idea. Six years later, in 1845, Howe had invented a machine that would sew a seam.

What is Howe's invention called? Do you think it helped people in factories produce more goods? How?

Jan Matzeliger was born in Dutch Guiana. ▲ He was the son of a Negro woman and a Dutch engineer. When he came to the United States, Jan Matzeliger learned shoemaking. At that time, a machine could make the parts of a shoe. Most of the shoe, however, had to be put together by hand. For ten years, Matzeliger worked on a machine that could do this work. By 1883, he had invented such a shoe-lasting machine.

Do you think more shoes were made after this? Why or why not?

You have been studying division of labor and the growth of factories. Matzeliger and Howe are only two of the men whose ideas helped factories produce more goods. Try to find out what each of these men did and when they did it: Eli Whitney, Samuel Colt, and Henry Ford.

What did you find out when we gave you an imaginary fifty cents? You found that there were many things to buy. ● But you couldn't buy everything. If you bought some things, you couldn't buy others. We agreed that no one can have everything he wants.

There were a limited number of things you could do with fifty cents. So, you had to make choices. You could spend fifty cents in many different ways, or you could save it to spend later. We saw, too, that families and communities choose the ways in which they spend their money.

Can you imagine what it would be like if everybody could have everything that he needed and wanted? Perhaps you would like to live in a place where this was so. But you know that isn't possible. There is no such place.

Everywhere, people's wants are unlimited, but their resources are limited. Everybody has to make choices. In this unit, you have come to this understanding of the concept of **resources: The resources of peoples and regions are limited.**

Because resources are limited, families try to make the best use of their resources. So do communities and countries. Often, people and groups make plans. One kind of plan is a family budget. Another kind of plan is made by communities when they divide their tax dollars. Communities also plan how to use their land.

Plans help people use their limited resources well. You have, then, come to another understanding of the concept of **resources: Planning helps people use their resources wisely.** Planning helps them share resources efficiently—without wasting them.

Sharing Resources

Recall the maps of the United States that you studied (pages 123 and 147). You saw that the United States has many different kinds of resources. But no region has all the kinds of resources it needs. People in each region need the resources of other regions. People in different regions of the country are interdependent.

All people are interdependent. People share their resources. They may barter, as the early settlers did. In bartering, people exchange goods or services for other goods or other services. You saw that, if many people want to trade together, it is easier to use money than to barter. Each piece of money is worth just as much as any other piece that has the same face value. For example, every dime will buy just as much as every other dime.

We may trade by bartering or by using money. People produce services. They produce goods. ● They build homes, cut forests, and grow crops. People are one of the great resources of our nation.

Today, machines do much of the work that was once done by human hands. But men still plan, build, and sometimes run the machines. ▲ The resource that gives us machines is still people. People share their knowledge and skills. ■ They share their knowledge of how to act and interact. Thus, you have come to a better understanding of the concept of **resources: People share resources when they trade goods and services. They also share resources when they teach others.**

In this unit, you learned that resources are limited, or scarce. You saw that people must act and interact in order to share these limited resources. Perhaps everything you have learned in this unit can be summed up by this statement about the concept of **resources: People interact to use the resources available to them.**

AN ANALYSIS OF VALUES

How were "labor credits" a form of money?

In 1825, a man named Robert Owen bought a little town in Indiana. ● He named the town New Harmony. Everyone was welcome to come to New Harmony. Owen promised to pay for food and to supply shelter. In exchange, each person was expected to work on the farms or in the factories. Over one thousand people came.

A small committee decided what the people of the community could and should do. For his work, each person received "labor credits," which could be exchanged for food and other goods.

New Harmony had a kindergarten, a free public school, a free public library, and a school where children could learn how to do certain jobs. They were all supported by the community of New Harmony.

From the beginning, there were problems. New Harmony did not have enough skilled workers. Homes were small. One year after the town began, Owen said that the members must share *everything*, even their homes. No one could own property. Everything would belong to the people together. People who were not happy about this talked and argued. Meanwhile, the farms and factories produced very little.

After a year, Robert Owen could no longer pay for food. He had not finished paying for the land that they were living on, and he was running out of money. The community had failed.

Now try to answer these questions:

1   How was New Harmony different from your community?

2   What were some values of the people there?

3   Did everyone agree on all the values?

4   Could New Harmony have worked? Why?

What does the year 1776 mean to you? Like most Americans, you probably think of the Declaration of Independence. But, in 1776, another revolution was starting—a revolution in ways of thinking about our needs and wants. A book, instead of a gunshot, began this revolution. The book was called *The Wealth of Nations*. Its author was Adam Smith. ●

Adam Smith wrote about the ways in which a nation could produce more goods. The goods in a nation depend on labor, or workers. Therefore, Smith said, the number of goods could be increased by increasing the number of workers. But Smith knew that this would be hard to do. (Recall that human resources are limited.) Another way to increase the number of goods was for each worker to do more work. How could this be done?

In *The Wealth of Nations*, Smith gave an example of the way in which division of labor increased the number of pins each worker could make in a pin-making factory. He wrote that one man working alone,

> could scarce, perhaps . . . make one pin in a day, and certainly could not make twenty. But in the way in which this business is now carried on . . . it is divided into a number of branches . . . One man draws out the wire, another straights it, a third cuts it, a fourth points, a fifth grinds it . . .

By dividing the labor in this way, Smith said, ten men "could make among them upwards of forty-eight thousand pins a day."

What Adam Smith wrote in 1776 was important. He started people thinking in a new way. That is why he is called "the father of modern economics."

A NEW VIEW
OF
RESOURCES

You know now that resources fill our needs and wants. You know, too, that resources are limited. Therefore, people must make choices like these: Which needs do I want most to fill? Which resources are available to me to fill those needs? Which ways of acting may I use to fill my needs?

When people answer the last question, they choose their **economic behavior**. Everyone behaves in economic ways. But is all economic behavior the same?

Study the map. ● Then look at the pictures which were taken in Israel. ▲ Which ones show ways in which the people of Israel use two of their basic resources: land and water? Which ones show ways in which Israelis interact to share their resources?

How are Israelis acting like the people of the United States? How are their actions different?

AN INVESTIGATION FOR YOU

If you don't remember what **hypothesis** means, look up the word in your Social Science Dictionary.

Can you make a **hypothesis** about the people in Israel? How is the economic behavior of Israelis like that of people in other countries?

You might test your hypothesis. Choose a country in Europe or Africa, and compare it with Israel. Collect pictures showing how the people of the country you chose act. Look for magazine and newspaper articles that will help you answer these questions:

1 How do the people of the country you chose use their resources to get what they need?
2 How do they share resources? For what goods and services do they depend on other countries?
3 Do the people trade? Do they sell goods? Are they consumers? Does the law of supply and demand work in the country you chose?

Is the economic behavior of the people in the country you chose like the economic behavior of people in the United States? Write your answers under these headings: "Likenesses" and "Differences."

ISRAEL

RULES FOR INTERACTION

UNIT FIVE

Introduction

In the 1800's, Walt Whitman would write this about the different people who were building the United States:

I hear America singing, the varied carols I hear,
Those of mechanics, each one singing his as it should be blithe and strong,
The carpenter singing his as he measures his plank or beam,
The mason singing his as he makes ready for work, or leaves off work,
The boatman singing what belongs to him in his boat, the deckhand singing on the steamboat deck,
The shoemaker singing as he sits on his bench, the hatter singing as he stands,
The wood-cutter's song, the plow-boy's on his way in the morning, or at noon intermission or at sundown,
The delicious singing of the mother, or the young wife at work, or of the girl sewing or washing,
Each singing what belongs to him or her and none else . . .

How did all the different people who built the United States learn to live together? ● What did they have to help them? To find out, begin reading on the opposite page.

1. Government in a New World

In 1492, Columbus landed on the shores of America. The news of his discovery spread across Europe. Soon, other people followed him. English, French, Dutch, and Spanish explorers came to the New World. As they explored, they each claimed the lands they found for their countries and their kings. ●

After the explorers, traders came. The traders carried gold and furs from the New World to Europe. Soon, people began to come to America to stay. These people wanted to start a new life. They came to get land, to build homes, and to start farms. Most of them settled along the east coast. And most of the people who settled there were from England.

**LAND CLAIMS
ABOUT 1650**

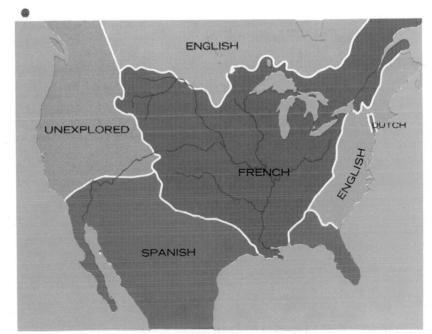

ENGLISH

UNEXPLORED

DUTCH

FRENCH

ENGLISH

SPANISH

LAND RIGHTS IN THE NEW WORLD

Like other kings, the king of England gave the lands he claimed to his people. He gave land to British companies, like the Hudson Bay Company. He also gave land to men, like William Penn. In turn, these companies and men gave part of their land to settlers. Usually, a colonist did not have to give much in return. He had to agree to live on the land and farm it.

The people who came from England believed that they had a right to own property. They expected people to respect property rights. The colonist worked hard on his land to clear it. On the cleared land, he built a home which looked like this rebuilt cabin. ● He worked hard to plant his crops.

The colonist wanted to protect his property from anyone who tried to take it from him. Most colonists were even willing to use force. But there was a better way to protect property. That was through **government**.

SETTING UP A GOVERNMENT

Some of the Pilgrims sailed to the New World on the *Mayflower*. The ship looked like this rebuilt model. ▲ Before the Pilgrims left the *Mayflower*, they signed an agreement. They agreed to obey a government that would be set up in the new colony. A government is made up of leaders who have authority that is accepted by the people they govern.

After landing in Massachusetts, the Pilgrims formed a government and elected a governor. The Pilgrims met in town meetings. ■ In these meetings, all the men who had signed the *Mayflower* agreement voted on each law. A government in which each man votes on every law is called a **direct democracy**.

Later, the Massachusetts colonists elected a group of lawmakers to represent them. These lawmakers met in a **legislature** (lej′is·lā′chər). The men in the legislature had the authority to make laws for everyone.

What is **authority**? If you don't remember, look the word up in your Social Science Dictionary.

The word **represent** means to act and speak for.

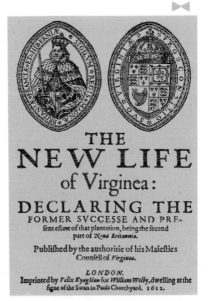

THE
NEW LIFE
of Virginea:

DECLARING THE
FORMER SVCCESSE AND PRE-
sent eſtate of that plantation, being the ſecond
part of Noua Britannia.

Publiſhed by the authoritie of his Maieſties
Counſell of Virginea.

LONDON,
Imprinted by Felix Kyngſton for William Welby, dwelling at the
ſigne of the Swan in Pauls Churchyard. 1612.

Thus, the colonists gave up some of the authority they had over themselves. They gave some of this authority to people who would act for them. A government in which people choose who will represent them is called a **representative** (rep′ri·zen′tə·tiv) **democracy**.

Of course, each of the thirteen colonies was English. ▶◀ As Englishmen, the colonists were expected to obey many of England's laws. The king of England could use his authority over the colonists. For example, after 1624, the king chose the governor of Virginia.

However, the colonists were a long way from England. Between England and America stretched the Atlantic Ocean. In every colony, people had to make many laws for themselves. These laws were often like English laws. In Massachusetts, for example, there was a law against any man taking another man's property. A person accused of taking something was given a trial. If he was found guilty, he was punished.

What is a **norm of behavior**? If you don't remember, look it up in your Social Science Dictionary.

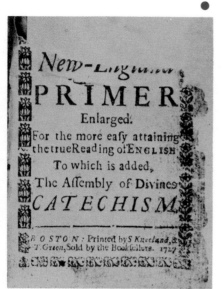

Recall that **social** refers to people living and working together in groups.

Honesty had been a norm of behavior in England. It had been so important that it had been made into a set of laws. When they went to the New World, the colonists took with them the norm of honesty. They also took ideas of English laws about honesty.

Sometimes, laws made norms stronger. The Massachusetts colonists believed that children had a right to learn to read and to learn a trade. ● This right was soon protected by a school law. Massachusetts was the first colony to pass a law ordering towns to hire teachers.

Other important norms were made into laws, too. For example, when the colonies broke away from England, the right to speak freely became a law. So did the right to worship freely.

NORMS AND LAWS AS SOCIAL CONTROLS

Remember that norms are the ways that people expect each other to act. Norms are one kind of **social control**. Laws are another. Members of a group learn the social controls of the group. Recall the Blackfoot boys who learned the norms of behavior of a warrior. In their culture, they learned how to act. They also learned how *not* to act.

People who do not obey laws are usually punished. What happens to someone who breaks the law and takes something which belongs to you? People who do not follow norms are often punished, too. What might happen to a plumber who wore a bathing suit to his job?

Norms and laws have something to do with the behavior of every person. They make it easier for members of a group to get along with each other. How do laws about taking another person's property help all the people in a community?

To find out more about norms and laws, try the investigation on the opposite page.

What are some norms of behavior in your class? ● One norm might be: *We expect class members not to push other class members around.* List the norms, and choose one by voting.

Now think of a law which will help make the norm stronger. In writing the law, make these parts:

1 A part that tells what the law is. One law could be: *Class members must not push other class members around on the playground.*

2 A part that tells the punishment for those who do not obey the law. Here is an example: *Class members who are found guilty of pushing people around will have to stand in one spot on the playground during recess.*

During the next five school days, try to carry out part 2 of the law. Do most children obey the law? Is there a reward for obeying it?

Do all lawbreakers accept their punishment? Why or why not?

A Problem on Your Own

Can your class pass laws for the whole school? Can it pass laws for your community or your nation? ▲ Why or why not?

What do you need to get people to obey laws?

191

THE COLONISTS' BAGGAGE

The colonists who left the Old World and sailed westward took their families with them. When they could, they also took the things that were most useful to them. ● Clothes and tools were part of their baggage.

The colonists carried other things to the New World, too. They took their norms of behavior. They also took their values. One of the things that the colonists valued was the idea that men should choose their own leaders. They believed that elected leaders should have the authority to make rules for everyone. Do Americans today still believe in these values? How do you know?

AT THIS POINT IN YOUR STUDY

Do these statements seem correct?

1   The colonists chose to make laws.

Why did the colonists make that choice? Do we make laws that govern the way we act? Why?

2   The colonists brought law with them to the New World.

How did the colonists know about law and government?

Do you have some social controls wherever you are? What are they? How did you learn them?

Choose the ending for each of these sentences.

1. Laws and norms
   (a) make it hard for people to get along
   (b) are social controls

2. In town meetings, laws were made
   (a) by voting
   (b) by leaders only

3. In representative democracy, leaders
   (a) are chosen by the voters
   (b) are born with the authority they have

USING WHAT YOU KNOW

1. People who follow norms of behavior are rewarded. People who do not follow them are punished. If someone who loses a game is not a "good sport," how might he be punished? Is there only one way?

   There are certain punishments for breaking laws. For example, any person who is caught driving his car too fast must pay a fine. Who makes sure that laws are obeyed? Are they the same people who make sure norms are followed?

   Do you think norms become stronger when they are made into laws? Why or why not?

2. These are some norms of behavior in most communities today:
   stop at red lights
   pay taxes
   say "please" and "thank you"
   keep sidewalks and streets clean
   send children to school
   Which of these norms have been made into law? Why? Which norms have not been made into law? Why not?

ON YOUR OWN

In some colonial settlements, there were laws against stealing. In other settlements, there were no such laws. But, even in settlements without laws against stealing, the custom was not to steal. Why do you think few people stole even when there were no laws against it?

Which works best: norms of behavior or law? Why do you think so?

IN TRANSIT

As more people came to the colonies, the first settlements grew larger. Hungry for land, the colonists moved west.

Would the customs they had learned help them live together in new lands? Would they need to make laws and build governments? To find out, turn to the next section.

2. Moving Beyond the Frontier

As they searched for new land, British colonists began to leave the thirteen colonies. They began to move westward across the Appalachian Mountains. Find these mountains on the map on pages 296-297. Who owned the land west of the Appalachians?

WHOSE LAND?

Both the British and the French made claims to the Appalachian area. This conflict over the land broke out into a war. The French, together with some of the Indians, fought British and colonial troops. In 1763, the French and Indian War ended, and the French had to give up all their claims in North America. The map shows the land that the British won from the French. ● Compare it with the map on page 187.

After the war, the British government made a law to keep colonists from moving westward. This law ordered the colonists not to move across the Appalachians into Indian lands.

THE WESTWARD MOVEMENT GOES ON

The pioneers went on moving westward. The new British law did not stop them. Neither did the mountains. The Indians had lived on these lands for a long time. But the pioneers did not stop to think about the rights of the Indians.

At first, most of the pioneers who crossed the Appalachians were fur traders and explorers. The fur traders wanted to trade with the Indians. The explorers wanted to find out more about the western lands.

One of the explorers was Daniel Boone. In 1769, he started from North Carolina and crossed the mountains through the Cumberland Gap. He stayed for a long time in the great forests, hunting and exploring alone.

The fur traders and explorers prepared the way for other people. And there were many others who wanted some of the good land west of the Appalachians. Soon, farmers were moving west.

THE RIGHT TO MAKE LAWS

After the French and Indian War, the British government made several new laws for the colonies. One law ordered settlers not to move beyond the Appalachian frontier. Another law ordered the colonists to provide houses for British troops. These laws made the colonists angry.

The colonists also had to pay taxes to Britain. The tax money paid for British troops and for part of the cost of the French and Indian War. These new tax laws

LAND CLAIMS AFTER 1763

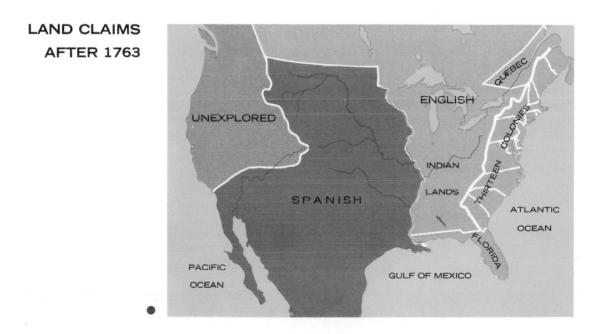

If you do not know what **representatives** are, look up **represent** in your Social Science Dictionary.

were not made by representatives of the colonists. They were made by lawmakers in Britain. This, said the colonists, was "taxation without representation."

Then the lawmakers in Britain passed more laws to tax the colonies. And the colonists became even angrier. For these and other reasons, many colonists no longer wanted to be British citizens.

You know that on July 4, 1776, the thirteen colonies broke away from Britain. In the Declaration of Independence, representatives from each colony said that the colonies were no longer part of Britain. ● Each man was now a citizen of one of the thirteen independent states. Each state had its own representative government. Each state was also part of a new nation, the United States of America.

But Great Britain would not give up the colonies without a battle. So, troops from each of the new states came together. For six years, George Washington led this national army against the British army. ▲ When the long battle was over, the states had won their freedom. Americans felt free to push westward.

The American West was being settled. But were all the problems solved? A few years later, the United States fought another war with Britain. Also, from the 1800's through the 1850's, a much bigger conflict was growing inside the United States itself. To find out about this, try the investigation on the next page.

BUILDING A FRONTIER GOVERNMENT

Study the map. It shows the borders of five present-day states. ■ What are their names?

When the Appalachian area was being settled, these states were part of the Northwest Territory. The British government did not want the colonists to move into these Indian lands. But pioneers settled the Northwest Territory, just as they had settled the Appalachian country.

The pioneers brought with them their norms of behavior and their ideas about law and authority. They knew that arguments could be prevented and settled through social controls. To protect themselves and

Recall that norms and laws are **social controls**.

Eighty-five years after the Revolutionary War began, another conflict broke out into war. What was this conflict? How did it begin?

In the late 1700's and the 1800's, most people in the North made goods. ● They did not use slaves. In the South, most people were farmers. ▲ They grew tobacco, cotton, sugar, and used Negro slaves to plant and harvest crops. The South sold some of its cotton to Europe. In exchange, Southerners bought goods made in Europe. Northerners wanted taxes put on the European goods. Americans, then, would be more likely to buy goods made in the North. Can you see why the South and the North argued about these taxes?

There was another argument, too. A large group of people in the North began to talk about freeing *all* slaves. They felt that slavery was wrong. But, to Southerners, slaves were property—not people. And the Constitution protected property.

As the westward movement went on, new states came into the Union. Should slavery be permitted in new states? Should it be forbidden?

As the arguments became more bitter, some Southerners began to talk of leaving the Union. Most Northerners felt that no state had the right to do this.

In 1861, shortly after Abraham Lincoln became President, many southern states did try to leave the Union. They banded together and set up their own government. To keep the country together, President Lincoln went to war.

1   What caused the Civil War? Was there more than one cause? Do you think that this is true of other wars? What evidence do you have?

2   How were the values of Northerners and Southerners different?

3   Are there other ways, besides war, to solve conflicts? Name some.

Who were the Founding Fathers? Why are they called that?

their property, they set up governments. These governments had the authority to pass and enforce laws.

The men in the new United States government thought that the pioneers needed help in governing the territory. Thomas Jefferson, who later became President, had some ideas on the way the territory should be set up. ● Some of his ideas were put into a law called the Northwest Ordinance, passed in 1787.

The law told how parts of the territory could become states. When there were sixty thousand free people within an area, the people could write a state constitution. The constitution was to be approved by the Congress of the United States. The area would then become a state. There could be no slavery in any state made out of the Northwest Territory.

The Northwest Ordinance also said that "schools and the means of education shall forever be encouraged." The Founding Fathers of our country believed that education was needed if people were to choose leaders wisely. Do you agree? Why or why not?

The Northwest Ordinance was an important law. It showed some ways other territories could become states.

AT THIS POINT IN YOUR STUDY

Do these statements seem correct?

1   Laws are made to protect rights.

The Northwest Ordinance protected the rights of settlers in the Northwest Territory. Are there laws today that protect your rights? Name at least two.

2   Governments help people do things that they cannot do by themselves.

What did the pioneers' government help them do?

How does your community government help people do things? Name at least two things your community government does that people could not do by themselves.

BEFORE YOU GO ON

Choose the ending for each of these sentences.

1 Many colonists wanted
(a) to keep British troops in their homes
(b) to move beyond the Appalachian Mountains

2 Colonists said that British tax laws
(a) gave the Indians too much land
(b) were "taxation without representation"

3 As they moved westward, the pioneers took with them
(a) their ideas about social control
(b) their families only

USING WHAT YOU KNOW

Not all colonists agreed to break away from Great Britain. Many hoped that the problems with Great Britain could be settled without war. Colonists who did not want to break away from England called themselves Loyalists. When war came, many Loyalists fled to Canada.

Today, Americans sometimes disagree. Find an example in a newspaper. How was the disagreement solved? Did government help? Did laws help? Did norms help?

ON YOUR OWN

The British tried to stop settlers from moving west of the Appalachians. But the settlers didn't obey the law the British had made. Why didn't the settlers obey this law?

In what way did the British government have a right to make such a law? In what way did it not have that right?

IN TRANSIT

We have seen how more and more pioneers moved westward over the Appalachians. Soon, they reached the Mississippi River and moved down the great river valley. ●

Did the pioneers need laws? Did they need government? To find out, begin reading the next section.

3. Government and New Lands

In 1800, Louisiana was made up of all the land from the Mississippi River to the Rocky Mountains. New Orleans was a busy port. Down the Mississippi floated steamships and the flatboats of the farmers. At the port, the farmers unloaded their goods. Then ship captains bought the goods and sold them at ports in the United States or Europe.

WHO OWNED LOUISIANA?

Spain owned Louisiana. The Spanish allowed Americans to store or sell their goods in New Orleans without paying taxes. Then, in 1800, Spain secretly agreed to turn Louisiana over to the French. In 1802, Spain said that American farmers could no longer store their goods in New Orleans without paying taxes.

President Thomas Jefferson had heard that Spain had secretly agreed to give Louisiana to France. He knew that France could keep Americans from using the lands along the eastern Mississippi. And he was worried about what would happen to American farmers.

Jefferson made an offer to the French. Could the United States buy New Orleans and the part of Florida next to it? The answer he got was a surprise. How much would the United States pay for *all* of Louisiana? The price set was about 15 million dollars.

Then Jefferson had a problem. As you know, the United States Constitution is the highest law in the land. It gives the President and other leaders the right to do certain things. But nothing in the Constitution gives the President the right to buy land from another nation.

The Constitution does give the President the right to make treaties. Jefferson thought this right might permit him to make a treaty to buy land. But Jefferson did not want to claim more power for the national government. He had always believed that the government should *not* try to grow too powerful.

Should Jefferson ask to have an amendment added to the Constitution so that the President could buy land? This would take time, and the French might change their minds. In 1803, Jefferson bought Louisiana by using the President's power to make treaties. The map shows the size of the Louisiana Purchase. •

A QUESTION OF MEANING

Did the national government have the right to buy land? That question is part of a bigger one: Just what powers does the national government have? There are two ways of thinking about our Constitution. One way of thinking is that the government can do *only* those things which the Constitution says it can. The other is

What is an **amendment**? If you don't know, look it up in your Social Science Dictionary.

LOUISIANA PURCHASE 1803 •

that the government can do everything *except* what the Constitution says it *cannot* do.

What happens when people disagree about meanings of the Constitution? To find out, try the investigation on the next page.

THE IMPORTANCE OF THE NEW LAND

Before he had any idea of buying Louisiana, Jefferson had wanted to find out what resources were in the lands west of the Mississippi River. He had also wanted someone to find a route to the Pacific Ocean.

Trace Lewis and Clark's journey on the map on pages 296-297.

In 1803, Jefferson had asked two men to explore the western lands. These men were Meriwether Lewis and William Clark. ● Lewis and Clark set out from St. Louis. They traveled along the upper Missouri River and along the Snake and Columbia rivers. One of their guides was a Shoshoni Indian woman. Finally, they reached the Pacific Ocean. As they traveled, they kept records of furs, mineral resources, and plant and animal life.

The explorers' records told Americans something about Louisiana. But people still did not know exactly

AN INVESTIGATION into meanings of the Constitution

After a certain law has been passed, people may think that it is **unconstitutional**. That is, people sometimes believe that a law has been passed which does not agree with the Constitution. As you know, the Constitution is the highest law of the land. No law may disagree with it.

Set up a committee to find out how a law is tested. You might ask a lawyer to visit your class. Here are some questions you might ask:

1 Who decides whether or not a law is unconstitutional?

2 How can one person get a law tested?

3 If someone with very little money wants a law tested, what can he do about it?

4 Can someone who is not a United States citizen test a law?

A Problem on Your Own

The Supreme Court is made up of nine justices, or judges. They are appointed by the President of the United States. This court is the highest court in the United States. It makes the final decision on whether or not laws are constitutional.

Over the years, justices have changed their ideas about the meaning of the Constitution. You have learned that environments change. New ways of acting are learned. Why might justices of one Supreme Court disagree with justices of past Supreme Courts?

what had been bought. The boundaries were not even clear. In fact, it would be a long time before people knew how valuable Louisiana really was.

What would the United States be like today without the land that was Louisiana? Look back at the map on page 147. What resources are in the land that was bought? ● How is this land valuable today?

● ● ● ● ● ● AT THIS POINT IN YOUR STUDY ● ● ● ● ● ●

Do these statements seem correct?

1   The Constitution gives the President the right to make treaties.

President Jefferson made a treaty to buy Louisiana. Why didn't he just go ahead and buy it?

2   The Constitution has been given different meanings at different times.

The Constitution was written about two hundred years ago. Why couldn't the men who wrote it plan far enough ahead so that it would always be given the same meaning?

Why are amendments added to the Constitution?

BEFORE YOU GO ON

Choose the ending for each of these sentences.

1 Jefferson wanted the western farmers to be able to
   (a) store their products at New Orleans
   (b) travel to Europe on ships

2 By buying Louisiana, Jefferson helped
   (a) only a small number of farmers
   (b) the whole country

3 When Jefferson bought Louisiana,
   (a) he acted in a way that the Constitution says the President cannot act
   (b) he decided what the writers of the Constitution had meant

USING WHAT YOU KNOW

To buy Louisiana, Jefferson had to act against a value he had always held. He thought that the national government should not grow too strong. But he also valued the good of the nation as a whole.

Why did he decide to buy Louisiana? Which value did he place first?

ON YOUR OWN

The first two Presidents of the United States, George Washington and John Adams, believed in a strong national government.

As you know, Thomas Jefferson believed that the national government should not grow too powerful.

Do you think that John Adams would have worried about buying Louisiana? What is your reasoning?

IN TRANSIT

In 1803, the border of the United States went as far west as the Rocky Mountains. There were many Indians in the new western lands. ● Their environment was changing. They had to learn new ways of acting.

How did the Indians feel about the growing nation? How did the people of the United States behave toward them? To find out, begin reading the next section.

4. Nations Against Each Other

The United States is not small. It is a very large country. Yet, even a very large country can become crowded. Long ago, it became crowded for the Indians who lived in it. Their hunting lands became filled with settlements. Their woods were cleared for farms. The animals they needed for food and clothing were destroyed. The pioneers took over the lands that were the home of the Indians.

The Indians did not have the same customs that the pioneers did. They did not have the same ways of acting or the same norms of behavior. To them, land that was needed and used by everyone belonged to everyone in a tribe. Sharing land was a norm of behavior of the Indians.

At first, most Indians did not try to keep settlers from the land. Most were willing to share their resources with others. The Indians wanted only what they had always had: the right to use the land to supply their needs. They did not understand that owning property meant something else to the settlers. They did not understand that they would not be able to use lands which they gave to others.

As more colonists settled along the east coast, the Indians, too, began to move west. Some tribes moved by agreement. That is, a treaty was made between the tribes and the colonists. These treaties usually gave Indian lands to the settlers.

Even when members of the tribe were still allowed to hunt and fish on the land, they were not always able to do so. Can you guess why? The physical environment was no longer the same. The woods were changed. The water was used by many people. Old ways of acting did not work in the new environment. The Indians had to adapt to the changes in their environment or find other places to live.

Once the colonists had settled along the east coast, they began to explore the lands west of them. Soon they began to move west. This did not always happen peacefully.

To whom did the frontier lands belong? Often the settlers and Indians clashed in war. At such times, many of the settlers on the frontier lived in daily fear of Indian attacks. Forts, such as Boonesboro, in Kentucky, were built to protect settlers.

JUSTICE FOR ALL?

Recall that, in 1763, the British tried to stop the settlers from moving westward. But the pioneers kept on moving west. Then the Indians decided that they would have to stop the settlers. They began to raid and to burn homes and farms on the frontier.

One leader of the Indians was the Shawnee Tecumseh (ti·kum′sə). ● In the early 1800's, he traveled among the tribes of the Northwest Territory. Tecumseh asked the Indians to unite under one government. He thought that all the Indians together might be able to stop the settlers. Tecumseh did not want war. He wanted only to stop strangers from taking Indian lands.

The Indian groups did not unite, however. They had different languages and leaders. They had different ways of living. Because they had different customs, they were not always friendly toward each other. All these things made an Indian union seem impossible. And so the settlers went on moving over the land, claiming it as their own.

In 1830, the government of the United States passed a law. It was called the Indian Removal Act.

What does **unite** mean? Why is our country called the United States?

As a result of this law, many tribes were forced to move from their homes. The Choctaws (chok'tôz) were moved to the Oklahoma Territory. The Chickasaws (chik'ə·sôz) in Mississippi were moved there, too. By 1846, most of the eastern Indians had been moved west of the Mississippi River.

To learn more about what happened after the Indian Removal Act was passed, try the investigation on the next page.

THE PLAINS INDIANS

Many Indian tribes once lived on the Great Plains of the United States. The buffalo herds were important to all of them. Recall your study of the Blackfoot Indians. The buffalo was their basic source of food, clothing, and shelter. This is how the buffalo looks to a modern artist. ▲

AN INVESTIGATION into law as a social control

Study this map. ● It shows where some of the Indian tribes lived before the Indian Removal Act. Study the other map. ▲ It shows where some of the same tribes live today. Which tribes moved at least five hundred miles?

The way people act is sometimes changed by force. It is sometimes changed by norms of behavior or law. Law was used to get the Indians to give up their lands.

Why do you think most of the Indians obeyed the law? What do you think happened when the law was not obeyed?

A Problem on Your Own

Were the pioneers' laws also the Indians' laws? Whose laws did the Indians obey before the Removal Act? Whose laws do they obey today? ■

Which laws are groups most likely to obey: laws which they share in making or laws which others force them to obey?

SOME
INDIAN TRIBES
BEFORE REMOVAL

OJIBWA

OTTAWA

WINNEBAGO

ONEIDA

YANKTON
DAKOTA

SAC
FOX

SENECA

KICKAPOO

WYANDOTTE

IOWA

POTAWATOMI

MIAMI

ARAPAHO

SOUTHERN
CHEYENNE

SHAWNEE

CHEROKEE

QUAPAW

KIOWA

CHICKASAW

CHOCTAW

CREEK

TONKAWA

SEMINOLE

0   300   600 miles

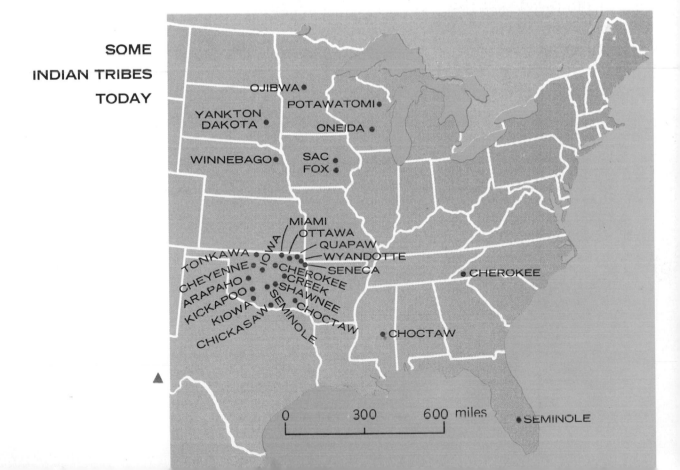

SOME
INDIAN TRIBES
TODAY

OJIBWA

POTAWATOMI

YANKTON
DAKOTA

ONEIDA

WINNEBAGO

SAC
FOX

MIAMI
OTTAWA
QUAPAW
WYANDOTTE

TONKAWA

IOWA

CHEROKEE

SENECA

CHEYENNE

CHEROKEE

ARAPAHO

CREEK

KICKAPOO

SHAWNEE

KIOWA

CHICKASAW

SEMINOLE

CHOCTAW

CHOCTAW

SEMINOLE

0   300   600 miles

Then the Plains Indians—the Blackfeet, Cheyenne (shī·en′), Crow, and Pawnee—saw the wagon trains begin to move along the trails to the Far West. They saw the railroad being built across the plains, splitting the buffalo herds. They saw hunters kill thousands and thousands of buffalo until the animal they needed was gone. The Indians could no longer live in the old way.

Treaties had taken away much of their land. The settlers were destroying their resources. What could the Indians do? Of course, they could choose to fight. And many tribes did.

INDIAN WARS

From 1790 to 1915, different groups of Indians and settlers were fighting almost all the time. Perhaps you have already heard about one of the famous battles in the Indian wars. Maybe you have seen something about it in the movies or on television. In 1876, the United States Army fought against the Sioux at the Little Bighorn River in Montana. ● In this one battle, General Custer and all his soldiers were killed.

The wars did not bring justice to the Indians. At that time, the people of the United States did not give the Indians the same rights they valued for themselves. The United States made many treaties with the Indians. Too many times, the treaties were broken.

New treaties were made which reserved, or set aside, certain lands for the Indians. These lands were called **reservations**. Only Indians were permitted to live on them. But, often, even these lands were taken from the Indians. Many times, settlers, railroad men, and miners claimed parts of the reservations.

The environment of the Indians was changing very quickly. ▲ Both Indians and settlers wanted the land. Each group wanted to use the resources in its own way. Could the conflict have been settled without fighting? How?

▲

This is the way an Indian called Kicking Bear pictured the Battle of the Little Bighorn.

══════ AT THIS POINT IN YOUR STUDY ══════

Do these statements seem correct?

1   The Indians' norms of behavior and laws were different from those of the settlers. ■

Recall what you have learned about the Blackfeet (pages 3-12). How were their norms different from those of the settlers?

Why didn't the Indians have the same laws and norms of behavior as the settlers?

2   The environment of the Indians changed.

How did the social environment change? Was the government of the Indians one of the changes? Name some other changes. How did the physical environment change? Name some changes.

Choose the ending for each of these sentences.

1 Reservations for Indian tribes were

(a) set up by the United States government

(b) never claimed by settlers

2 The Indians made treaties with the government that were

(a) never broken by others

(b) often broken by others

3 When the Indian wars ended, the Indians

(a) were sent to England

(b) were forced to obey the settlers' laws

USING WHAT YOU KNOW

Chief Joseph was a Nez Percé Indian. The United States government ordered the Nez Percé to move to a reservation. The tribe would not go. Chief Joseph led them in a flight toward Canada. They covered more than thirteen hundred miles in two months. When they were almost in Canada, they were surrounded by United States soldiers.

Chief Joseph said, "I am tired of fighting. The old men are all dead. It is cold and we have no blankets. The little children are freezing to death. Hear me, my chiefs, I am tired. My heart is sick and sad. From where the sun now stands, I will fight no more, forever."

Why do you think the tribe ran away? Why didn't the Nez Percé think of the United States government as *their* government?

ON YOUR OWN

When the government of Georgia tried to take the Cherokees' land, the Indians went to court. Finally, the Supreme Court of the United States decided that the land belonged to the Cherokees. But the government of Georgia did not pay any attention to the Supreme Court. Neither did President Jackson. The Cherokees were forced to move.

Could laws made by the United States government have helped the Indians keep their land? Why weren't such laws made? What were the values of Americans at that time?

If such laws had been made, how could they have been enforced?

IN TRANSIT

Nothing could stop the wave of pioneers from flowing west. The pioneers carried little with them. But they did take what they had learned. They did take with them ideas about how people in a group can interact without conflict. To find out about this, begin reading the next section.

5. Government on the Move

In the 1840's and 1850's, many people predicted that all of the West was going to be part of the United States. They thought that the country would go on growing until it reached the Pacific Ocean. Were these people right?

Do you have dreams of good things that you hope will happen? Many of the pioneers who went west had dreams, too. They dreamed about owning land and living well. To these people, the way west was the way to a new life.

Some of the pioneers sailed around South America and up to California and Oregon. ● Some followed the western trails. At first, there were only a handful of people. But then the great wagon trains began to come over the trails to Oregon, California, and Utah.

THE WAGON TRAIN

In the spring of 1843, a thousand people with one hundred twenty wagons met at Independence, Missouri. With them, they had five thousand animals. The goal of these people was to reach the Oregon country.

A very heavy wagon, the Conestoga (kon'is·tō'gə), was used by many pioneers. ▲ But the most common one was an ordinary farm wagon with very sturdy wheels. Both kinds of wagons were usually pulled by oxen. The Oregon Trail was long and hot and dusty. In either kind of wagon, riding was so uncomfortable that many chose to walk.

The pioneers planned to hunt for some of their food along the way. They couldn't take everything with them. Here is a list of some of the things which each wagon carried:

a barrel of flour ●
half a bushel of beans
ten pounds of rice
twenty pounds of sugar and coffee ▲
one hundred and fifty pounds of bacon
a ten-gallon water keg
spare shoes for oxen
a year's supply of woolen jeans
extra shoes
two woolen blankets ■
farm tools ▶◀

LEADERS FOR THE WAGON TRAIN

Before a wagon train like this one started, a government was set up, and laws were made. A group of people who would act as leaders were elected. They were called the council of elders. The council of elders had the authority to make new rules. They also had the authority to punish members of the wagon train who broke the rules.

Often, the council of elders hired a scout to help find the way. The scout was a man who had traveled the trail many times before. His job was to lead the train across the plains, over the mountains, and through the forests. The scout also chose places to camp along the way. ●

The council of elders might decide that each man should have a rifle and a supply of powder and bullets. They might say that each man should have a canteen, a hunting knife, and an ax. All problems were brought before the council. The council's decisions were the laws of the wagon train.

Many of the people in the wagon train had never met before the train was formed. Many would never meet again after the train reached the end of its journey. But, for many long months, the people in the wagon train were a group. They were a traveling community. The wagon train community had a government. The members of the community chose their own leaders. The leaders made rules. They also had the authority to make people obey the rules.

In what ways did the wagon train government help people on the trails? How was it easier for them to interact after they had chosen leaders? How was it easier for the group to reach its goal? ▲

To learn more about the way government helps groups reach their goals, try the investigation on the next page.

217

AN INVESTIGATION into law and travelers

Study the map. ● With the eraser of your pencil, follow the routes of the three main wagon trails west. Now find the Rocky Mountains. Follow them from north to south.

Try to answer these questions:

1 How long was each of the trails? (Use your ruler to measure the scale of the map.)

2 What rivers did each of the trails cross?

3 Where did the Oregon Trail cross the Rocky Mountains?

4 What present-day states did each of the trails go through?

5 Why did the people who traveled in wagon trains need leaders and laws?

6 Why was traveling dangerous? What hardships were caused by the physical environment? ▲

A Problem on Your Own

Some people believe that laws about transportation should be made by each community or state government. Some people believe that the national government should make them. Which view do you agree with? Why?

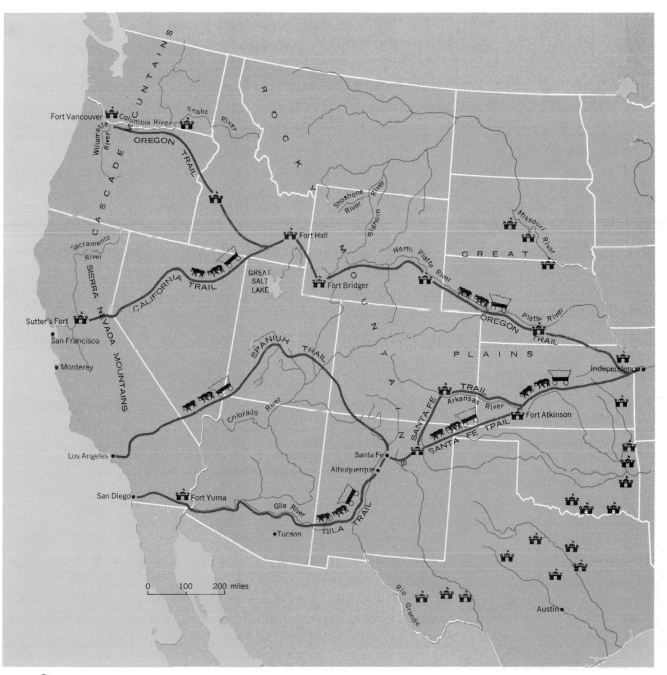

Trails  Forts and settlements

WAGON TRAILS TO THE WEST

219

AT THE END OF THE TRAILS

As you learned from your investigation, most of the wagon trains used one of three main trails. One was the Oregon Trail. Another was the California Trail, which followed the Oregon Trail almost to Fort Hall, in Idaho. The Santa Fe Trail was the third.

Indians had used the Santa Fe Trail long before the settlers came. Later, Mexican and American traders traveled along it. The traders brought needles, pins, knives, spoons, tools, hand mirrors, cotton cloth, thread, and thimbles from Independence, Missouri, to Santa Fe. Santa Fe was in a different country then. It was part of Mexico.

When the traders returned to Independence, they carried raw wool from the Mexican sheep ranches. They also carried tallow, beaver skins, and gold and silver. Do you recall what this kind of trading is called? If a social scientist had been asked to name this center of trade, he might have called it *Inter*dependence, Missouri! Can you see why? (You might want to look up **interdependent** in your Social Science Dictionary.)

The dreams of new lands came true for many who followed the trails west. But for all, the trails west brought hardship and suffering. There was the heat and the dust. There was sickness and death. There were broken wagons and worn-out mules and oxen. Yet, many groups of pioneers made the long journeys. Many achieved their goal of reaching new lands. ●

When wagon train communities ended, new communities were built. ▲ New groups were formed in a new environment. In western towns, new governments were set up and new laws made. How was this possible?

Like the colonists, the pioneers carried with them all that they had learned before. They took with them their values and ideas about government and law. With these, they tried to set up peaceful communities wherever they went.

Do these statements seem correct?

1   Government and law make interaction among people easier.

Why did the people in the wagon trains decide they needed government? Would the move west have been different without it? How?

How would life in your community be different without law and government? Name two ways.

2   People model their governments and laws after ones they have known before.

In the thirteen colonies, people modeled their governments and laws after those they had known in England.

Where did the pioneers who moved westward get their ideas about government and law?

Where do you get your ideas about government and law?

BEFORE YOU GO ON

Choose the ending for each of these sentences.

1 People in wagon trains
    (a) made all new norms of behavior
    (b) kept many of the norms they had known before
2 A wagon train
    (a) set up a government for all
    (b) permitted each family to make its own laws
3 Each member of a wagon train was
    (a) independent
    (b) interdependent

USING WHAT YOU KNOW

Elijah (i·lī′jə) Lovejoy lived in Illinois in 1837. He published a newspaper. Mr. Lovejoy did not believe that men should be slaves. In his newspaper, he wrote that there should be laws against slavery.

Many people in the town where Mr. Lovejoy lived did not agree with him. Once, they burned his shop and threw his printing press into the river. But Elijah Lovejoy kept printing his paper. He kept on with his fight against slavery. One day, people came, full of anger. While trying to defend his building, Elijah Lovejoy was killed.

Why did Elijah Lovejoy keep on printing his newspaper when he knew he was in danger? Was he a pioneer? How was he like other pioneers? How was he different?

ON YOUR OWN

After the Civil War, a group of black people who had been slaves traveled to Manzanola, Colorado. They had heard of rich farmland in eastern Colorado.

When the black pioneers arrived in Manzanola, they faced many hardships. First, they found that lumber was scarce. So, like other pioneers in prairie country, the Manzanola settlers made their first homes by digging into the earth. These homes were called dug-outs.

Because rainfall was light, farming in Manzanola was not easy. But one neighbor let the new settlers use his well. After that they could raise beans, corn, sorghum, and squash.

When there were about one hundred black settlers in Manzanola, a schoolhouse was built. For a while, the schoolhouse was also used as a church and a meeting place for the community. Slowly, the town began to grow.

Why did the black settlers move to Manzanola?

What were some of the settlers' norms of behavior? How do you know?

What were some of their values?

Every group has its own ways of acting. It has its own values. It has its own norms of behavior and customs. Although the norms and customs are not written down, the members of the group understand them. ●

Long before the first colonists came to the New World, they had learned the meaning of law and government. The colonists brought with them their ideas about honesty and liberty. People were punished who did not follow the norms in which the group believed. They were rewarded if they did follow them. People were punished if they disobeyed laws, too, because many norms were made into laws.

Norms and laws are both forms of social control. The colonists used social controls to make interaction easier.

When the pioneers crossed the Appalachians, they took tools with them. They took their axes and guns. They also took government and their belief in law. At first, there were no written laws. People were expected to behave according to certain norms of behavior. They were expected to behave in peaceful ways and to respect the property of other settlers.

Later, the pioneers made laws to make sure that people would follow these norms. They made their social controls stronger. Perhaps we may make this statement, then, about the concept of **social control: Some norms of behavior are made stronger by laws.**

Recall that the colonists made laws like those they had learned in England. As they pushed westward, the pioneers built communities with representative governments. Their laws were based on laws which they had known in eastern communities. You have reached, then, another understanding of the concept of **social**

control: New laws are modeled after those that are already valued.

Many laws and treaties are made to stop conflicts between groups of people. Sometimes they are made to prevent them. The British and French made a treaty after the French and Indian War. This treaty stopped conflict. Recall, too, the treaty that President Jefferson signed for the Louisiana Purchase. This treaty probably prevented fighting over New Orleans. Why might France and the United States have fought over New Orleans?

Laws are also made to prevent conflicts within groups of people. ● Sometimes they are made to end conflicts within groups. Recall that the Pilgrims made laws to protect property rights. Do you see how laws about property rights could prevent conflict?

Laws made by the wagon train communities prevented conflict, too. The people elected a council of elders. The council of elders punished those who broke the rules.

What you have learned in this unit about laws has given you more understanding of the concept of **social control: Laws are a form of social control. They help settle conflicts between groups. They also help settle conflicts within groups.**

People interact with each other. Interaction sometimes brings conflict. In this unit, you have studied conflicts that broke out into war. You have studied some of the wars which the people of the United States have fought.

Most of the time, though, people interact peacefully. Why is this so?

Knowing how others will act makes interaction easier. That is why groups have social controls, such as norms of behavior and law. Some norms and laws are found in all groups. This statement tells us the importance of the concept of **social control: People's peaceful interaction depends on their social controls.**

Focus on the Concept

A. A PROBLEM IN ANALYSIS

The first ten amendments to the United States Constitution are called the Bill of Rights. ● Here is the first amendment in the Bill of Rights. Read it carefully. If you find it hard to read, look at the paragraph to the right of it. This paragraph uses easier words to explain what the amendment means.

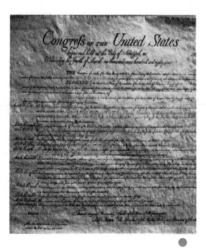

Amendment 1
Congress shall make no law respecting an establishment of religion, or prohibiting the free exercise thereof; of abridging the freedom of speech, or of the press; or the right of the people peaceably to assemble, and to petition the government for a redress of grievances.

Congress may not pass a law that favors one religion or that limits freedom of religion. Congress may not pass a law that limits freedom of speech or freedom of the press (newspapers, television, and so on). Congress may not pass a law that limits people's right to have peaceful public meetings or their right to ask the government to correct wrongs.

After you have studied the first amendment, try to answer these questions:

1 What rights are protected in the first amendment?

2 What does "freedom of speech" mean? Why is it valued?

3 What does "freedom of worship" mean? Why is it valued?

4 What does "freedom of the press" mean? Why is it valued?

5 What does "freedom of assembly" mean? Why is it valued?

6 The men who wrote the Constitution protected these rights by putting them in the first amendment. Was it important to write them down? Why?

Here is an article of a United Nations document, called the Declaration of Human Rights. ● This document was written almost two hundred years after the Bill of Rights. Read the article carefully. Then read the sentence to the right of it. This sentence explains the article.

Article 4

No one shall be held in slavery or servitude; slavery and the slave trade shall be prohibited in all their forms.	Slavery and the slave trade shall not be allowed.

After you have studied the article, try to answer these questions:

1 In the Bill of Rights, there is no amendment like Article 4 of the Declaration. Would all the Founding Fathers have agreed with Article 4? Would some of them have agreed?

2 Is there a later amendment to the Constitution like Article 4 of the Declaration? How can you find out?

3 What has changed from the time that the Bill of Rights was written?

B. ANALYSES OF VALUES

Ways of behaving change. Values change. You have seen evidence, too, that laws change. Predict some laws that the United States government may make in the future.

Which of the following do you think will become laws? What values does each of these statements show?

1 Everyone eighteen years old or over may vote.

2 Property rights on other planets belong to the person or the group who paid for the first landing. They do not belong to those who took part in the exploring.

3 People who dump litter from spaceships must pay a fine.

4 The taxes of all citizens shall be used to pay for hospitals which shall be free to everyone.

UNIVERSAL DECLARATION OF HUMAN RIGHTS

UNITED NATIONS

Focus on the Social Scientist

Some social scientists study the way governments work. They are called **political scientists**. **Political** means "of government."

One political scientist, Glendon Schubert, studied a part of our government, the Supreme Court. ● As you may know, there are nine Supreme Court justices. The justices vote on each case. If five or more justices vote for one decision, it becomes the decision of the Supreme Court. Have all the different Courts understood the Constitution in the same way? For example, have they all agreed on which powers are given to the national government by the Constitution? How do the different justices decide the cases they must judge?

Dr. Schubert tried to answer these questions by using the methods of social science. He studied the decisions made by different Courts at different times. He recorded his observations and analyzed them.

How did each justice decide a case? His values and all that he learned before helped him to decide. Schubert learned that justices of different Supreme Courts had different values and norms because they had lived at different times.

Perhaps you know that justices are appointed to the Supreme Court by the President. If they wish, they may be justices for the rest of their lives. But no matter how long they are justices, the values of each justice usually do not change.

The values of different Supreme Courts do change, however. How can this be? Different men with different values become part of the Supreme Court. When this happens, the decisions of the Supreme Court change, too.

Will the Supreme Court keep on changing? What do you predict?

UNIT SIX

INTERACTING
AS A NATION

Introduction

In 1790, the United States was not a large nation. Most people lived east of the Appalachian Mountains. (Look at the map on page 232.) At that time, the land west of the Appalachians was on the frontier. A frontier is settled land at the edge of land where no one lives.

In the 1800's, people settled the Appalachian lands. But they did not stop there. They pushed farther and farther west. As they pushed westward, they found new ways of interacting in new environments.

By 1890, there was no longer a frontier. (Look at the map on page 233.) People from many different countries had come to the United States. They had spread across the nation, from coast to coast. Wherever they went, they learned to interact with new groups of people.

What had Americans learned that helped them interact in new environments? How could so many people — with so many different customs — build the new nation? ● To find out, begin reading on the opposite page.

1. Government in California

California has a long history. Long before explorers saw the coastline of California, Indians lived on the land. One of the first Europeans to set foot in California was the English explorer Sir Francis Drake. In the 1500's, he sailed around the world. Along the way, he stopped on the coast of California to repair his ships. But California was not settled by the English.

In the 1500's and early 1600's, the Spanish explored the California coast. In the 1700's, Spanish priests traveled north from Mexico to set up missions. Then the Spanish government sent men from Mexico to govern California.

What does **independence** mean? If you don't know, look up the word in your Social Science Dictionary.

Although the Spanish settled and claimed California, other people were also interested in this new land. In the 1800's, the Russians built Fort Ross, which has now been rebuilt. ● Fort Ross was a fur-trading post north of San Francisco. The Spanish did not want more Russians in California. But they did let Americans go there. At that time, the Spanish did not think that the Americans would be a threat to Spanish power.

A NEW GOVERNMENT FOR CALIFORNIA

The Spanish governed California until 1821. In that year, Mexico won its independence from Spain. California was then ruled by the Mexican government. At first, the Mexican government did not allow Californians to trade with people in other countries. But trade went on anyway. Californians needed goods from the United States. New England shoe factories needed

231

NUMBER OF PEOPLE IN THE UNITED STATES IN 1790

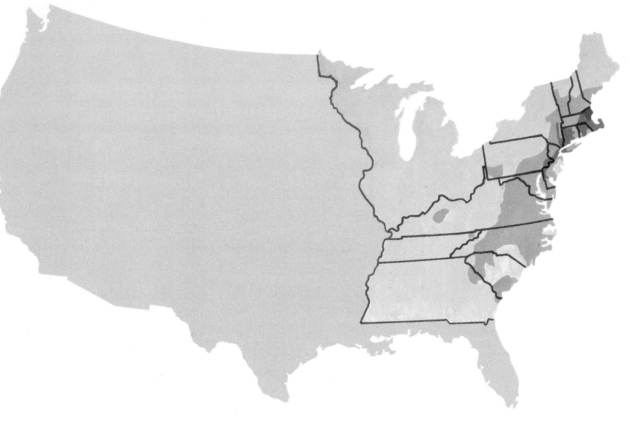

Legend

Fewer than 6 people for each square mile

6 - 45 people for each square mile

45 - 90 people for each square mile

More than 90 people for each square mile

Not part of the United States in 1790

hides from California cattle. Ships came around Cape Horn, at the tip of South America. The ships left goods in exchange for hides that California ranchers stacked on the beaches.

Little by little, American farmers began to come to California. By 1840, there were about three hundred Americans there. Many of these Americans did not want California to be governed by Mexico.

Some people thought that California should not be part of either Mexico or the United States. In 1846, these people tried to make California independent by setting up the Bear Flag Republic. But, in the same year, something else happened. Mexico and the United States went to war. At the end of the Mexican War, California became a territory of the United States.

NUMBER OF PEOPLE IN THE UNITED STATES IN 1890

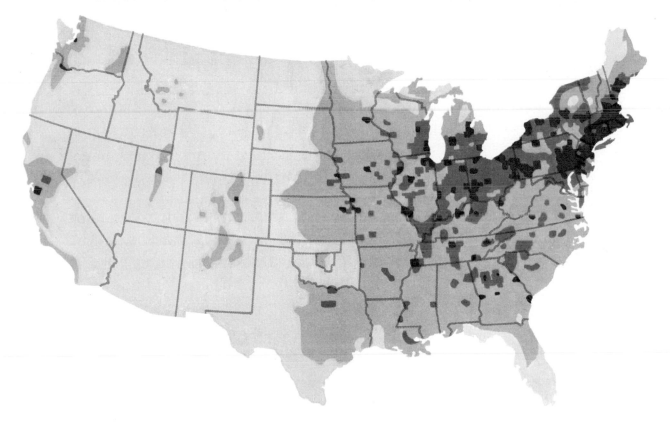

This new territory grew quickly in the 1840's and 1850's. People from all over the world rushed to California. What started this rush? And what happened in California as more and more people came?

THE GOLD RUSH

John Sutter had come all the way from Switzerland to settle in the Sacramento Valley of California. In 1848, a carpenter who worked for Sutter saw something glittering in a stream. He bent over and picked up a small yellowish chunk of metal. It did not take him long to realize what he had found. It was gold!

The news of gold spread all over the world. Soon, gold-seekers began to arrive in California. They came from St. Louis and Philadelphia, from Mexico City, and even from faraway London and Paris. Some came by sea—sailing around South America or to Panama. Some came overland—on foot, by horse, or in wagon trains.

Why were many of the gold miners called "Forty-Niners"?

There were not many people in California before the gold rush began. But, after 1848, people poured in. They had all caught gold fever! ● By the middle of 1850, there were already about 100,000 people in California. And, by 1852, there were about 250,000 people—almost a quarter of a million.

California grew so fast that, at first, many people lived in camps or very crowded settlements. Towns sprang up overnight. In these new towns and settlements, there were often conflicts. And there were no laws and no policemen to keep the peace.

SOCIAL CONTROL: THE MINERS

Study the picture. ▲ It shows a mining camp called Dry Diggings. Are there shelters for the miners? Does Dry Diggings look orderly? Does it look planned? Dry Diggings looks like many mining towns that sprang up during the gold rush.

In towns like Dry Diggings, miners made claims to land they wanted to work for gold. A miner drove a stake into each corner of the land he wanted. That is, he "staked his claim." This showed other people that the land belonged to him. No one else was supposed to take it.

If someone did try to take another man's claim, the group of miners punished him. After the miners in Dry Diggings punished three men for claim jumping, the camp was called Hangtown. What had happened to the three men? Can you guess?

At the mining camps, there was usually no community government. No representatives were elected, and no laws were passed. Can you imagine what it would be like to be without government and laws?

Perhaps you have played ball with someone who didn't follow the rules. What did you do? Of course, if there was an umpire, you did not have a problem. But if there was no umpire, how could you and your friends make sure everyone followed the rules?

Most of the miners who came to California knew how they were expected to behave. Most of them valued law and peace. Most of them lived by the norms of behavior they had learned.

In the camps, the miners agreed on the rules and how to enforce them. The miners used social controls. But most mining camps did not have governments like the one in your community. What would happen if your community enforced laws the way the miners did? How would your life be different?

SOCIAL CONTROL: THE VIGILANTES

In the East, many towns had grown up around bays along the coast. This was true in the West, too. San Francisco grew up at the entrance to a large, deep bay. ● The entrance is called the Golden Gate.

During the gold rush, the small town of San Francisco suddenly became a large city. It seemed as if thousands of people had moved there overnight. Many people broke the law, and crimes often were not punished.

Most San Franciscans thought that the city needed better government. Most of them wanted laws that would be enforced. But fourteen men didn't wait for the city government to do something. They set up a committee. The members of the committee were called vigilantes (vij′ə·lan′tēz). ▲ With the help of some other San Franciscans, the vigilantes tried to protect lives and property.

Remember the town meetings in Massachusetts. In their meetings, the Pilgrims talked about town problems and voted on laws and decisions. Every person

who had signed the *Mayflower* agreement was given the chance to vote on each law. Recall that government in which every person votes on each problem or law is called direct democracy.

Did the vigilantes use direct democracy? How many San Franciscans were vigilantes?

Both the California miners and the vigilantes needed social controls in their new environment. Both groups knew the importance of enforcing laws. They also knew that justice is an important part of law. If laws are just, they apply to every person in the same way. Everyone has to obey them. Everyone has the same rights.

But the justice of the miners and vigilantes was often harsh. In your community, would a person be hanged for taking someone else's property? Do you suppose the miners or the vigilantes ever punished the wrong person? Why might this have happened?

The methods which the miners and the vigilantes used would not work in our communities today. But both these groups knew something you have learned: Without social controls of some kind, men cannot live together peacefully and safely.

THE STATE OF CALIFORNIA

What is the Congress? If you can't remember, look it up in your class dictionary.

The thousands of people who came to California wanted to build a lasting government. They wanted California to become a state. So, in September of 1849, the people chose representatives to write a constitution. ● The constitution said that there could be no slavery in California. It also said that elections would be held for a governor and for lawmakers.

In October 1850, the Congress of the United States approved the state constitution. California had become the thirty-first state of the United States.

LIVING TOGETHER

Wherever towns and cities sprang up, new groups were formed. The people who had gone to California to build a new life had the same needs as people everywhere. They needed the feeling of belonging to a group. They needed to interact with other people. They needed social controls—norms of behavior and law. ▲

AT THIS POINT IN YOUR STUDY

Do these statements seem correct?

1 Every group needs some form of social control.

The miners in Dry Diggings needed social controls. So did the San Franciscans. How is property protected in your family? in your community? in your country?

Is there any group whose members may do what they please? Name one.

2 People who govern themselves choose some kind of social control.

Did the miners choose ways of governing themselves? Did the San Francisco vigilantes?

Do people who elect representatives choose some kind of social control?

BEFORE YOU GO ON

Choose the ending for each of these sentences.

1 In 1848 and 1849, the number of people in California grew quickly because of the
   (a) good soil
   (b) discovery of gold

2 The social controls of the miners
   (a) were always just
   (b) protected property

3 The vigilantes were formed
   (a) to build a government
   (b) to enforce laws

USING WHAT YOU KNOW

1 The vigilantes decided what laws were to be enforced. Then they punished those who broke them. Do our policemen *decide* what our laws are? How are our policemen different from vigilantes?

2 Is a law just if one person has to obey it and another person doesn't? Is a law just if it protects everyone's rights? Why?

ON YOUR OWN

Like California, Texas was under Spanish authority. Then Mexico won its independence from Spain. Texas became part of Mexico.

In the 1820's, many settlers from the United States moved to Texas. There was a Mexican law against slavery. But because this law was not enforced, many settlers brought their slaves with them to Texas.

Then Mexico decided to enforce the law. It also began to tax goods made in the United States and sold in Texas. Finally, Americans were told to stop settling in Texas.

In 1836, the Texans fought against Mexico. They won their independence and formed the Republic of Texas. Then, in 1845, Texans decided to join the United States. Texas became a state.

Now try to find out the answers to these questions:

Who was Stephen Austin?

Who was General Santa Ana?

What happened at the Alamo?

What happened at the Battle of San Jacinto?

Why is Texas sometimes called the Lone Star State?

IN TRANSIT

Like people everywhere, Californians tried to settle conflicts by using different kinds of social controls. Did other people use the same ways to settle their problems? To find out, turn to the next section.

2. Groups, Conflicts, and Government

One of the tall-tale heroes of the West is Pecos Bill. ● Have you heard about him? He was a giant cowboy who had a wildcat for a pet. Pecos Bill was so strong that he could ride a cyclone from one part of the West to another. He was so brave and clever that, for a long time, he thought that he was a coyote, rather than a man.

There were other tall-tale heroes. John Henry, Paul Bunyan, and Old Stormalong, were also huge, strong, and smart. Any one of them could do more than any man on Earth. By making up tales like these, the pioneer storytellers seemed to be saying, "This is a big country—so big that there is room enough in it for giants, with room left over."

The land was big indeed, but there were many different groups of people who wanted to use it. You have already learned that some of these groups had conflicts with the Indians. Were there other conflicts? How were they settled?

USING LAND: THE CATTLEMEN

Long before the colonists came to the New World, buffalo had grazed on the Great Plains. By the 1860's, most of the buffalo had been killed off by hunters. When the buffalo were almost gone, another grazing animal came to the plains—the longhorn. ▲

First the Spanish and later the Mexicans raised longhorn cattle in Texas. In 1860, some Texas cattlemen drove longhorns to southern ports, such as Galveston and New Orleans. From the ports, the cattle were carried by ship to the East. There, they were sold as beef.

The great cattle drives, however, began after the railroad came to the West. Then, cattle were driven north to be fattened on the Great Plains. The railroad carried the cattle from the plains to the East. Cowboys rode out of Texas, driving great herds to Kansas City or Dodge City. Sometimes, herds were driven as far north as Colorado or Wyoming. ■

USING LAND: THE SHEEPMAN

There was a market in California and on the east coast for lamb and wool, too. So sheep, as well as cattle, began to graze on the Great Plains. The sheep were driven from New Mexico to Colorado. Sometimes, they were driven as far north as Montana. Many sheep were raised in Utah, as they are today.

What happened when sheepmen moved their flocks onto land already claimed by cattlemen? The cattlemen said that the sharp hoofs of the sheep destroyed the range grass. Where the sheep grazed, they ate the grass down to the roots. There was none left for the cattle. The cattlemen also claimed that cattle would not drink at a water hole where sheep drank.

The cattlemen were on the land first. Because they were first, they thought that they alone had a right to the land. Would the Indians have agreed?

USING LAND: THE FARMERS

In cattle drives, cowboys sometimes took their herds across land that belonged to other people. When this happened, the farmers became angry. They did

CATTLE TRAILS 1870

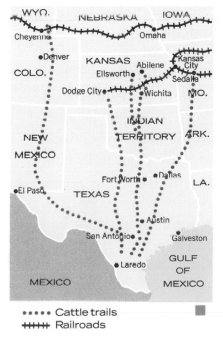

••••• Cattle trails
╫╫╫╫ Railroads

not want thousands of head of cattle trampling their land. Kansas farmers sometimes banded together and met cattle drives at the state border. ● Then the cowboys had to turn back and find new trails farther west. How were the farmers enforcing norms about property rights?

Much of the western land belonged to the United States government. Cattlemen and sheepmen let their animals graze on this public land. And many of the pioneers who went west settled on public land. They farmed it and built homes on it, without worrying about who owned it. The cattlemen called these farmers "squatters." Farmers claimed that they had "squatter's rights." They felt that people had more right to live on the land than animals had to graze on it.

You can understand why there were conflicts. Each group had its own interest in the land. Who had the right to use this public land—the farmers or the cattlemen or the sheepmen? How would you have settled these conflicts?

To find out more about the conflicts on the Great Plains, try the investigation on the opposite page.

Cattlemen fattened their herds on open ranges.  When the cattle were sold and shipped east on the new railroad, they brought high prices.

People in the East learned of this new way to make money easily. There was a rush to the Great Plains. Men bought land, stole it, or fought for it. Land on the plains became valuable.

Then sheepmen moved onto the Great Plains. ▲ Sheepmen and cattlemen fought over the use of the land. Later, farmers built barbed wire fences. ■ Fences stopped cattle from grazing freely.

1 How was the cattle rush like the California gold rush? How was it different?

2 The cattlemen wanted the range to be left open — to be left unfenced. Did they have a right to use all the land for grazing their cattle?

3 How did the farmers want to use the land? How did the sheepman want to use the land? Which group was right?

4 Could social controls have helped? ▻◅ How?

A Problem on Your Own

Do conflicts arise in your community? Do people in your community have different ideas about the way they want to use land or tax money? How does government help settle these conflicts?

The number of people on the Great Plains had grown quickly during the cattle rush. Because different groups of people wanted different things, there were conflicts. In most communities, peace officers had been elected. The peace officers tried to protect people's rights and property, but there was still lawlessness.

Sheepmen and cattlemen argued with each other. Both of these groups argued with farmers. There was trouble with outlaws. On the ranges, there were no fences. And many cattle were not branded. Can you see why it was easy for outlaws to steal cattle?

The national government decided to help bring order to the Great Plains. To enforce laws, the President of the United States appointed marshals. ●

In the 1840's, the government also began to sell much of the public land in the Great Plains. The squatters felt that they had first claim to the land. So, many of them, like the farmers in Iowa, set up claim clubs.

Each claim club elected officers and kept a record of land claimed by the members of the club. When the public sale of land was held, the club members went to the sale. ▲ The secretary of the club offered $1.25 for each acre that a member claimed. Usually, there were no bids from outsiders. In this way, the squatter got legal right to his farm. Most people agreed that a man had a right to land he had plowed and planted himself.

In 1841, the Congress of the United States made this norm of behavior into a law. The government was helping the farmers. According to the law that was passed, a squatter had first chance to buy the land on which he had settled. For each acre he bought, he was to pay $1.25.

This is another example of the way that norms of behavior sometimes become law. As you go on in your

study of the social sciences, you will find many other examples. What is the difference between a norm, such as honesty, and a law, such as one which forbids stealing?

MORE REQUESTS FOR LAND

In 1862, Congress passed another land law, called the Homestead Act. It granted up to one hundred sixty acres of farmland to any citizen who was twenty-one years of age or older. The homesteader, or settler, paid only $10 for all this land. After five years, he paid another small amount of money. Then the land belonged to him.

A few years later, the Civil War ended. The Negroes had been freed from slavery. Many Negroes wanted to start farms. They asked the national government to give them forty acres and a mule. Most of them asked for their forty acres in the southeastern part of the country. But, by then, there was very little public land east of the Mississippi River. Since the govern-

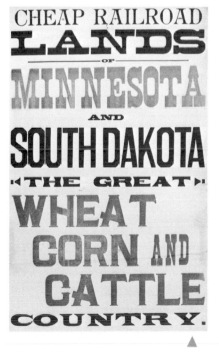

CHEAP RAILROAD
LANDS
OF
MINNESOTA
AND
SOUTH DAKOTA
THE GREAT
WHEAT
CORN AND
CATTLE
COUNTRY.

ment could not give them land there, Negro pioneers began to make the journey westward. ● There was much more land available in the West.

In the 1870's, the cattlemen began to feel that their needs were being overlooked by the government. The government had helped the squatters. ▲ But ranchers needed much more than the one hundred sixty acres granted to farmers by the Homestead Act. They asked the government to help them. In 1877, the national government agreed to sell any person six hundred forty more acres for twenty-five cents an acre.

Can you buy land for twenty-five cents an acre today? Why or why not?

By 1900, the Great Plains were settled. Towns had grown up across the land. ■ Great fields of wheat, surrounded by barbed wire fences, were growing in Kansas, Nebraska, and the Dakotas. Cattle and sheep grazed on the open plains where the buffalo had once lived. Throughout the country, new resources were being used. New laws made new ways of behaving easier. The frontier was gone, and the nation was settled from coast to coast.

▬▬▬ AT THIS POINT IN YOUR STUDY ▬▬▬

Do these statements seem correct?

1   Laws sometimes state norms which people already have.

The law passed by Congress gave squatters first claim to land where they lived and farmed. But most people had already agreed that the squatters had a right to the land. Why was the law made anyway? Is it helpful to write norms down as laws? Why or why not?

2   Representatives in the national government have to plan for the needs of many different groups of people.

Did the Homestead Act please the cattlemen as well as the farmers? Will every national law please all the different groups in the country? Explain your answer.

BEFORE YOU GO ON

Choose the ending for each of these sentences.

1 Cattlemen and farmers had conflicts because
   (a) they lived in different parts of the country
   (b) they wanted to use the same land in different ways

2 Congress passed land laws
   (a) to protect the rights of settlers
   (b) to keep cattlemen from moving

3 The national government looks after the interests of
   (a) one group only
   (b) many different groups

USING WHAT YOU KNOW

Farming was not easy on the frontier of Kansas and Nebraska. Many farmers built their homes of sod because there were no trees for lumber. (Sod is soil with grass growing in it.)

Grasshoppers often ate the crops. Seasons without rain caused crops to fail. Winds dried out what little water was in the soil. The farmers worked from early morning to dark. Their work sometimes seemed useless.

One historian said that sometimes there were as many farmers returning to the East as moving to the West. Why did anyone choose to stay?

ON YOUR OWN

Abraham Lincoln said that free land grants were good for the poor farmer. Therefore, he said, they were good for the country. Do you agree? Why?

IN TRANSIT

The government passed laws to help the sheepmen, the cattlemen, and the farmers. But there were many other groups across the nation who needed help, too.

How did they let their leaders know what laws they wanted? Did the government always listen? To find out, begin reading on the next page.

3. Groups and Their Government

The westward movement is the story of pioneers, Indians, gold miners, and cattlemen. It is the story of groups and their search for ways to live together in peace. It is the story of the settling of a large part of the country.

The westward movement is also the story of groups and their government. The people who moved westward had different goals. They worked to reach their goals in different ways. Many of them felt that they could reach their goals only if they worked together as a group. Working together, they could make the national government understand their needs. These people wanted to change the government's ways of acting. They wanted to **influence** (in'floo·əns) the government. How did groups go about this?

Influence means to change people's ways of behaving.

TRYING TO UNITE THE INDIANS

Do you remember how the United States government tried to stop conflicts between settlers and Indians? Indian reservations were set up. Many tribes were moved from their homes to the reservations. But even the reservations were not spared.

The railroad builders and the gold and silver miners made claims on Indian lands. And the government often gave Indian lands to these people.

The Indians believed that they had been treated unjustly. Some of them decided to try to change what the government was doing. Sequoya (si·kwoi'ə) was a Cherokee Indian. He believed that, if all his people

If you do not remember the meaning of **communicate**, look up the word in your Social Science Dictionary.

Cherokee Alphabet.

worked together, they could influence the government. He thought that only if they were united could they plan their goals and agree on their needs.

As you remember, the Shawnee Tecumseh had already tried to unite the Indian tribes. But Tecumseh had found that it was very hard to bring tribes with different customs and different languages together. He had not been able to do it.

Sequoya had a new idea for bringing the Indians together. Like other Indian tribes, the Cherokees had a spoken language, but no written language. Cherokees in one area were not able to communicate with Cherokees in another area. Without writing, the Indians could not work together as a group.

Sequoya was a gifted man. He worked twelve years to invent a Cherokee alphabet. When the alphabet was finished, it showed the sounds of the Cherokee language. Using this alphabet, thousands of Cherokees learned to read and write their own language. ● By 1828, the Cherokees had started their own newspaper. And they were planning to send their own representatives to Washington, D.C.

The Indians were not able to influence the national government. Along with other tribes, the Cherokees were moved westward to Oklahoma. (See the map

on page 211.) Sequoya left the reservation and traveled for many years. He went through the Southwest to California. As he traveled, he studied languages of different Indian groups. It had become his dream to make a common language for all Indians. ▲

Was Sequoya's idea a good one? How does a common language help unite people? How can groups use language when they try to influence government?

To learn more about the ways in which groups try to influence the government, try the investigation on the next page.

GOVERNMENT AND THE RAILROAD MEN

During the gold rush, thousands of people went to California. They traveled over the trails or on the seas. For those who traveled by ship, the journey was very long. It took them more than three months to get from New York or Boston to San Francisco on a ship that looked like this model. ■ The first gold-seekers who went overland from the East had a long journey, too. They could go only as far as the Mississippi River by railroad. There, the railroad ended. For the rest of the journey, many of them rode stagecoaches that looked like this model. ▶◀ But stagecoaches were slow and uncomfortable.

AN INVESTIGATION into influencing the government

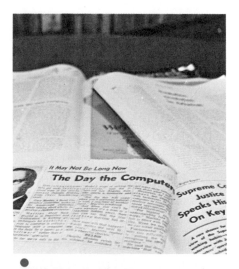

Look at newspapers to find out about some of today's problems. ● What law would the members of your class like to have passed? Would you like a new law about education? a new law about conserving resources? a new law about voting for leaders?

1 In your class, choose one new law that you think the people of the United States should have.

2 Did you all agree on the law at the beginning of the discussion?

3 Could you reach an agreement without a discussion?

4 After you have reached an agreement, write a letter to your Congressman and to the two Senators of your state. ▲ Tell them about your discussion. Describe the law that your class thinks is needed. Ask your representatives if they will help to make such a law.

5 How do representatives in Congress know what kinds of laws the voters want? Why do they pay attention to what the voters want?

A Problem on Your Own

The government, said Abraham Lincoln, was made "by the people and for the people." What did he mean?

Americans began to see that a coast-to-coast railroad would make traveling easier. Also, food, clothing, lumber, and metals could be carried to many different regions. Farm products, such as beef, lamb, and fruit could be carried, too. Letters could be delivered more quickly. Even by the fastest pony express, mail took ten days to get from Missouri to California.

The national government had already sent men to explore a route for a coast-to-coast railroad. More help from the government was needed. The group of men who wanted to build the railroad needed land and money. The government passed laws to lend railroad men money and to give them land. With this help, men began to build the railroad. ● In passing laws to help the railroad men, the government was helping the whole nation.

The first cross-country railroad was really two railroads. One began in Sacramento, California, and was built eastward. The other began in Omaha, Nebraska, and was built westward. On May 10, 1869, the two lines met at Promontory, Utah. The final spike, a golden one, was driven into the track. ▲ In the next few

Most people in the West wanted the railroad to go through their town. Can you explain why?

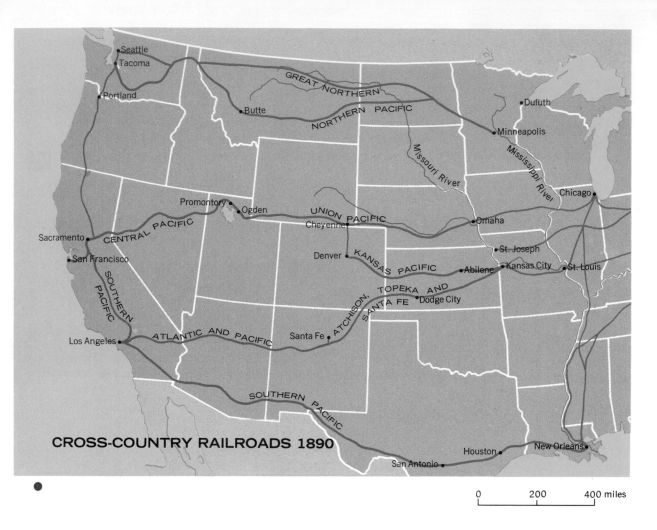

CROSS-COUNTRY RAILROADS 1890

0   200   400 miles

1869. May 10th. 1869.
GREAT EVENT
Rail Road from the Atlantic to the Pacific
GRAND OPENING
OF THE
Union Pacific
RAIL ROAD
PLATTE VALLEY ROUTE
PASSENGER TRAINS LEAVE
OMAHA
ON THE ARRIVAL OF TRAINS FROM THE EAST
THROUGH TO SAN FRANCISCO
In less than Four Days, avoiding the Dangers of the Sea!
Travelers for Pleasure, Health or Business
LUXURIOUS CARS & EATING HOUSES
ON THE UNION PACIFIC RAIL ROAD
PULLMAN'S PALACE SLEEPING CARS
GOLD, SILVER AND OTHER MINERS!
CHEYENNE for DENVER, CENTRAL CITY & SANTA FE

years, more railroads were built. By 1890, four railroads crossed the country.

The environment was changing. People were working to influence the government. They wanted the government to help bring about more changes. Could the group of people who wanted the railroads have built them without the government's help?

OTHER GROUPS

In the 1860's and 1870's, many of the farmers who had settled in the West came into conflict with railroad owners. The farmers depended on the railroads to ship farm products to other parts of the country. ▲ But shipping prices were higher in some places than they were in others. The farmers thought that this was unfair.

254

American farmers formed groups called Granges. The Granges worked to influence the government. They helped to get laws passed that made shipping prices the same for farmers all over the country. ■

As time went by, railroad workers themselves formed groups called labor unions. By working together, railroad workers were able to get laws passed. Some of these laws gave the workers higher wages. Others gave them shorter work weeks.

■

The railroad builders, the farmers, and the railroad workers found out that, through government, they could reach their goals. But they are not the only groups that have worked to influence the government. Through government, many Americans have been able to get the help they need to reach their goals.

AT THIS POINT IN YOUR STUDY

Does this statement seem correct?

Through the groups to which they belong, people may influence the government.

Why do lawmakers pass laws that some groups want? Can one person get any law passed? Can any group?

Choose the ending for each of these sentences.

1. Conflicts between groups can be settled
   (a) through government and law
   (b) by building railroads
2. The railroads helped bring cattlemen and farmers
   (a) more open land
   (b) faster service to more markets
3. A group can influence the government
   (a) if its members fight about what they want
   (b) if its members agree on what they want

Is there a group in your community or state that wants to change a law? How is the group trying to bring about the change? Use newspapers, magazines, or television to help you answer these questions.

Many buffalo were shot to feed the men who built the railroad. But many were shot for no reason at all. People traveling on the railroad sometimes shot buffalo for fun and left them where they died.

Do you think the Indians were happy to see the railroad built? What changes did it bring to Indians like the Blackfeet? Explain your answer.

After the railroads were built, people traveled across country more quickly. ● News traveled faster, and goods were carried to all parts of the country. More and more settlements appeared on the once open plains. Settled territories became states.

Do you think that all the frontiers were gone forever? Did American ideas about law and government stay within the ocean borders of the United States? To find out, begin reading on the opposite page.

4. Government in Two New States

Would you say that $7,200,000 is a lot of money? That's how much it cost the United States to buy Alaska from Russia in 1867. For a long time, a great many Americans believed that it was too much to pay for such a faraway place.

What resources did Alaska have? To most people, the land seemed to be without value. They thought that Alaska was always cold and filled with ice and snow. They thought the Secretary of State William Seward was making a mistake when he wanted to buy the territory. Some people called Alaska "Seward's Folly" and "Seward's Icebox."

After the purchase, many people in the United States forgot about Alaska. To get there, people had to take a long voyage by sea. Most people thought that the long trip was not worthwhile.

However, some American settlers did make the journey to the new frontier. Like other pioneers, these settlers brought with them their norms of behavior. They thought that some kind of government should be set up. They thought that children should go to school. Soon, they started a town council and a school. Neither the council nor the school lasted for even five years. There were not enough people.

In 1880, gold was found near Juneau (joō′nō). After this discovery, some more people came to Alaska. ● Soon, there were enough people for the United States government to send a governor and other officials to the territory.

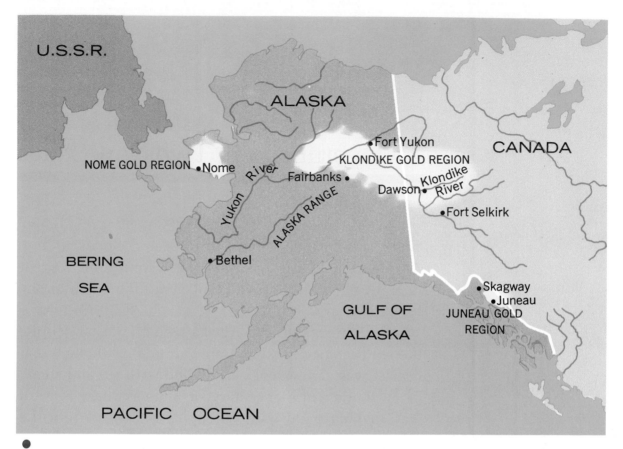

MAJOR GOLD REGIONS IN ALASKA

Study the map. ● Find the Klondike River. It is a small stream that runs into the Yukon River in Canada. In June of 1897, people in the United States heard that a great gold strike had been made on the Klondike. Gold was also found in parts of the Klondike that are in Alaska. Remember what you have learned about the history of California. Can you guess what happened in Alaska? ▲

Thousands of Americans and Canadians rushed to the Klondike. Later, more gold was discovered near Nome. Once again, mining towns sprang up in a territory of the United States. Do you suppose that people changed their ideas about Alaska? Did they begin to value the new territory? Or did they still think of it as "Seward's Folly"?

Recall the way that the miners had governed themselves in Hangtown, California. Skagway was like

Hangtown. It was a frontier town in Alaska where the miners got their supplies. Skagway and other Alaska mining towns had many of the same problems that the Wild West towns had once had. What do you think some of these problems were?

What does **adapt** mean? If you don't remember, look up the word in your Social Science Dictionary.

The Alaskans used what they had already learned about social controls. They adapted what they knew to their new environment. Their methods were like those used by the people in California during the gold rush. In Alaska, vigilantes tried to bring order to the towns. Claim jumpers and other lawbreakers were punished. But before the gold rush was over, the settlers set up more lasting forms of government. They elected lawmakers. They had mayors, marshals, and sheriffs. Soon, laws and law enforcers were preventing conflicts among the people in Skagway and other mining towns.

To learn more about social controls in United States history, try the investigation on the next page.

A NEW FRONTIER

Since the gold rush, Alaska has kept on growing. In January, 1959, the forty-ninth star was added to the flag of the United States. Alaska became a state.

Alaska's importance to the rest of the world has grown, too. Alaska has many natural resources. Other countries trade with Alaska for its gold and oil. Salmon that are caught and packed in cans are shipped all over the world. ● In the Matanuska (mat'ə·nōos'kə) and Tanana (tan'ə·nô) valleys, crops are grown. ▲ But, even today, food must be imported from other places. Why don't Alaskans grow more food? Why do they depend on farmers in other parts of the United States?

Today, Alaska is still not completely settled. There is room for many more people. There is land that can still be claimed by homesteading. Is the environment the same as it was in the days of the early settlements? Is government one of the ways it is different?

Recall that norms of behavior are the ways that people expect themselves and others to behave in their roles. Rules and laws tell how people should behave. Norms, rules, and laws are all forms of social control.

Make two columns on a piece of paper. Label one column, "People Who Enforced Social Controls." Label the other, "People Who Needed the Enforcement."

Which of the people below enforced social controls? Which people did not behave as they were expected to behave? Put each person under the correct heading.

cattle rustler	gunman ■
vigilante	thief
marshal	squatter ▶◀
claim jumper	judge ●
governor ●	outlaw
jury member ▲	sheriff

●

A Problem on Your Own

Study the list of people who enforced laws as social controls. Did they have to act according to norms and laws, too? Were social controls enforced for them, too? Explain your answer.

●

BEYOND THE FRONTIER

The Hawaiian Islands are more than two thousand miles from San Francisco. Look at the map on pages 292-293. Can you give one reason why pineapples and sugar cane are grown on these islands? ●

The first European to see the Hawaiian Islands was the British explorer James Cook. That was in 1778. From your earlier studies, you may remember that there were many kings in the Hawaiian Islands at that time. Most of the kings were fighting each other. But, by 1795, all the islands were under the government of King Kamehameha. (If you do not remember how this came about, reread pages 22-25.)

Recall the wagon trains that traveled to Oregon and California. At that time, some Americans left the east coast of the United States by ship. They sailed around South America to Hawaii. Many of these people wanted to teach the people of Hawaii to become Christians. Later, Chinese and Japanese went to Hawaii. Many of them became farmers and traders.

In 1894, Hawaii became a republic. There were to be no more Hawaiian kings. But Hawaii did not stay independent for very long. Only a few years afterward, Hawaii became a territory of the United States.

Do you know what a **republic** is? If you don't, look up the word in your Social Science Dictionary.

Do you remember what **influence** means? If you don't, turn back to page 249.

For sixty years, a group of Hawaiians tried to influence the United States government. They wanted Hawaii to become a state. Finally, in 1950, the people of Hawaii were permitted to hold a convention. Representatives wrote a constitution. What happened then? How had other territories become states in the past?

When Alaska became a state, the people of Hawaii gained new hope. At last, in 1959, Hawaii became the fiftieth state in the United States. The President signed the bill. ● On July 4, 1960, the United States had a new flag with fifty stars. ▲

▲

AT THIS POINT IN YOUR STUDY

Does this statement seem correct?
Groups change their governments.

When they became states, territories changed their kind of government. Why did they do so? What changes did they make?

Did your town or city always have the kind of government it has now? Try to find out.

Choose the ending for each of these sentences.

1   On the Alaskan frontier,
(a) people needed social controls
(b) each person did what he pleased
2   Today, the people in Hawaii
(a) elect representatives
(b) obey the rules made by kings
3   Alaska and Hawaii became states
(a) by saying they were states
(b) by doing the same things other territories had done

USING WHAT YOU KNOW

1   Oil was one of Alaska's resources. ● What were others? How do you think resources helped bring Alaska statehood?
2   The number of people in the world has grown and grown. Where on Earth might a pioneer go today to settle a frontier? What knowledge might he need to take with him?

ON YOUR OWN

Name three groups of people whose governments changed long ago. How did the governments change?

Have any national governments changed in the last twenty years? How can you find out?

Will any more governments change in the future? What do you predict?

IN TRANSIT

In the United States, the frontier closed, and two faraway territories became states. But the country kept on growing.

More and more groups of people have come to the United States — bringing with them their customs and their ways of acting. Who are these people? Where have they come from? To find out, turn to the next section.

5. We, the People

Carl Sandburg's mother and father came from Sweden to live and work in Illinois. Carl Sandburg's father did not know how to read or write, but Carl grew up to be a famous American poet. ● He wrote many poems about people like his father. He wrote about people who had come from other countries to live and work in the United States. In one of his poems, Carl Sandburg wrote,

> I am the people — the mob — the crowd — the mass.
> Do you know that all the great work of the world is done through me?
> I am the workingman, the inventor, the maker of the world's food and clothes.

The story of the United States is the story of people moving, working, and building. It is the story of people adapting to new environments. Hunters, gold miners, railroad builders, farmers, cowboys, sheepmen — all are part of the story. All these people — men, women, and children, leaders and followers — learned to take part in democratic government.

THE PEOPLE COME

Who are Americans? Where have they come from? Recall the European explorers who first came to the New World. Among them were the Spanish, the French, the Dutch, and the English.

After the explorers, the colonists came. The English came to Jamestown and Plymouth. The Dutch came to New York, and the Swedish to Delaware. German farmers settled on the good soil of Pennsylvania. The French came to South Carolina and, later, to Louisiana. African slaves were brought to work on the southern rice and cotton plantations. The Scottish came to the Appalachian frontier.

In the spring, the people of Holland, Michigan, hold a tulip festival. ● From which country did these people bring their customs?

Except for the Negroes, most people came to the colonies from Europe. From the colonies, they began to spread into the American West.

Later, people went west without first settling on the east coast. From about 1840 on, many of the people who came settled in all parts of the country. More Germans came to farm in Iowa and Pennsylvania. Irish helped build the first cross-country railroad. During the 1870's and 1880's, Swedish and Norwegians settled on farms in Illinois, Wisconsin, Minnesota, Nebraska, and the Dakotas.

Not all the people came from Africa and Europe. Many Chinese came during the California gold rush. Many others came to the United States to work on the railroad. Still later, Japanese came—many of them to farm in California.

Spanish and Mexican settlers moved into Texas, New Mexico, and California. ▲ Thousands of people came from Italy. During the past thirty years, many Polish and Russians have come, too. So have many people from Puerto Rico.

What kind of people have settled in the United States? We are people with many different customs and beliefs. We are people who brought with us ways of acting which we had learned somewhere else. We are people who have learned new ways of behaving in a new environment.

To learn more about who we are and why we came, try the investigation on the next page.

AN INVESTIGATION into the people of the United States

▲

From what countries did the families in your community come? ● With your parents' permission, choose three families in your neighborhood, and interview them. List the names of the families. Find out the countries from which they or their ancestors came. (Ancestors are great-grandparents and their parents and their parents before them.) Find out why their ancestors came to America.

Compare your list with your classmates' lists. Then, make a class chart to answer these questions:

1   From how many different countries did your neighbors or their ancestors come?
2   From what countries did they come?
3   For what reasons did they come?

A Problem on Your Own

You might want to use other ways to find out the countries from which the people in a community came. Here are three hints:

1   What is the name of the community?
2   For whom are the streets named? ▲
3   How might the community's telephone book help you?

266

NEW ROLES FOR A GROUP OF AMERICANS

The first black people arrived in Jamestown in 1619 as unpaid servants. They worked for a certain number of years to pay for their fare to the New World. After that, they were free to claim their own land.

By the late 1600's, most black people were no longer arriving in America as servants. They were arriving in chains, as slaves. By the early 1800's, there were large numbers of black slaves in the United States.

For over two hundred years, most American Negroes were slaves. ● Then, during the Civil War, Abraham Lincoln wrote the Emancipation Proclamation. The slaves were freed! Two years later, in 1865, the thirteenth amendment was added to the United States Constitution. This amendment made slavery against the law anywhere in the United States.

Before the Civil War, many black people worked for freedom for the slaves. In the 1820's and 1830's, men like Samuel Cornish and Philip Bell started the first Negro newspapers in America. They wanted to influence the government to free the slaves.

What is an **amendment**? If you don't remember, look up the word in your Social Science Dictionary.

Other free Negroes like Sojourner Truth and Harriet Tubman risked their lives to help escaping slaves reach freedom in the North. Many slaves in the South also helped their friends reach freedom.

One famous escaped slave was Frederick Douglass. ● After he came to the North, he worked to bring about the end of slavery. To help his cause, Frederick Douglass gave many speeches, wrote books, and even started his own newspaper. After the Civil War, he was sent to the Republic of Haiti to represent the United States government.

After the Civil War, black leaders kept on working for the good of their people. Some men, like George Washington Carver, became educators. ▲ George Washington Carver was also a well-known scientist.

Most Americans know that Negroes invented jazz and made it popular all over the world. Bessie Smith and W. C. Handy were two early jazz musicians. ■

Do you know the names of other famous black Americans? Perhaps you have heard of Leontyne Price, an opera star. Someday, you may read the books of Ralph Ellison and the poems of Gwendolyn Brooks.

You have probably heard of Martin Luther King, Jr., a minister who was killed while trying to get equal rights for all Americans. Perhaps you have heard of Ralph Bunche, a political scientist. Both Ralph Bunche and Martin Luther King, Jr., won the Nobel Peace Prize. ⋈

Like other Americans, some black Americans with great talents have become leaders. But it has not been easy for most black people to live in the United States. True, the law gives all Americans the right to own land, to run a business, and to learn a job. But black people have not always had justice. They have not always had their rights under the law. Not all Americans have always had the chance to learn. What happens when people are not free to learn? Are they free to find new roles for themselves?

HUMAN RIGHTS AND THE LAW

Recall how much the American pioneers valued law and government. They believed that, through law and government, they could protect their property and rights. They believed that laws made it easier for people to interact peacefully. Frontier settlements set up governments. Territories became states with their own governments. Of course, the state governments were under the national government.

Roughly 60 million people came to America from the time Jamestown was settled in 1607 to the closing of the frontier in 1890. The rights of everyone who lives in or comes to this country are protected by law.

The first ten amendments to the Constitution are the Bill of Rights. More amendments have been added to the Constitution since the Bill of Rights was written. Recall that Lincoln freed the slaves. ● After the Civil War, the thirteenth amendment was added. It made slavery against the law anywhere in the United States.

The fourteenth amendment makes all citizens equal under the law. It gives Negroes citizenship. It also protects the rights of naturalized citizens. Naturalized citizens are people who were not born in the United States but have decided to live here. In order to become a naturalized citizen, a person must learn his rights and duties as a citizen. He must also pledge his allegiance to the government of the United States.

The fifteenth amendment gives all male citizens the right to vote. No person can be refused the right to vote because of his race or color.

These amendments help protect rights. But even more laws have been needed to give each person the chance to use his rights. Slowly, these laws have been made. In the past few years, Congress has passed laws to make sure that American Negroes can use their rights to vote. ▲ It has also passed laws to make sure that black people have an equal chance to get an educa-

tion. Different presidents have signed these bills into law. ■

Over the years, some of our values have changed. Today, we value rights for every American. Norms have changed and new laws have been made. These laws help all the members of the group to which we belong—the United States of America.

AT THIS POINT IN YOUR STUDY

Does this statement seem correct?

Laws protect rights.

Laws protected the rights of the squatters to claim their land. Laws protect the right of all Americans to vote and to have an education. Laws protect the right of all Americans to live peacefully without fear for their lives or property.

What other rights do laws protect?

What rights would you like to see protected? Whose rights are they? Do they take away the rights of other people? Whose rights are most important?

Choose the ending for each of these sentences.

1 The people who came to the United States
(a) brought with them none of their own customs
(b) learned some new ways of behaving in a new environment

2 Some human rights are protected by
(a) law and government
(b) moving to a new environment

3 Norms and laws
(a) never change
(b) change when people's values change

●

1 Here is a statement: Except for Eskimos, Indians, and Hawaiians, everyone in the United States is a newcomer or has ancestors who were newcomers. (If you don't remember the meaning of "ancestor," turn back to page 266.) What does the statement mean? Do you agree with it? Why or why not?

2 Many of the people who came from Europe called the United States an asylum (ə·sī′ləm). ● An asylum is a safe place. Why did some people think of the United States in this way?

1 Not everyone who wants to come to the United States can do so.

Why can't some people come to the United States?

Should everyone be permitted to come?

Which of the questions above has to do with **fact**? Which has to do with **values**?

2 You have learned that most people in the United States believe that every American should have the same rights. Why do people believe this?

Focus on the Concept

In mining camps and other communities, people were expected to know how to act. ● Wherever they had lived, they had learned how they were expected to behave. But people need more than norms to prevent conflicts. They need law and government.

You have learned about the conflicts between sheepmen, farmers, and cattlemen. Each group had an interest in the land. Some of the farmers were squatters who lived on public land. The government passed a law that gave squatters the first chance to buy land on which they lived.

The cattlemen wanted to be able to buy more land, too. They worked together to get the government to pass laws that would help them.

The railroad men also worked to influence the government. The government gave them land. It also lent them money. Who was helped when the government helped the railroad men? In most cases, the whole country was helped. The railroad made it easier for people to settle the West. It also helped farmers get their goods to market.

You can see how government and law helped many groups of people in the West. In this unit, then, you have learned something about the concept of **social control: Laws are made to help different groups within a society.**

Laws that Stay the Same

As territories were settled, the people living in them wanted them to become states. Most state constitutions were modeled very closely after the Constitution of the United States. They set up the same forms of government. They gave people the same rights.

The nation which had begun as thirteen states grew until it spread from coast to coast. It grew still more when Alaska and Hawaii became states. As the nation grew, Americans carried their ideas of law and government far beyond the first thirteen states. They spread these ideas throughout the nation.

You now have learned a little more about the concept of **social control: People often model their social controls after those that other people have used in the past.**

Laws that Change

Today, there are fifty states. Most American customs are shared by everyone in the country. Where did these customs come from? From all over the world. As people came to America from Europe, Africa, Asia, and South America, they brought with them their own ways of acting. The newcomers interacted with people who were already here. Old ways of acting were changed, and new customs were learned.

Over many years, some values and norms changed. Laws were passed which showed these changes. The thirteenth, fourteenth, and fifteenth amendments grew out of new values and norms. These amendments helped to give people the same rights under the law. What change in law do these pictures show? ●

The men who wrote the Constitution believed that people should be able to add amendments to it. They believed this because they knew an important concept of **social control: As values and norms of behavior change, so do laws.**

The Founding Fathers of our country knew the importance of social control. So did the miners and vigilantes in California and Alaska. Do you remember the statement that was made in Unit Five? It tells us this about the concept of **social control: Man's peaceful interaction depends on social control.**

A PROBLEM IN ANALYSIS

Dred Scott was a Negro slave who was bought by a man in Missouri in 1833. ● In 1834, Dred Scott's master took him to Illinois. There, slavery was against the law. Then his master took him to a part of the Louisiana Purchase where slavery was also against the law. In 1838, Dred Scott was taken back to Missouri. Of course, slavery was permitted in Missouri.

Dred Scott said he had a right to be a free man because he had lived on free soil. He took his case to Missouri state courts. They ruled against him. At last, Scott's case went to the highest court in the United States. Which one is that?

In 1857, the Supreme Court decided against Scott. The Court said that Scott was not a citizen of the United States. To the men who wrote the Constitution, a citizen was a free, white man over twenty-one years old. As a slave, Dred Scott was property, rather than a person. Therefore, he couldn't even take his case to a United States court. The Supreme Court said that he was still a slave and still the property of his master.

The Court added that it was unconstitutional for Congress to make a law against slavery. Slaves were property. No law in the United States could take property away from a man without a fair trial.

Now try to answer these questions:

1 Why did the Supreme Court say that Dred Scott was property?

2 Why couldn't a law take away property?

3 In Dred Scott's time, did the Supreme Court value property rights more than human rights? Why do you think so?

4 Give some evidence that people are valued more today than they were when Dred Scott lived.

Focus on the Historian

How do we know what happened long ago? People have kept records. Historians have studied the records.

A historian does not have to take part in an event to write about it. He can study records left by people who did take part. Then he can decide what happened. Historians study more than facts. They try to find out the *meaning* of facts.

You have studied the people who came to the United States to live. The early colonists who settled on the east coast were very much alike. Most came from the same culture and had the same customs.

From the 1840's to about 1919, many people arrived in this country. These people were different from the early colonists. They came from different cultures and different countries. Often, they did not speak English. Often, their customs were different from those of people already here.

Oscar Handlin is a historian who has studied these newcomers. ● He has studied why it was sometimes hard for them to adapt to the new environment. Many newcomers had lived in small villages in Europe, where they had known everyone. Everyone had had the same customs. Life in the United States, says Handlin, was different. The kind of government was different. Farming was different from the kind of farming they had known. Life in big cities, too, was different.

Oscar Handlin calls these people "the uprooted." He says, "The ocean forever separated them from the old home, from the church, the village, and above all, the kinfolk . . ." They had lost their old way of life. But, without them, the nation could not have grown as it has. They were the human resources who helped to build this country.

What does **culture** mean? If you don't remember, look up the word in your Social Science Dictionary.

A NEW VIEW

OF

GOVERNMENT

Who makes the rules at home or at school? Who settles quarrels? You may not have thought of these people as being part of government, but they are. As you have learned, some people have the authority to govern others. They are expected to govern. It is one of the norms for their role. These people are called leaders. The leaders in your home and your school make rules and enforce them.

You have studied many groups of people. All of them had leaders. Recall the leaders of a Blackfoot tribe and the leaders of early Hawaii. Recall, too, the leaders who were chosen at constitutional conventions in which territories were working to become states.

How were those leaders like leaders chosen in the United States today? How were they different? What leaders are chosen in your state and your community? How are these leaders chosen?

You know that, throughout the United States, many leaders are elected. Some of these leaders are expected to make rules. Some of them are expected to enforce the rules.

ANOTHER KIND OF BEHAVIOR

Earlier in your studies, you learned about **social behavior**. Social behavior is the way in which we act and interact in groups. You also learned about **economic behavior**—the way in which we act to use and share our resources. In the last two units, you have begun your study of another important kind of behavior: **political behavior**.

What does **influence** mean? If you do not remember, look it up in your Social Science Dictionary.

To most political scientists, political behavior means all the ways in which people act to influence the government. Look at the pictures. ● Explain what the people in each picture are doing. Then explain what each picture shows about political behavior. Are the people in each picture trying to influence the government? Tell some ways.

When you looked at the pictures on page 278, you saw some of the ways in which people try to influence the government. These are some ways:

1 Talking about what leaders decide
2 Writing letters to leaders
3 Voting, that is, helping to elect leaders
4 Running for office

What other ways of acting might help change the government? Name some. Name some changes that you think should be made. If you were grown up, how would you go about influencing the government to make these changes?

ACTING IN A DEMOCRACY

What is a **democracy**? If you don't remember, look up the word in your Social Science Dictionary.

Because the United States is a republic, Americans give authority to leaders who represent them. We can also say that the United States is a representative democracy because it is a republic with federal and state constitutions that provide for regular elections of representatives. At election time, if the government leaders have not done what people want, the people can vote for other leaders.

Some groups of people do more than vote. Some of them write letters to newspapers. Some go on television. How else can they let people know about the changes they think should be made?

In your community, find one group of people which is trying to influence the government. How did you find out about this group? Perhaps they use the telephone or go from house to house, ringing doorbells. Why do they want other people to know what they are doing?

As you grow older, you will want to know many things about the government in your community, your state, and your country. You, too, will behave politically. You will be a voter. Perhaps you will work in other ways to influence the government.

THE END AS BEGINNING

A First Research into Records

THE PEOPLE OF MEXICO

This year you have added to your understanding of some important concepts about people. You have studied behavior. These are some of the concept statements which have been important to your studies:

People's social behavior is learned from the groups of which they are members.

People are born with some ways of behaving. But they learn most of their ways of behaving.

People use their environment to get what they need to live.

People interact to use the resources available to them.

People's peaceful interaction depends on their social controls.

In your studies, you have looked at evidence for each of these statements. You have investigated norms of behavior in the United States. Do the concept statements above seem to be true of Americans?

You also investigated some of the ways in which people behave in Japan and Israel. Do the concept statements seem to be true of them?

How do people in Canada and Mexico behave? Begin your investigation by studying the map. ● It is a record. It will show you that Canada and Mexico are the countries to the north and south of the United

160°W

140°W 80°N

120°W

100°W 20°W

80°W 60°W

40°E

20°E

60°N

Hudson
Bay

40°N

NORTH

AMERICA

40°N

PACIFIC

ATLANTIC

20°N

20°N

Gulf of Mexico

OCEAN

Caribbean Sea

OCEAN

0°

SOUTH

0°

0°

AMERICA

20°S

PHYSICAL MAP OF
NORTH AND SOUTH AMERICA

40°S

20°S

140°W

120°W

100°W

80°W

60°W

40°W

20°W

States. Photographs are also records. All the photographs in this book are records of observations. If you visit other countries, you may be able to test these observations. Perhaps you will make records of your own to compare with them.

Begin your research into Mexico by studying each photograph. ● The photographs are records. Then analyze each question. In your answers, use what you have already learned from your studies so far.

1   (a) What kinds of behavior are the people of Mexico born with?

    (b) Do you think that they make some inborn responses? Which ones?

    (c) What are some of the ways of acting that Mexicans learn? From whom do they learn them?

2   (a) From whom do Mexicans learn to act as members of a group?

    (b) Does everyone in a group have the same role?

    (c) How do you know that the people in the photographs share meanings?

    (d) How are they interacting?

3   (a) How do the people of Mexico use their environment to get what they need to live?

    (b) What basic resources do they use?

    (c) Do they have all the resources they want?

4   (a) In what ways do Mexicans interact to share their resources?

    (b) Who are the consumers? the producers?

    (c) Find evidence of planning in pictures. Why do the people of Mexico need to plan?

    (d) Does price in Mexico depend partly on supply and demand? How can you find out?

5   (a) Why do Mexicans need social controls?

    (b) Where did the social controls of the Mexican people come from?

    (c) What kinds of social controls do they use? One of them begins in a building shown in one of the pictures. Which one is it?

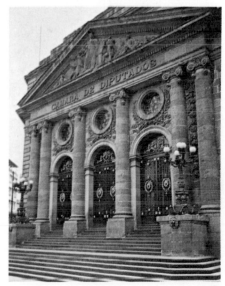

23,000,000

22,000,000

People living in cities

People living in towns and villages ●

38,300,000

3,600,000

1,800,000

Indian-speaking only

Spanish and Indian-speaking

Spanish-speaking only ▲

In answering the questions on page 284, you were using what you already know about the behavior of all people. You were also using records about the behavior of Mexicans. How is their behavior like the behavior of people elsewhere? How is it different?

If you wish to know more about the ways in which Mexicans act, you can find out for yourself. How will you begin your research? First, you must decide what you want to know. Then you can make a list of questions or problems which you would like to investigate. Here are some questions that you might want to answer. You may think of others.

1 Do children in Mexico learn in a school group? Are most Mexican people part of a small community group or a large community group? Study the graph. ● It will give you some evidence that will help you answer the question.

2 What is the environment of Mexico? What language do Mexicans speak? ▲ What kinds of transportation do they use? Are their shelters like those in the United States?

3 What kinds of games do Mexicans play? What kinds of dances do they have? What kind of music? What kind of art?

4 What form of government does Mexico have? Is it like that of the United States?

5 How do the people of Mexico earn income? How do they spend their income?

6 Who are the people of Mexico? Is Mexico's past like that of the United States? How do graphs like this one give you evidence that will help you answer your questions? ▲

Whatever you want to learn about Mexico, you will need to use records. Begin by visiting a place where records are stored—the library. Look for books and magazines to help you find out what you want to know.

THE PEOPLE OF CANADA

Look back at the map on page 283. Where is Canada? Where is the United States? Can you find the boundary between them? Not unless you already know where it is! Much of the physical environment of Canada is like that of the United States. In some places, the countries seem to run into each other.

Here is part of the map you studied before. ● You may use this part or the map on page 283 to answer these questions:

1 Where do the western plains of the United States end to the north?

2 Where do the Rocky Mountains you see in Canada end to the south?

3 What part of the United States has a physical environment like northern Canada?

4 How are eastern Canada and the northeastern United States alike?

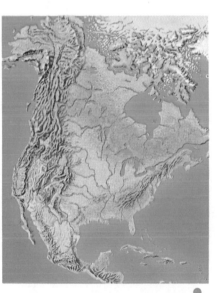

A region is an area that has likenesses. A **geographic region** is one in which the physical environment is almost the same everywhere. Look at the map again. You can see that parts of the United States and Canada form geographic regions. Which parts of the United States and Canada are alike?

Most of Canada and the United States form another kind of region, too. Social scientists call this kind of region a **cultural region**. Recall that culture means all the ways of acting and believing that groups have. When different groups of people share many of their ways of acting and believing, they probably live in a cultural region. Together, Canada and the United States are sometimes called Anglo-America. "Anglo" means "English." The cultures of the United States and most of Canada come from England. Why?

You have already learned something of the likenesses and differences in the behavior of people in Mexico and people in the United States. Since Canada

and the United States are a cultural region, will there be many likenesses in the way the people in the two countries act and believe?

Recall that words that are printed or written are records. Recall that photographs are records, too. They can be used as evidence. But if they are to be evidence, they must be done carefully.

Study these records. ● Use the eraser end of your pencil to point to each Canadian. Next, point to each American. Name the groups to which each Canadian or American belongs. Name the roles he or she has.

Now what is your answer to this question: Are Canadians and Americans alike? In what ways?

What other records can you use to find likenesses and differences among the people of these two countries? You can find phonograph records of Canadian music. Books which tell about life in Canada will help you. So will newspaper articles. Perhaps your class would like to exchange newspapers with a class in Canada.

Before you begin your research, try to write a statement about each of the customs listed below. Your statement should be a careful guess that is based on what you already know.

1 The language most Canadians speak
2 The kinds of clothes most Canadians wear
3 The kinds of shelters most Canadians use
4 The ways in which Canadians act in groups
5 Some ways in which Canadian children learn
6 Some ways in which resources are used
7 Some ways in which resources are shared
8 Some kinds of social controls which Canadians have

Write down your statements. Then write down what you learn about the people of Canada. Perhaps your evidence will be written records. Perhaps it will be photographs or your own careful observation. Make a list like the one on the next page.

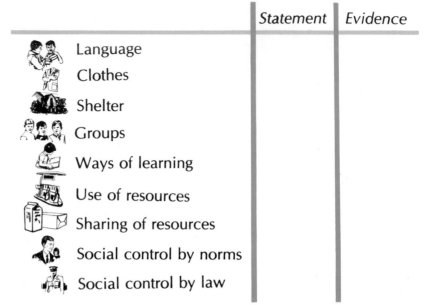

	Statement	Evidence
Language		
Clothes		
Shelter		
Groups		
Ways of learning		
Use of resources		
Sharing of resources		
Social control by norms		
Social control by law		

What are **resources**? What is a **norm**? If you don't remember, look up the words in your Social Science Dictionary.

You have now made some statements based on what you've learned about Anglo-America. But perhaps by now you have discovered that some Canadians have another culture. They are French-Canadians whose children sing songs like *Un Canadien Errant*— a French song about a wandering Canadian who misses his friends at home. They eat French foods. Many of them are Roman Catholics and go to Roman Catholic schools.

In fact, the first settlements in Canada were French. French settlers, like English settlers, brought their customs with them to the New World. The laws of the province of Quebec, for example, are based on French, rather than British, law.

Provinces are like American states

Study the graph. ● In 1871, there were 3,689,257 people living in Canada. How many people live there today? Canada has two official languages: French and English. How many Canadians speak only French? ▲ Many of these French-speaking people live in the province of Quebec. They think of themselves as a group. Have their customs changed since the French first came to Canada? What do you think? What records from the past can you use for evidence?

21,000,000

3,689,257

Number of
people in 1871

Number of
people in 1970

14,000,000

4,000,000

2,500,000

French- *and*
English-
speaking

French-
speaking
only

English-
speaking
only

This year you have made your own investigations, too. You have learned to look for evidence. Just as the social scientists go on adding to what they know, you, too, will go on learning.

Some Things Change, Some Things Last

The American frontier is closed. From ocean to ocean—and beyond—the land has been settled. In places where the environment makes it hard for man to live, there are still a few frontiers. Will all frontiers soon be gone forever?

Soon, we may live under the sea, in the polar regions, or on the moon. The geographic frontiers may soon be gone. But the frontiers of learning will last. Think for a moment about some things we do not yet know about our **physical environment**:

> how to live in great heat or cold
> how to control the weather
> how to prevent certain diseases
> how to produce food without growing it

There are many things we don't yet know about our **social environment**, too:

> how to make sure no person goes hungry
> how to make sure that every person gets an
>   education
> how to live in peace

When will we need to stop exploring these frontiers? When will we need to stop learning?

In the past, we learned how to adapt to changing environments. We learned how to change our environment, too. Your grandmother probably had to learn about wonder drugs and jet airplanes.

Learning is the road to the future. It is how we have learned to act today that shapes tomorrow. Some things change and some things last. But one thing goes on, day in, day out. Wherever we are, we go on learning.

195 180 165 150 135

ALASKA

60

Juneau

45

PACIFIC OCEAN

30

400   200   0 miles
                60°
              30
              0°

⊙ Honolulu

HAWAII

15

THE UNITED STATES, CANADA, AND MEXICO

0

195 180 165 150 135

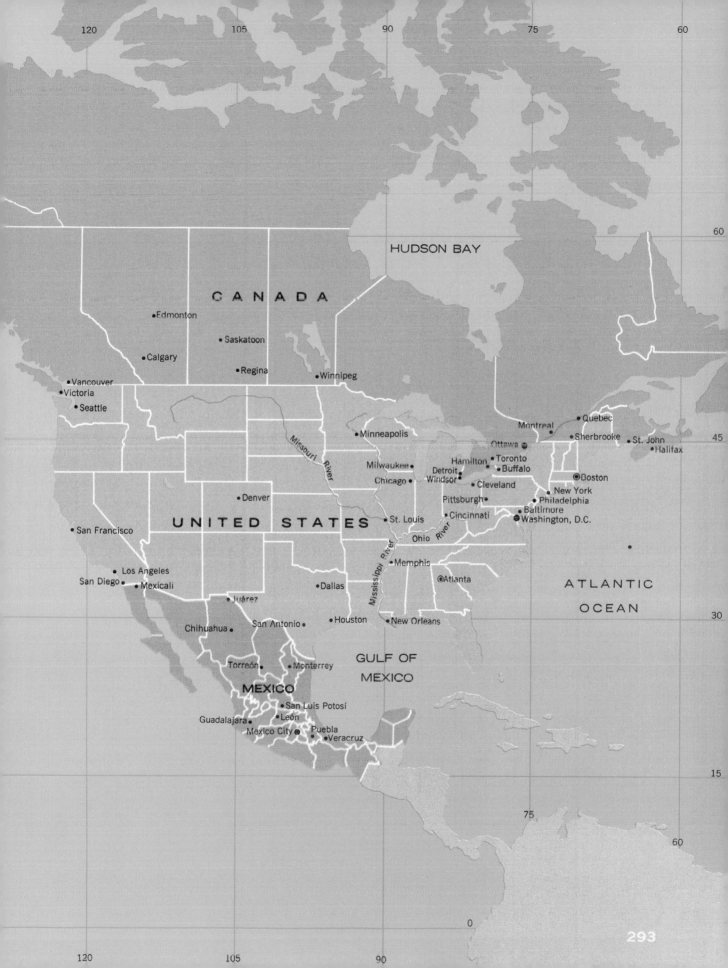

120 105 90 75 60

60

HUDSON BAY

CANADA

•Edmonton

•Saskatoon

•Calgary

•Regina •Winnipeg

•Vancouver
•Victoria
•Seattle

Missouri River

•Minneapolis

Montreal •Quebec
•Sherbrooke
Ottawa ◎ •St. John
•Halifax

45

Hamilton •Toronto
Milwaukee• Detroit• •Buffalo
Chicago• Windsor •Cleveland
•Denver Pittsburgh• •New York
•Philadelphia
UNITED STATES •St. Louis •Cincinnati •Baltimore
Washington, D.C.
•San Francisco Ohio River

Mississippi River •Memphis

•Los Angeles •Dallas •Atlanta
San Diego• •Mexicali
San Diego•

ATLANTIC

OCEAN

30

•Juárez •Houston
Chihuahua• San Antonio• •New Orleans
•Torreón •Monterrey GULF OF
MEXICO MEXICO

•San Luis Potosí
Guadalajara• •León
Mexico City ◎ •Puebla
•Veracruz

15

75

0 60

293

120 105 90

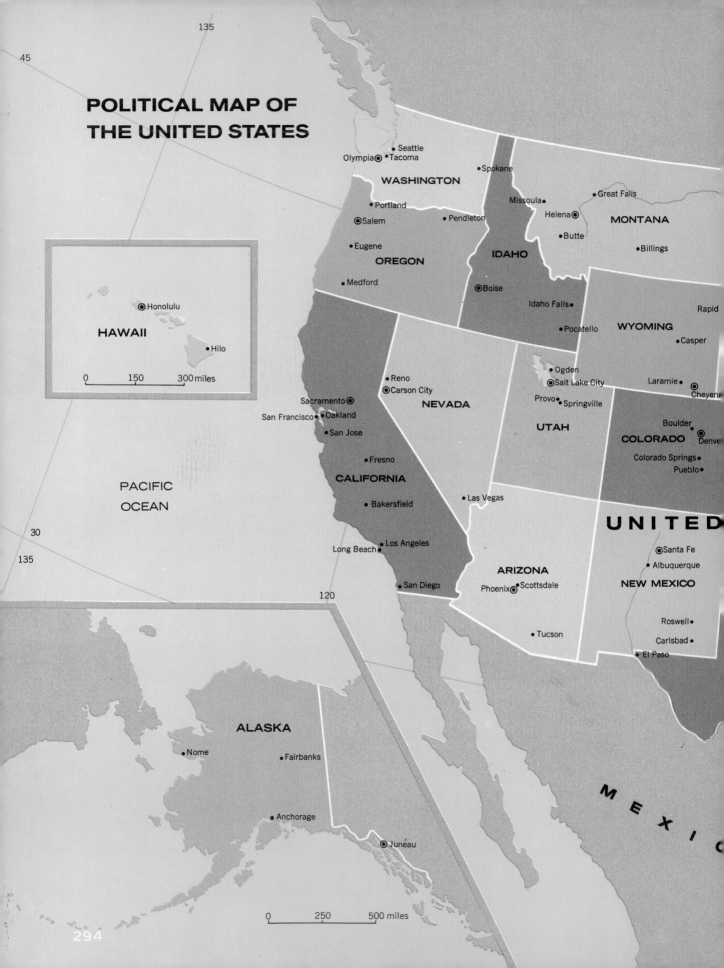

POLITICAL MAP OF THE UNITED STATES

135
45

• Seattle
Olympia◉ • Tacoma
• Spokane
WASHINGTON
Missoula• • Great Falls
• Portland Helena◉
Salem◉ • Pendleton **MONTANA**
• Butte
• Eugene • Billings
OREGON **IDAHO**
• Medford
Boise◉
Idaho Falls• Rapid

◉Honolulu • Pocatello **WYOMING**

HAWAII • Hilo
• Casper
0   150   300 miles

• Reno •Ogden
◉Carson City ◉Salt Lake City Laramie• Laramie•
◉Cheyenne
Sacramento◉ Provo• **NEVADA** •Springville
San Francisco• •Oakland **UTAH** Boulder
•San Jose •◉Denver
COLORADO
PACIFIC • Fresno Colorado Springs•
Pueblo•
OCEAN **CALIFORNIA**
30
135 • Bakersfield • Las Vegas
U N I T E D
• Los Angeles
Long Beach• ◉Santa Fe
• Albuquerque
• San Diego **ARIZONA** **NEW MEXICO**
120 Phoenix◉• Scottsdale

Roswell•
• Tucson Carlsbad•
• El Paso

ALASKA
• Nome M
E
• Fairbanks X
I
C
O
• Anchorage

◉Juneau

0   250   500 miles

294

CANADA

NORTH DAKOTA
• Grand Forks
◉ Bismarck • Fargo

• Duluth

Sault Sainte Marie

MINNESOTA

MAINE
• Bangor
◉ Augusta

Burlington ◉ Montpelier • Portland
VT. N.H.
Concord • Manchester
◉ Boston
Albany ◉ Worcester
Syracuse ◉ Providence
Hartford ◉ R.I.
New Haven CONN.

Minneapolis ◉ St. Paul

WISCONSIN • Green Bay

MICHIGAN

SOUTH DAKOTA
◉ Pierre
• Sioux Falls

Missouri
River

NEW
YORK

Rochester
• Buffalo

Grand Rapids • Flint
Madison ◉ ◉ Milwaukee ◉ Lansing
Racine Detroit

IOWA
Cedar Rapids •
Rockford • Chicago •
Toledo

PENNSYLVANIA

Newark • • New York
◉ Trenton
• Philadelphia
N.J.

NEBRASKA

Grand Island •
Hastings •
◉ Lincoln

• Omaha
Des Moines ◉ • Davenport Gary
• Peoria
• Fort Wayne

Cleveland ◉
◉ Akron
Harrisburg ◉
• Pittsburgh

OHIO
◉ Columbus

Baltimore ◉
Washington, D.C. ⊛ Dover
DEL.
Annapolis
MD.

INDIANA
◉ Springfield ◉ Indianapolis
ILLINOIS

WEST
VIRGINIA
• Cincinnati
Huntington • ◉ Charleston

Richmond ◉

Kansas City
Topeka ◉ ● Kansas City
Jefferson City ◉ • St. Louis

KANSAS
• Wichita

MISSOURI

Louisville •
• Frankfort
• Lexington
Ohio River

KENTUCKY

VIRGINIA
• Norfolk

STATES

OKLAHOMA • Tulsa
◉ Oklahoma City • Fort Smith
• Lawton

ARKANSAS
• Little Rock
Pine Bluff •

TENNESSEE
◉ Nashville
• Knoxville

Winston-Salem • • Greensboro
NORTH ◉ Raleigh
Charlotte • CAROLINA

• Memphis
• Chattanooga
Greenville •
SOUTH CAROLINA
◉ Columbia
• Charleston

Forth Worth • • Dallas
Shreveport • • Monroe
TEXAS

MISSISSIPPI
Meridian •
Jackson ◉
ALABAMA
Montgomery ◉

• Birmingham
◉ Atlanta
Augusta •
• Macon
• Columbus

GEORGIA
• Savannah

◉ Austin
• San Antonio
• Houston

LOUISIANA
◉ Baton Rouge • Biloxi
• Lake Charles • New Orleans
• Mobile

• Jacksonville

◉ Tallahassee

FLORIDA

ATLANTIC
OCEAN

Rio Grande
• Corpus Christi

GULF OF MEXICO

St. Petersburg • • Tampa

• Miami

CUBA

0   250   500 miles

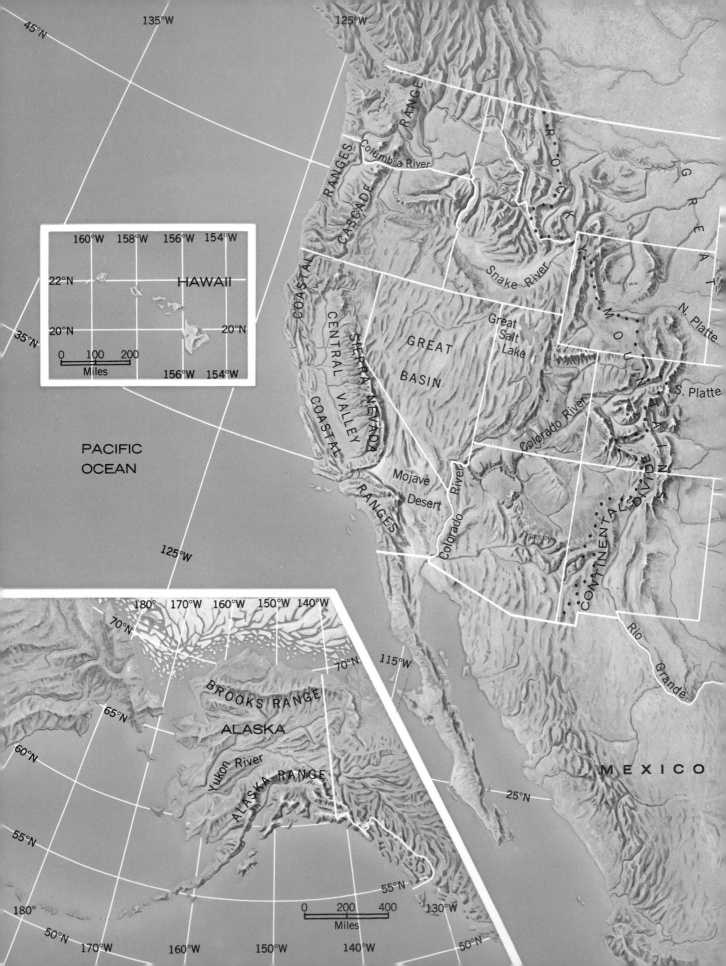

45°N

135°W

125°W

RANGE

R
O
C
K
Y

COASTAL
RANGES

CASCADE

Columbia River

160°W 158°W 156°W 154°W

22°N

HAWAII

G
R
E
A
T

20°N

20°N

Snake River

M
O
U
N
T
A
I
N
S

N. Platte

35°N

0 100 200
Miles

156°W 154°W

Great
Salt
Lake

COASTAL

CENTRAL VALLEY

SIERRA NEVADA

GREAT
BASIN

S. Platte

PACIFIC
OCEAN

COASTAL

Mojave
Desert

River

Colorado River

Colorado

CONTINENTAL DIVIDE

RANGES

125°W

Rio

Grande

115°W

180° 170°W 160°W 150°W 140°W

70°N

70°N

M E X I C O

65°N

BROOKS RANGE

ALASKA

60°N

Yukon River

ALASKA RANGE

25°N

55°N

55°N

50°N

0 200 400
Miles

130°W

180°

170°W

160°W

150°W

140°W

50°N

SOCIAL SCIENCE DICTIONARY

These are first definitions. As you go on in your work, the words will grow in meaning and in use. The page numbers after the words tell you where you can find more information about the word.

adapt (76), to change one's behavior in order to adjust to changes in the environment; to learn new ways of acting.   The pioneers who traveled westward had to **adapt** to new environments.   Why is it important for people to be able to **adapt** to their environment?

agriculture (ag′rə·kul′chər) (83), the raising of plants and animals.   As more and more machines are used in **agriculture**, fewer farmers are needed. Why is soil conservation important to **agriculture**?

amendment (202), a change; a change in the United States Constitution.   In 1920, an **amendment** to the Constitution gave women the right to vote.   Why is it important for Americans to be able to make **amendments** to the Constitution?

analysis (86), the breaking up of something into its parts in order to study or describe it.   A soil scientist often makes an **analysis** of a soil sample. When you are asked to **analyze** a map, what should you do?

authority (ə·thôr′ə·tē) (24), the right to make decisions and enforce rules for a group of people.   Leaders have the **authority** to make sure that people obey rules.   How do the leaders of the United States get their **authority**?

barter (154), the trading of goods or services for other goods or services. The Indians **bartered** with the settlers by giving animal furs and skins in exchange for blankets, cloth, and guns. When your mother buys clothes for you, does she **barter**?

behave (36), to act; to do something. Your **behavior** is made up of all the things you do, such as going to school, reading, watching television, and playing with your friends.   How are your ways of **behaving** different from those of the other members of your family?

census (100), a counting of all the people in a city, state, or country, with information about their age, sex, and job.   In the United States, a **census** is made every ten years.   What might be some of the differences in the **censuses** of 1790 and 1970?

communicate (58), to use language to exchange information.   Telephones, television, and air mail letters are all means of **communication.**   How do written symbols help people **communicate**?

community (6), a group of people who live near each other, help each other, and are interested in the same things. Blackfoot tribes were made up of **communities** called bands. What are some differences between a Blackfoot band and your **community** group?

concept (57), a putting together of the ideas you already have about something. The **concept** of "person" puts together the many likenesses shared by people. Why are **concepts** useful?

conditioning (39), a kind of learning in which a person or an animal is taught to respond, without thinking, to a certain stimulus. A dog can be **conditioned** to come when called if he is rewarded. Why isn't shivering in a cold wind a **conditioned** response?

conserve (kən·sûrv) (115), to save or protect from waste or loss; to use wisely. American farmers had to learn to **conserve** the soil. Why is **conservation** of water important today?

consumer (131), a person who uses goods and services. Your mother is a **consumer** because she buys food, has her washing machine repaired, and so on. Are most people both producers and **consumers**? Why?

culture (3), all the ways of believing and acting of people in a group, including customs, ideas, and tools. In the Blackfoot **culture**, most men had the role of warrior. Name three ways in which the Blackfoot **culture** was different from your culture.

custom (8), a habit followed by most members of a group, a way of doing something that people in a group have followed for years and years. You have the **custom** of eating with a knife and fork. From whom are **customs** learned?

data (148), information (facts or figures) that has been carefully collected. If you wanted to know how many people live in your community, you would have to find **data** about your community. If you wanted to know more about an African country, where might you find **data**?

demand (165), the wish to buy something (goods and services) and the money to buy it. Rock-and-roll records are in **demand** by teenagers but are often not in **demand** by their parents. Name two things for which there might be a great **demand** in summer but a low **demand** in winter.

democracy (188), a form of government in which the people choose their own leaders and make some decisions, either by voting directly or by voting for people to represent them (*see also* direct democracy *and* representative democracy). In a **democracy**, each person has a say in government. Name one kind of government that is not a **democracy**.

direct democracy (188), a government in which each man votes on every law (*see also* representative democracy). **Direct democracy** was used in the Pilgrims' town meetings, where each voter could vote on all laws and decisions. What form of **democracy** is used in your state today? Why isn't **direct democracy** used?

division of labor (172), the dividing up of work so that each worker does only part of a job. No worker makes a complete television set. Instead, **division of labor** is used in factories producing television sets. Can all goods be made by **division of labor**? Why or why not?

economist (i·kon′ə·mist) (137), a social scientist who studies the way goods and services are produced, used, and divided. A study of the way people earn and spend money is part of **economics**. Do your parents, your friends, and the leaders of your country sometimes act like **economists**? How?

environment (35), everything around you —people, weather, animals, plants, and so on (*see also* physical environment *and* social environment). The **environment** of the Blackfoot Indians was made up of plains, horses, tepees, buffalo, and many other things. Describe your school **environment**.

erosion (i·ro′zhən) (90), the wearing away of soil by water, wind, air, and ice. The Grand Canyon was caused by **erosion**. How does *erosion* cause gullies?

frontier (frun·tir′) (104), unsettled land at the edge of lands where people live; a new or unexplored area. By the late 1800's, the American West had been settled, and there was no longer a land **frontier**. Are the oceans and outer space **frontiers** today? Why?

geographer (127), a scientist who studies the Earth's surface and may study its peoples, natural resources, climates, and so on. A human **geographer** studies population, the movement of people from place to place, and the ways people change the environment. Why are maps important to the study of **geography**?

goal (14), a purpose. The **goal** of a soccer team is to win soccer games. What is the **goal** of one of your groups?

goods (131), things produced or made by people. Department and grocery stores are filled with **goods**. Are canned tomatoes **goods**? Why?

government (188), the control of the affairs of a nation, state, city, and so on; the people who have this control. Before they left the *Mayflower*, the Pilgrims agreed to form a **government**. Why does your community have a **government**?

group (15), sociologists say that a group is made up of two or more people who have a purpose, interact, are interdependent, and share meanings. You belong to many **groups**: your family, your school, your community, and your society. People sitting in a ball park watching a baseball game are not a **group**. Why aren't they a **group**?

habit (47), a learned act which a person does over and over. Most people in the United States have the **habit** of brushing their teeth two or three times a day. From whom did you learn the **habit** of going to bed at a certain time?

hypothesis (hī·poth′ə·sis) (27), an informed guess based on what a scientist has observed. After he makes a **hypothesis**, a scientist works hard to find out whether or not his **hypothesis** can be proved. How does a scientist go about proving a **hypothesis**?

income (131), all the money a person receives. Some boys and girls earn **income** by delivering newspapers or selling homemade cookies. Does a person who rents his house earn **income**?

independence (231), the state of being free; the state of not being under the authority of another person or nation. The United States won its **independence** from Great Britain after the American Revolution. What was the Declaration of **Independence**? Why was it called that?

influence (249), to change the ways of acting of a person, a group, or a government. Today, many people try to **influence** the government by voting and writing letters to their Congressmen. In the 1800's, why did some Indians try to **influence** the government?

insight (52), a kind of learning in which a person or animal "sees the whole picture" at once. After working on a math problem for a long time, a boy gained **insight**. Suddenly the boy "saw the whole picture," and the way to solve the problem became clear to him. Tell about a time that you learned by **insight**.

interact (15), to act with others so that what one person does can change what other people do. At school, you learn from your **interaction** with your teachers and the other students in class. Do people who **interact** always agree?

interdependent (14), dependent on each other. If a baseball player doesn't pay attention, his team may lose, because the players on the team are **interdependent**. In what ways are the members of your family **interdependent**?

irrigate (ir′ə·gāt) (93), to give water to land by using pipes, canals, or ditches. In places where there is not much rain, farmers may **irrigate** their crops. In what parts of the United States is there the most **irrigation**?

law of supply and demand (167), a law which states that if there is a great supply of a good or service and a low demand, the price tends to be low. If there is a low supply and a great demand, the price tends to be high. The price of goods and services depends partly on the **law of supply and demand**. How might the price of ice skates depend on the **law of supply and demand**?

legislature (lej′is·lā′chər) (188), a group of people who make laws. The Congress of the United States is a **legislature**. In the United States, how are people in **legislatures** chosen?

limited (132), not boundless, not endless; having limits. If you have two dollars, you are **limited** in what you can buy. If you have a million dollars, are you still **limited**?

manufacturing (172), the making of goods, most often by using machines in a factory. In the United States today, more people work in **manufacturing** than in agriculture. Name someone you know who works in **manufacturing**. What does he or she help to **manufacture**?

medium of exchange (161), anything that is used as money; a tool for making trade easier. Pigs were once used as a **medium of exchange**. Why is a nickel a **medium of exchange**?

middleman (164), a person why buys goods in large amounts from factories and then sells them to stores or consumers. A **middleman** earns income by producing a service. How does a **middleman** make a profit?

migrant laborer (109), a farm worker who travels from place to place to harvest, or pick, crops. **Migrant laborers** travel through most of our states. In what ways do farmers and growers depend on **migrant laborers**?

norms of behavior (4), a way that people in a group expect themselves and others to act. Among the Blackfeet, bravery was a **norm of behavior** for the role of warrior. In your culture, what are two **norms of behavior** for football players?

physical environment (111), that part of the environment which has to do with nature; that part of the environment which man has not made (*see also* social environment). Buffalo were part of the Blackfeet's **physical environment**. Name two resources found in your **physical environment**.

political scientist (227), a social scientist who studies governments and how they work. Some **political scientists** have studied how people vote and why they vote the way they do. Why have some **political scientists** studied the Supreme Court?

population (148), the number of people in a town, state, nation, or the world. Since the first colonists settled on the east coast, the **population** of the United States has grown and grown. Is the **population** still growing?

producer (131), a person who makes goods or does services. A doctor, a newspaper boy, and a farmer are all **producers**. Name some of the people you know who are **producers**, and tell what they produce.

profit (163), the money left over after goods or services are sold and the cost of producing them has been paid. It cost a girl seven cents to make doll dresses which she sold for ten cents. Her **profit** on each dress was three cents. Why must people who produce goods and services make a **profit** ?

psychologist (sī·kol′ə·jist) (36), a social scientist who studies how people behave and why they behave the way they do. Some **psychologists** study the ways in which people learn. Why do **psychologists** often study the behavior of animals?

represent (188), to act and speak for. In the United States, people vote for people who will **represent** them. Why do you think that one branch of the United States Congress is called the House of **Representatives**?

representative (rep′ri·zen′tə·tiv) **democracy** (189), a government in which people choose who will represent them (*see also* direct democracy). When your parents vote for a United States Senator or a governor for your state, they are taking part in **representative democracy**. Explain the differences between direct democracy and **representative democracy**.

republic (261), a government in which authority is given to leaders elected by and representing the people.   In 1894, Hawaii became a **republic**, and the people voted to elect representatives.   Is the United States a **republic**? Why?

reservations (212), lands reserved, or set aside, for Indians.   In Oklahoma today, there are many Indian **reservations**.   Why did the United States government set aside **reservations** for the Indians?

resource (101), anything that is useful. Natural resources are those **resources** found in the physical environment. What are human **resources**?

response (35), an action which is made in reply to some change in the environment.   When something suddenly comes near your eyes, you blink your eyelids quickly. This is an inborn **response**.   Is answering the telephone a **response**? Is it an inborn **response**?

role (3), all the ways of acting which make up one of the parts a person plays in life.   A Blackfoot man had the **role** of warrior.   Name some of the ways a Blackfoot man was expected to act in his **role**.

services (131), the work of people who do not produce things that can be touched. Television repairmen and teachers produce **services**.   Name some people in your community who produce **services**.

social (127), having to do with people as they live and work together in groups. Slavery was once a **social** problem in the United States.   Why are some scientists called **social** scientists?

social controls (190), the norms, laws, rules, and so on, which affect people's behavior.   People are rewarded for acting according to **social controls** and are punished for not acting according to them.   Why do groups of people have **social controls**?

social environment (48), that part of the environment which has to do with people—their customs, roles, ideas, government, and other things (*see also* physical environment).   The custom of riding horses and the norm of sharing were part of the **social environment** of the Blackfoot Indians. Name two places which have like **social environments** but different physical environments.

social scientist (127), a scientist who studies people living and working together.   One kind of **social scientist** studies the ways people earn and spend money.   What kind of **social scientist** is he?

society (sə·sī′ə·tē) (6), the largest group to which people belong in which they share their way of life.   The Blackfoot **society** was made up of smaller groups: tribes, bands, and clubs.   Name some of the groups which make up your **society**.

sociologist (so'sē·ol'ə·jist) (6), a social scientist who studies how people act in groups.   A **sociologist** studies people's roles and norms.   Try to act like a **sociologist** by using norms and roles to tell about a group to which you belong.

stimulus (stim'yə·ləs) (35), a change in the environment to which people or animals respond.   An alarm clock is a **stimulus** to which many people respond every morning.   Is a television show a **stimulus**?

supply (165), an amount of something that can be used.   In a department store, there is a great **supply** of goods. Is there a great **supply** of unused land in your community?

Supreme Court (121), the highest court in the United States, made up of nine judges.   The **Supreme Court** decides meanings of the Constitution. What happens if the **Supreme Court** decides that a law does not agree with the Constitution?

symbol (sim'bəl) (58), a sign or thing that stands for something else. Words are written **symbols** because they stand for ideas.   Of what is the American flag a **symbol**?

theory (52), an explanation of the known facts that scientists have observed. The **theory** of conditioning is one way of explaining some kinds of learning. What is the **theory** of insight?

trading (152), the act of giving something you have for something you want even more.   People who collect stamps sometimes **trade** with each other.   How is your mother **trading** when she buys food?

transportation (153), a way of traveling from place to place.   Airplanes are one kind of **transportation**. Name two kinds of **transportation** used by your family.

treaty (207), an agreement between two or more nations about peace, trade, and so on.   At the end of the Revolutionary War, Great Britain and the United States signed a peace **treaty**.   Why did the settlers make **treaties** with the Indians?

unconstitutional (204), contrary to the Constitution.   The Supreme Court decides whether or not a law is **unconstitutional**.   What happens if the Supreme Court decides a law is **unconstitutional**?

value (26, 30), to think highly of something; a belief or an idea.   Most Americans **value** freedom.   Why was bravery one of the **values** of the Blackfeet?

weathering (80), the part played by weather (sun, rain, and wind) in breaking down rocks.   It may take a million years for the peaks and edges of a mountain to be worn down by **weathering**.   Name two things, besides mountains, which can be worn down by **weathering**.

westward movement (102), the movement of the people of the United States from the east coast to unsettled lands to the west.   The **westward movement** began in the late 1700's and ended in the late 1800's, when the country had been settled from coast to coast.   How did farmers from worn-out lands in the East take part in the **westward movement**?

INDEX

A **boldface** number (like **103**) means a page with a picture.

consumers, **130**, 131, **137**, **164**
contour plowing, 101, 116, **116**, **117**, 118, **118**, 119, **119**
Cook, Captain James, 261
Cornish, Samuel, 267
covered wagons, 102, **103**, **105**
crop rotation, 101
Crow Indians, 212
cultural region, 287
culture, 3; of Blackfoot Indians, 3–10; of Canada, 287–90; of Mexico, 282–86
customs, 8–9, 11, 13, 24, 28, 29; language customs, **45**, 45–47, **46**, **47**, **48**

Declaration of Human Rights, 226, **226**
Declaration of Independence, 196, **196**
delta, 90, 92, **92**
demand, 165, **165**
democracy: direct, 188, **189**, 237; political behavior in a, **277**, **279**, 280; representative, 189
De Quesada, Jorge, 144, **144**
direct democracy, 188, **189**, 237
division of labor, 172, 173, 180
Douglass, Frederick, 269
Drake, Sir Francis, 231
Dred Scott decision, 275, **275**
Dry Diggings, 234, **235**
Dust Bowl, **114**, 114–15, **115**, **124**

earning income, 131–32; *see also* income
economic behavior, 182, 278
economics, 137
economists, 137, **138**, 180, **180**
education, right to, 69, **69**
efficient, 172
Egyptian hieroglyphics, **59**
Eisenhower, Dwight D., **270**
Ellison, Ralph, 269
Emancipation Proclamation, 267, 270
environment: changed, of Indians, 212, **212**; changes with use, 123–24; *see also*

adaptation to new environment
erosion, *see* soil erosion
exchanging, *see* trading

face value, 163
factories and mills, 171, **171**, **172**
fallow fields, 101, **101**
farmers, formation of Granges, 254–55, **255**
farming, **74–75**, **76**, **82**, 82–84, **85**, 98–104; clearing the land, **100**, 100–01; and conservation methods, 101, **101**; farm products, 122, **122**, **123**; farmland, **74–76**, 122–23
fertilizers, use of, 82, **82**, 101
floods, 125, **126**
Fong, Senator Hiram W., **26**
Fort Ross, 231, **231**
French-Canadians, 290
French and Indian War, 194
frontiers, 104, 291

Gandhi, Mohandas K., **31**
geographic region, 287
geologists, 81
goal, of group, 14
gold rushes: in Alaska, **257**, 257–59, **258**; in California, 233–37, **234**, **235**, 251, **251**
goods, *see* producing goods
government, 278; groups trying to influence, 249–55; *see also* social control
Granges, 255, **255**
graphs, **286**, **291**
Great Plains, 102; conflict over land use, 240–47, **243**; land sales, 244–45, **245**; U.S. government and land laws, **243**, **244**, 244–47; U.S. marshals, **243**, 244, **244**
groups, 2, 28, 29, 58; trying to influence the government, 249–55; of the Blackfoot Indians, 3–9, 11–12; customs, 24, 28, **28**, 29; definition of a group, 14–15, 17; examples, **1**, **2**, **10**,

12, 14–16, **16**, **17**, **18**, 18–19, **58**; investigation into, 17, **17**; leaders, 22–25, 29, 278; norms of behavior, 28, 29; purpose, 14, 15
gully, 90, **90**

habits, 47
Handlin, Oscar, 276, **276**
Handy, W. C., **268**, 269
Hangtown, *see* Dry Diggings
Hawaiian Islands, 23, **23**, **24**, **97**, **261**, 261–62; customs, **24**, **25**; statehood, 262, **262**
Heidbreder, Edna, **64**, 65
Henry, Patrick, 121
historian, 276
Homestead Act, 245
Hong Kong, 148, **149**
Howe, Elias, 176, **176**
human geographers, 127, **127**
human resources, 169–75; changing job roles, 174–75, **175**; during colonial time, 170–71; newcomers to the U.S., 171, **171**, 264–66, 276; sharing, 174, **174**
human rights and the law, **270**, 270–71, **271**
humus, 79, 81
hydrologic cycle, 87
hydrologist, 87
hypothesis, 27

Icarus, 56, **56**
Ikechukwu (boy of Nigeria), 14, 14–16, 18–20
immigrants: cultural changes of, 276; countries from which they came, 264–66, **265**, **266**, **272**
inborn response, **35**, 35–36, **36**, 66, **66**
income, 131; community, 141–42; family, 139–41; family budget, 140; *see also* earning income *and* spending income
Independence, Missouri, starting point for wagon trains, 215, 220

needs, 53; shared, 72

Negroes: black pioneers, 245, **246**, 247; civil rights for, 270–71; history in America, 267–69; slavery and freedom of, 170, 171, 265, **267**, 267–70

New Harmony, 179

New Haven, Conn., community planning, 144, **144**

New World, 187; land claims, **187**, **195**; land rights, 188; setting up a government, 188–89, **189**

Nez Percé Indians, 214

Nigeria, 14, **15**, **19**, **20**; Ikechukwu and his soccer team, 14–16, **16**, 18–20

Nixon, Richard M., **138**, **262**

Nobel Peace Prize, 269

norms of behavior, 4, 10, 28, 29, 46–47; of Blackfoot Indians, 4–5; and laws, 190, **190**, 191, **191**, 223–24, 274; of a team, 18

Northwest Ordinance, 199

Northwest Territory, 105, **197**, 197–98

oil production, **156–57**, **205**

Oklahoma, land rush, 77; *see also* Dust Bowl

Operation Bootstrap, 62

Oregon Trail, 215–17, **219**, 220

Owen, Robert, 179

Panama Canal, 160, **160**

parks: Muir Woods, **224**; Point Reyes, 152, **152**

Pavlov, Ivan, 68

Pawnee Indians, 212

Pecos Bill, 240, **240**

Pennsylvania Dutch, 99, **99**, 265

Pilgrims, 99; *see also* Plymouth colony

pioneers, **184–85**, 215–20, 221, **223**, *see also* wagon trains *and* westward movement

Plains Indians, 209, **209**, 212, **212**; *see also* Blackfoot Indians

Plymouth colony, **188**, 188–89, **189**, 192, **192**

political behavior, 277, 278–80, **279**

political scientists, 227

population, 148, **232**, **233**

practice, in learning, 41, **41**, **42**, 43, 43

prairies, 102, **103**, 106

Price, Leontyne, 269

price, 163–65, 168; *see also* supply and demand

producing goods, 130, **130**, 131; services, 131, **132**, **133**, **135**

profit, 163

Promontory, Utah, 253, **253**

psychologists, 36, **41**, 41, 43; social psychologist, **64**, 65; theories of learning, 52–54

Puerto Rico, Operation Bootstrap, 62

Quebec, Canada, 290

railroads, **152**, 251, 252–54, **253**, **255**, **256**; coast-to-coast, 253, **254**; labor unions, 255

rainfall, 88, **89**, 93

records, 282–91, **288**, **290**

representative democracy, 189

reservations, Indian, **210**, 212

resources, 177–78; human, 131–37, 169–75; land, **74–76**, 77–84, **85**, 122; man-made, 146; natural, 146, **146**, **147**, 148, **205**; sharing of, 178, **178**; water, 86–94

response: conditioned, 36–37, **37**, **38–39**; inborn, **35**, 35–36, **36**

rewards and learning, 37–39, **38**, 41, 43, 45; *see also* conditioning

roles: changing job roles, 174–75; definition, 3; examples of, **10**

Roosevelt, Franklin Delano, 31

Roosevelt, Theodore, 85

rotation of crops, 101

Sandburg, Carl, 264, **264**

San Francisco: city planning, 144, **145**; vigilantes, **236**, 236–37, **237**

Santa Fe Trail, **219**, 220

scale, 95; an investigation into, 96, **96**, 97, **97**

Schubert, Glendon, 227, **227**

Scott, Dred, 275, **275**

Sequoya, 249–51, **250–51**

services, *see* producing services

Seward, William, 257

shared meanings in groups, 16, 48

sharing resources, 178, **178**; *see also* trading

sheep grazing, **85**, 241, **243**

ships, **215**, 251, **251**

Sioux Indians, and Custer's army, 212, **213**

skills, **169**, 170, **173**

Skinner, B. F., **64**, 65

slashing and burning, **100**, 100–01

slavery and freedom of Negroes, 265, **267**, 267–69

Smith, Adam, 180, **180**

Smith, Bessie, 269

social behavior, 278

social controls, 260, **260**, 273–74; by miners, 234–36, **238**, 258–59; by norms and laws, 190, **191**, 223–24, **224**; reasons for, 273; by vigilantes, 236–37, **237**, 259

social environment, 48, 291

social scientists: economists, 137; human geographer, 127; political scientists, 227, **227**, 278; psychologists, 36, **64**, 65; social psychologists, **64**, 65; sociologist, 6, 31; *see also* entries for different social scientists

society, 6

sociologist, 6, 31

sod houses, **103**, **246**, 248, **248**

soil, 78, **80**, 80–84; layers, **78**, 78, **79**; minerals, 81–82, **82**; *see also* soil erosion

FULL PRONUNCIATION KEY[1]

Each symbol, or letter, below stands for a sound, a sound you can recognize in the short, common words following it.

The heavy mark, ′, shows that the syllable it follows is given the strongest, or primary, stress, as in **sis·ter** (sis′tər). A lighter mark, ′, shows that the syllable it follows is given stress but a secondary, lighter stress, as in **tax·i·cab** (tak′sē·kab′).

a	add, map	m	move, seem	u	up, done
ā	ace, rate	n	nice, tin	û(r)	urn, term
â(r)	care, air	ng	ring, song	yōo	use, few
ä	palm, father	o	odd, hot	v	vain, eve
b	bat, rub	ō	open, so	w	win, away
ch	check, catch	ô	order, jaw	y	yet, yearn
d	dog, rod	oi	oil, boy	z	zest, muse
e	end, pet	ou	out, now	zh	vision, pleasure
ē	even, tree	ōo	pool, food	ə	the schwa
f	fit, half	ŏo	took, full		an unstressed vowel representing the sound spelled
g	go, log	p	pit, stop		a in above
h	hope, hate	r	run, poor		e in sicken
i	it, give	s	see, pass		i in possible
ī	ice, write	sh	sure, rush		o in melon
j	joy, ledge	t	talk, sit		u in circus
k	cool, take	th	thin, both		
l	look, rule	th	this, bathe		

[1]From *The Harcourt Brace School Dictionary,* published by Harcourt, Brace & World, Inc., 1968.